I0031974

ASIA BOND MONITOR
SEPTEMBER 2021

ASIAN DEVELOPMENT BANK

ADB

Creative Commons Attribution 3.0 IGO license (CC BY 3.0 IGO)

© 2021 Asian Development Bank
6 ADB Avenue, Mandaluyong City, 1550 Metro Manila, Philippines
Tel +63 2 8632 4444; Fax +63 2 8636 2444
www.adb.org

Some rights reserved. Published in September 2021.

ISBN 978-92-9269-043-4 (print), 978-92-9269-044-1 (electronic), 978-92-9269-045-8 (ebook)
ISSN 2219-1518 (print), 2219-1526 (electronic)
Publication Stock No. SPR210338-2
DOI: http://dx.doi.org/10.22617/SPR210338-2

The views expressed in this publication are those of the authors and do not necessarily reflect the views and policies
of the Asian Development Bank (ADB) or its Board of Governors or the governments they represent.

ADB does not guarantee the accuracy of the data included in this publication and accepts no responsibility for any
consequence of their use. The mention of specific companies or products of manufacturers does not imply that they
are endorsed or recommended by ADB in preference to others of a similar nature that are not mentioned.

By making any designation of or reference to a particular territory or geographic area, or by using the term "country"
in this document, ADB does not intend to make any judgments as to the legal or other status of any territory or area.

This work is available under the Creative Commons Attribution 3.0 IGO license (CC BY 3.0 IGO)
https://creativecommons.org/licenses/by/3.0/igo/. By using the content of this publication, you agree to be bound
by the terms of this license. For attribution, translations, adaptations, and permissions, please read the provisions
and terms of use at https://www.adb.org/terms-use#openaccess.

This CC license does not apply to non-ADB copyright materials in this publication. If the material is attributed
to another source, please contact the copyright owner or publisher of that source for permission to reproduce it.
ADB cannot be held liable for any claims that arise as a result of your use of the material.

Please contact pubsmarketing@adb.org if you have questions or comments with respect to content, or if you wish
to obtain copyright permission for your intended use that does not fall within these terms, or for permission to use
the ADB logo.

Corrigenda to ADB publications may be found at http://www.adb.org/publications/corrigenda.

Note:
ADB recognizes "China" as the People's Republic of China; "Hanoi" as Ha Noi; "Hong Kong" and "Hongkong"
as Hong Kong, China; "Korea" as the Republic of Korea; "Saigon" as Ho Chi Minh City; "Siam" as Thailand; and
"Vietnam" as Viet Nam.

Cover design by Erickson Mercado.

Contents

Emerging East Asian Local Currency Bond Markets: A Regional Update

Executive Summary

Recent Developments in Financial Conditions in Emerging East Asia

Between 15 June and 27 August, financial conditions in emerging East Asia remained stable amid accommodative policy stances, with some headwinds observed due to looming uncertainty on recovery paths.[1] Some weakening was observed in most regional markets as currencies depreciated versus the United States (US) dollar, equity markets retreated, and foreign portfolio investments intermittently flowed outward. Local currency (LCY) bond yields fell on the back of weakening economic fundamentals.

All emerging East Asian economies posted positive year-on-year (y-o-y) gross domestic product (GDP) growth in the second quarter (Q2) of 2021, with some markets rebounding from contractions in prior quarters. However, rising COVID-19 cases led to the reintroduction of mobility restrictions in some markets in emerging East Asia, casting a shadow over the region's economic growth trajectory.

The risk outlook in emerging East Asia's financial sector is largely tilted to the downside. Uncertainty regarding the region's economic recovery, combined with a strong US economic rebound and possible earlier-than-expected monetary policy normalization in the US, could lead to domestic currencies weakening further and increased capital outflows from the region. Currency depreciations would increase the debt burden on foreign currency borrowings. A continued strong economic recovery in the US could push up US bond yields and have spillover effects, raising financing costs in the region even for LCY borrowing. Lastly, existing high levels of private debt in some regional markets could pose risks to financial stability if financial conditions worsened.

Recent Developments in Local Currency Bond Markets in Emerging East Asia

Regional LCY bond markets continued to expand as governments tapped LCY bonds to support recovery measures and contain the negative impacts of rising COVID-19 cases. Outstanding LCY bonds in emerging East Asia rose to USD21.1 trillion at the end of June, with accelerated growth of 2.9% quarter-on-quarter (q-o-q) in Q2 2021, up from 2.2% q-o-q in the first quarter (Q1) of 2021. LCY bond issuance in Q2 2021 reached USD2.2 trillion on growth of 14.6% q-o-q, reversing a decline of 1.6% in Q1 2021.

The government bond segment led the regional bond market's expansion in Q2 2021. Outstanding government bonds in emerging East Asia reached USD13.1 trillion at the end of June, posting growth of 3.3% q-o-q in Q2 2021 versus 2.1% q-o-q in Q1 2021, while corporate bond market growth moderated to 2.2% q-o-q in Q2 2021 from 2.4% q-o-q in Q1 2021.

LCY bond markets have provided governments in the region with access to long-term financing during the pandemic, particularly in Association of Southeast Asian Nations (ASEAN) markets.[2] By the end of June, 62.5% of LCY government bonds in ASEAN markets had a tenor of more than 5 years. Regional bond markets exhibited reasonable market capacity as bond yields continued to fall amid ongoing market expansions. Domestic financial institutions, particularly banks, supported LCY bond market growth throughout the region in Q2 2021.

ASEAN+3 sustainable bond markets reached a size of USD345.2 billion at the end of Q2 2021, posting continued rapid growth of 13.1% q-o-q and 53.5% y-o-y in Q2 2021.[3] ASEAN+3 sustainable bonds markets comprised 19.0% of the global sustainable bond stock at the end of June. Strong growth momentum in ASEAN sustainable bond markets was also observed, with outstanding bonds of USD23.6 billion at the end of June on growth of 30.4% q-o-q, up from only 0.6% q-o-q in Q1 2021.

---

[1] Emerging East Asia comprises the People's Republic of China; Hong Kong, China; Indonesia; the Republic of Korea; Malaysia; the Philippines; Singapore; Thailand; and Viet Nam.
[2] LCY bond statistics for the Association of Southeast Asian Nations include the markets of Indonesia, Malaysia, the Philippines, Singapore, Thailand, and Viet Nam.
[3] For the discussion on sustainable bonds, ASEAN+3 includes ASEAN members Indonesia, Malaysia, the Philippines, Singapore, and Thailand, plus the People's Republic of China; Hong Kong, China; Japan; and the Republic of Korea.

Special Topics on Emerging East Asian Local Currency Bond Markets

The September issue of the *Asia Bond Monitor* features five boxes discussing special topics relevant to LCY bond markets in emerging East Asia.

Box 1: Economic Outlook—Strong but Divergent Global Economic Recovery

Despite the progress in global vaccination campaigns, there exists a divide between advanced and developing economies. The regions and economies with the highest income levels are vaccinating their populations more than 20 times faster than those with the lowest income levels. Such a gap is also reflected in economic growth forecasts. The International Monetary Fund's July GDP growth forecasts for advanced economies were upgraded to 5.6% for 2021 and 4.4% for 2022, while those for developing economies were downgraded to 6.3% for 2021 and modestly upgraded to 5.2% for 2022. Within emerging East Asia, such a divergence was also evident in the revised forecasts of the *Asian Development Outlook Supplement* released in July. Relatively richer economies such as the People's Republic of China; the Republic of Korea; and Hong Kong, China are projected to grow a combined 7.5% in 2021 and 5.1% in 2022. Among ASEAN member economies, many of whom have suffered major COVID-19 resurgences in 2021, the aggregate growth forecast was downgraded to 4.0% for 2021 and marginally upgraded to 5.2% for 2022.

Box 2: Market Capacity and Asset Purchase Programs in Emerging East Asian Bond Markets

Since the onset of the COVID-19 pandemic, many regional governments, particularly ASEAN member economies, have tapped the LCY bond markets to finance budget deficits. The region demonstrated robust market capacity with declining bond yields amid rising bond issuances. While foreign capital flows have been volatile, domestic financial institutions have supported regional LCY bond markets during the pandemic. To maintain liquidity in LCY bond markets, some regional central banks implemented modest asset purchase programs for the first time, which helped keep long-term bond yields low and complemented conventional monetary policy. Favorable market conditions in emerging East Asia have contributed to the effectiveness of these programs.

Nonetheless, regional authorities should still be aware of the possible risks associated with these unconventional monetary measures.

Box 3: Debt Buildup during the Pandemic in Emerging East Asia

Emerging East Asia experienced a rapid debt buildup in 2020, particularly public debt. The surge in public debt in 2020 reflected the need of governments to fund economic recovery measures and provide basic services during the pandemic. External debt also increased but remained much smaller compared to domestic debt due to the overall development of LCY bond markets. The share of short-term external debt continued to decline across the region in 2020, showing an improving debt maturity profile. Overall, the debt buildup in emerging East Asia is not too concerning but constant monitoring is necessary.

Box 4: Opening the Pandora's Box of Social Risks—Consequences for Investors

COVID-19 exposed how systemic shocks can have catastrophic consequences on unequal and less-resilient societies, bringing social risks to the spotlight. Social risks, defined as all risks arising from social factors that can have material impacts on a company and its stakeholders, are expected to become increasingly important in the post-pandemic world. Thus, investors should start incorporating social risks into their investment value chain. This box discusses a stakeholder-based approach to assess material social risks from an investment perspective. It then outlines how consideration of social risks can be integrated in an investment value chain—from analysis to engagement and voting. Firms with positive social practices are expected to provide attractive investment opportunities in the coming years, as the social pillar in environmental, social, and governance investing becomes even more salient.

Box 5: Social Bond Issues for Developing Asia

The COVID-19 pandemic has created an opportunity for social bonds to address underlying social issues. Given the exponential growth in the issuance of social bonds in 2020 and the first half of 2021, both globally and regionally, the challenge now is for policy makers and issuers to consider how to better utilize social bond markets to solve social issues that are most relevant to Asia. The pandemic has generated a significant shift in social bond issuance to more pandemic-related projects and socioeconomic crisis alleviation. In developing Asia, the social bond market is still at a nascent stage, addressing relatively narrow social areas such as small and medium-sized enterprise financing, transportation, training, and education.[4] More social areas can be supported via projects related to health care, clean water, food security, and gender equity. Clearly defined impact measurement methods and disclosure requirements will help further develop the market and maximize the impact of social bonds.

---

[4] Developing Asia refers to the 46 developing member economies of the Asian Development Bank.

Global and Regional Market Developments

Financial conditions remain robust with some weakening signs amid heightened uncertainty on recovery prospects.

From 15 June to 27 August, financial conditions in emerging East Asia were largely robust amid accommodative policy stances, but some weakening signs were observed as a rise in COVID-19 cases cast a shadow on the pace of economic recovery (**Table A**).[1] Bond yields declined, equity indexes dropped, and currencies depreciated in emerging East Asia. While liquidity conditions remained accommodative, a decrease in long-term bond yields signaled that the region's economic activities and outlook had been negatively affected by the rising COVID-19 cases and looming uncertainties in the economic recovery.

From 15 June to 27 August, 10-year government bond yields in major advanced economies trended downward (**Figure A**). This tracked investor concerns about the uneven global recovery amid rising cases worldwide (**Box 1**).

The United States (US) Federal Reserve affirmed that the US economy had made substantial progress toward recovery. The unemployment rate fell to 5.2% in August from 5.4% in July and 5.9% in June. However, nonfarm payroll additions fell to 235,000 in August from 1,053,000 in July and from 962,000 in June. US gross domestic product (GDP) growth also accelerated to an annual rate of 6.6% in the second quarter (Q2) of 2021 from 6.3% in the first quarter (Q1) of 2021 and

Table A: Changes in Global Financial Conditions

	2-Year Government Bond (bps)	10-Year Government Bond (bps)	5-Year Credit Default Swap Spread (bps)	Equity Index (%)	FX Rate (%)
Major Advanced Economies					
United States	5	(19)	–	6.2	–
United Kingdom	4	(18)	(0.7)	(0.3)	(2.3)
Japan	0.7	(2)	0.8	(2.8)	0.2
Germany	(6)	(19)	(0.5)	0.8	(2.7)
Emerging East Asia					
China, People's Rep. of	(26)	(27)	(2)	(1.0)	(1.0)
Hong Kong, China	3	(7)	–	(11.3)	(0.3)
Indonesia	(31)	(23)	(2)	(0.8)	(1.3)
Korea, Rep. of	9	(15)	(0.5)	(3.8)	(4.5)
Malaysia	(5)	(4)	3	0.6	(1.8)
Philippines	(7)	25	3	(2.7)	(3.8)
Singapore	3	3	–	(3.0)	(1.4)
Thailand	(2)	(23)	(2)	(0.7)	(4.2)
Viet Nam	(3)	(11)	(4)	(4.0)	0.8
Others					
Brazil	(49)	21	2	5.3	(0.5)
India	188	111	15	(7.2)	(3.0)
Mexico	55	28	(5)	3.0	(0.9)
Russian Federation	31	(23)	(8)	1.7	(1.7)
South Africa	(11)	3	4	0.5	(6.5)
Turkey	(5)	(81)	(18)	1.4	2.5

( ) = negative, – = not available, bps = basis points, FX = foreign exchange.
Notes:
1. Data reflect changes between 15 June 2021 and 27 August 2021.
2. A positive (negative) value for the FX rate indicates the appreciation (depreciation) of the local currency against the United States dollar.
Source: Bloomberg LP.

---

[1] Emerging East Asia comprises the People's Republic of China; Hong Kong, China; Indonesia; the Republic of Korea; Malaysia; the Philippines; Singapore; Thailand; and Viet Nam.

Figure A: 10-Year Government Bond Yields in Major Advanced Economies (% per annum)

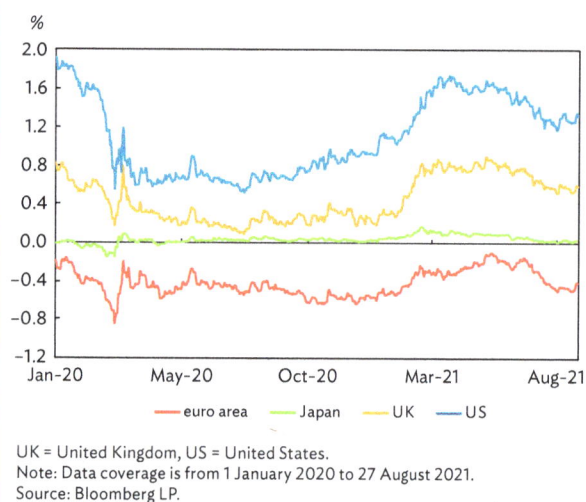

UK = United Kingdom, US = United States.
Note: Data coverage is from 1 January 2020 to 27 August 2021.
Source: Bloomberg LP.

4.5% in the fourth quarter of 2020. The Federal Reserve upgraded its March forecasts for 2021 GDP growth from an annual rate of 6.5% to 7.0% at its Federal Open Market Committee meeting in June. The projection for personal consumption expenditure inflation was adjusted from 2.4% year-on-year (y-o-y) to 3.4% y-o-y. It also forecast a 50 basis points (bps) rate hike in 2023, which was earlier than markets had been expecting. During its July meeting, the Federal Reserve implied there would be further discussion on tapering the current asset purchase program at subsequent meetings. While the current policy rate and asset purchase program remained unchanged, the 2-year yield rose 5 bps on the hawkish statement from the Federal Reserve.

Despite the strong rebound in the US economy, an unchanged federal funds target range, and possible tapering either later this year or early next year, the 10-year yield declined significantly by 19 bps from 15 June to 27 August. The decline in the bond yield partly reflected heightened concerns over the global economic recovery amid the surge of COVID-19 cases and the reimposition of mobility control measures in some markets. Also, the University of Michigan's consumer sentiment index fell from 81.2 in July to 70.3 in August, the lowest reading since December 2011.

In the euro area, GDP growth surged to 14.3% y-o-y in Q2 2021 from a decline of 1.2% y-o-y in the previous quarter. The European Central Bank (ECB) upgraded

its 2021 and 2022 GDP forecasts in June to 4.6% and 4.7%, respectively, from its March forecasts of 4.0% and 4.1%. The ECB's inflation forecasts were also adjusted higher in June to 1.9% for 2021 and 1.5% for 2022 from the March forecasts of 1.5% and 1.2%, respectively. More importantly, the ECB adjusted its forward guidance and shifted its inflation target from close to 2.0% to a symmetric inflation target of 2.0%. This shift offers the ECB the flexibility to allow inflation to temporarily run above 2.0% to sustain the economic recovery. Nevertheless, long-term bond yields declined during the review period over concerns about the trajectory of the global economic recovery. Meanwhile, the ECB has maintained an accommodative monetary stance and the liquidity conditions necessary to support economic recovery. At its 22 July monetary policy meeting, it maintained key policy rates and left the existing asset purchase program unchanged. The ECB also reiterated that it expected to conduct asset purchases at a higher volume in the third quarter of 2021 than in prior quarters.

The Bank of Japan (BOJ) noted that while the domestic economy was recovering, growth remained fragile. Japan recorded an annualized GDP growth of 1.3% in Q2 2021, reversing a contraction of 3.7% in Q1 2021. During its June meeting, the BOJ left unchanged its short-term policy rate target of −0.1% and its 10-year Japan Government Bond yield target of 0.0%. It also maintained the current asset purchase program and extended the duration of the purchase of commercial paper and corporate bonds from September 2021 to March 2022. The BOJ kept its monetary policies unchanged at its July meeting and slightly downgraded its 2021 GDP growth forecast to 3.8% from its April forecast of 4.0%, while it upgraded its 2022 forecast to 2.7% from 2.4%.

Similar to advanced economies, emerging East Asian markets witnessed declines in 2-year and 10-year government bond yields between 15 June and 27 August, as economic activity and the recovery outlook were affected by the reintroduction of mobility restriction measures amid rising COVID-19 cases in many regional markets (**Figure B**). As shown in Table A, all regional markets experienced a decline in 10-year government bond yields except for the Philippines and Singapore. The 10-year yield rose in the Philippines as the economy recorded 11.8% y-o-y GDP growth in Q2 2021 after a decline of 3.9% y-o-y in Q1 2021. On 10 August, the Bangko Sentral ng Pilipinas said that it had yet to consider reducing the reserve requirement ratio. Inflation in the

Box 1: Economic Outlook—Strong but Divergent Economic Recovery

COVID-19 vaccination campaigns are under way around the world, but there are substantial differences across regions and economies.[a] A global vaccine divide is emerging between advanced and developing economies, with the former making much faster progress on the vaccination front. However, due to the highly contagious nature of COVID-19, which can easily spread across borders, not even advanced economies will be immune from major renewed outbreaks until the world as a whole reaches a sufficient level of herd immunity. This strengthens the case for reinforcing international cooperation to increase the supply of vaccines to poor, developing economies.

Notwithstanding the stark global vaccine divide, there has been steady, albeit gradual, progress toward global herd immunity. As of 16 August, 4.71 billion vaccine doses had been administered across 183 economies, according to Bloomberg.[b] This was enough to fully vaccinate 30.7% of the global population. The global vaccination rate at the time of writing stood at around 38.2 million doses administered globally per day. At this pace, it will take until February 2022 for 75% of the global population to be vaccinated.

While the COVID-19 vaccination campaign is by far the largest in history, the impressive overall progress in global vaccination masks a lopsided gap in the global distribution of vaccines. Specifically, the regions and economies with the highest income levels are vaccinating their populations more than 20 times faster than the regions and economies with the lowest income levels.

Due to the progress in the global vaccination campaign against COVID-19, both business and consumer confidence have continued to strengthen. More concretely, while there have been some major outbreaks around the world in 2021, most notably in India in March, the overall COVID-19 landscape has become more benign. In response to the improving pandemic situation, in its latest July 2021 *World Economic Outlook Update*, the International Monetary Fund (IMF) projected global economic growth of 6.0% in 2021, following a contraction of 3.2% in 2020 and modest growth of 2.8% in 2019. In 2022, global growth is projected to moderate to 4.9%. The exceptionally high global growth forecasts for 2021 and 2022 reflect a large base effect (i.e., the fact that 2020 was an exceptionally bad year for growth due to the pandemic). The IMF's July gross domestic product growth forecasts for advanced economies are 5.6% in 2021 and 4.4% in 2022, which are 0.5 percentage points and 0.8 percentage points higher, respectively, than the IMF's April

forecasts. The sizable upgrading reflects the rapid progress of vaccination and the consequent normalization of the economy. The corresponding growth figures for emerging markets and developing economies are 6.3% in 2021 and 5.2% in 2022. The slower pace of vaccination in these economies rules out any substantial upgrade. In fact, there was a downgrade of 0.4 percentage points relative to the IMF's April forecast for 2021, while there was a modest upgrade of 0.2 percentage points for 2022.

The growth forecasts for emerging East Asia show a similarly mixed pattern. According to the Asian Development Bank's July 2021 *Asian Development Outlook Supplement*, developing Asia is poised to grow a robust 7.2% in 2021 before growth moderates to 5.4% in 2022. The 2021 and 2022 forecasts represent a downgrade and upgrade, respectively, of 0.1 percentage points each from the Asian Development Bank's April forecast. While many parts of developing Asia have suffered major renewed COVID-19 outbreaks in 2021, the overall impact on growth has been limited.

Within emerging East Asia, there is a clear dichotomy between East Asia and Southeast Asia. For example, the People's Republic of China; Hong Kong, China; the Republic of Korea; and Taipei,China are projected to grow a combined 7.5% in 2021 and 5.1% in 2022. In fact, the economy-level growth forecasts of the Republic of Korea and Hong Kong, China have been upgraded by 0.5 percentage points and 1.6 percentage points, respectively, relative to April forecasts. Both are export-driven economies that are benefiting greatly from the robust rebound in global trade. On the other hand, many member economies of the Association of Southeast Asian Nations (ASEAN) have suffered a major COVID-19 outbreak in 2021, forcing them to impose various social distancing restrictions. According to the *Asian Development Outlook Supplement*, the aggregate gross domestic product of ASEAN members is projected to expand 4.0% in 2021, a downgrade of 0.4 percentage points from April, and 5.2% in 2022, a marginal upgrade of 0.1 percentage points.

The short-term economic outlook for emerging East Asia is positive but fraught with a great deal of uncertainty. A surge in COVID-19 cases in major ASEAN economies—such as Indonesia, Malaysia, the Philippines, Thailand, and Viet Nam—has highlighted the vulnerability of economic recovery to renewed pandemic outbreaks. The region will enjoy a broad-based recovery in which strong domestic demand complements robust exports only when it brings the pandemic under some degree of control.

---

[a] This box was written by Donghyun Park (principal economist) in the Economic Research and Regional Cooperation Department of the Asian Development Bank.
[b] Bloomberg. COVID-19 Tracker. https://www.bloomberg.com/graphics/covid-vaccine-tracker-global-distribution/ (accessed 16 August 2021).

Figure B: 7-Day Smoothed New COVID-19 Cases per Million Population in Emerging East Asia

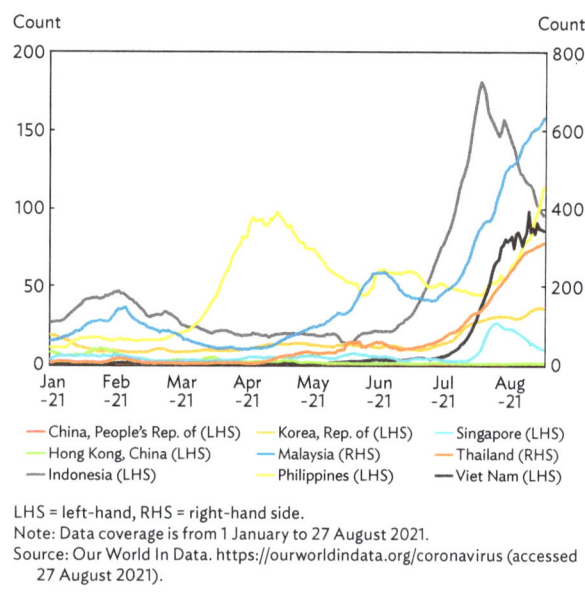

LHS = left-hand, RHS = right-hand side.
Note: Data coverage is from 1 January to 27 August 2021.
Source: Our World In Data. https://ourworldindata.org/coronavirus (accessed 27 August 2021).

Philippines also remains elevated, and while it has trended downward in June, it spiked again to 4.9% y-o-y in August. (**Table B**).

While regional liquidity conditions were kept largely accommodative and monetary stances remained unchanged, 2-year government bond yields were mostly stable except in the People's Republic of China (PRC) and Indonesia. The PRC recorded declines in both its 2-year and 10-year government bond yields despite reporting GDP growth of 7.9% y-o-y in Q2 2021. The declines were largely driven by a 50-bps reduction in the reserve requirement ratio on 9 July to help support the economy. Indonesia's 2-year bond yield declined following the announcement by Bank Indonesia that it would continue to purchase up to IDR215 trillion of government bonds directly from the government this year. The debt-burden sharing agreement will also be extended until 2022 with planned purchases of up to IDR224 trillion. Bank Indonesia's bond buying program aims to keep interest rates low, facilitate market liquidity, and support government financing.

Consistent with lower long-term bond yields, regional equities and currencies also weakened during the review period. All regional equity markets posted losses from 15 June to 27 August except for Malaysia, which recorded a marginal gain of 0.6% (**Figure C**). The largest equity market decline was in Hong Kong, China (11.3%) as its equity market was negatively affected by PRC regulators' crackdown on various industries such as technology, gaming, and education.

All regional currencies weakened versus the US dollar during the review period except for the Vietnamese dong, which gained a marginal 0.8% (**Figure D**). This, on the

Table B: Inflation in Major Advanced Markets and Emerging East Asia

Economy	Inflation Rate (%)												
	Jul-2020	Aug-2020	Sep-2020	Oct-2020	Nov-2020	Dec-2020	Jan-2021	Feb-2021	Mar-2021	Apr-2021	May-2021	Jun-2021	Jul-2021
United States	1.00	1.30	1.40	1.20	1.20	1.40	1.40	1.70	2.60	4.20	5.00	5.40	5.40
Euro Area	0.40	(0.20)	(0.30)	(0.30)	(0.30)	(0.30)	0.90	0.90	1.30	1.60	2.00	1.90	2.20
Japan	0.30	0.20	0.00	(0.40)	(0.90)	(1.20)	(0.70)	(0.50)	(0.40)	(1.10)	(0.80)	(0.50)	(0.30)
China, People's Rep. of	2.70	2.40	1.70	0.50	(0.50)	0.20	(0.30)	(0.20)	0.40	0.90	1.30	1.10	1.00
Hong Kong, China	(2.30)	(0.40)	(2.20)	(0.40)	(0.30)	(1.00)	2.60	0.50	0.60	0.80	1.00	0.70	3.70
Indonesia	1.54	1.32	1.42	1.44	1.59	1.68	1.55	1.38	1.37	1.42	1.68	1.33	1.52
Korea, Rep. of	0.30	0.70	1.00	0.10	0.60	0.50	0.60	1.10	1.50	2.30	2.60	2.40	2.60
Malaysia	(1.30)	(1.40)	(1.40)	(1.50)	(1.70)	(1.40)	(0.20)	0.10	1.70	4.70	4.40	3.40	2.20
Philippines	2.70	2.40	2.30	2.50	3.30	3.50	4.20	4.70	4.50	4.50	4.50	4.10	4.00
Singapore	(0.40)	(0.40)	0.00	(0.20)	(0.10)	0.00	0.20	0.70	1.30	2.10	2.40	2.40	2.50
Thailand	(0.98)	(0.50)	(0.70)	(0.50)	(0.41)	(0.27)	(0.34)	(1.17)	(0.08)	3.41	2.44	1.25	0.45
Viet Nam	3.39	3.18	2.98	2.47	1.48	0.19	(0.97)	0.70	1.16	2.70	2.90	2.41	2.64

( ) = negative.
Note: Data coverage is from July 2020 to July 2021.
Sources: Various local sources.

Figure C: Changes in Equity Indexes in Emerging East Asia

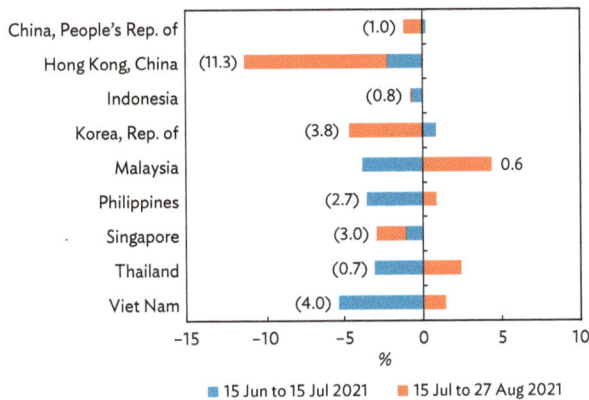

China, People's Rep. of (1.0)
Hong Kong, China (11.3)
Indonesia (0.8)
Korea, Rep. of (3.8)
Malaysia 0.6
Philippines (2.7)
Singapore (3.0)
Thailand (0.7)
Viet Nam (4.0)

%

■ 15 Jun to 15 Jul 2021   ■ 15 Jul to 27 Aug 2021

( ) = negative.
Notes:
1. Changes from 15 June to 15 July 2021 and from 15 July to 27 August 2021.
2. Figures on the chart refer to the net change between the two periods.
Source: *AsianBondsOnline* computations based on Bloomberg LP data.

Figure D: Changes in Spot Exchange Rates versus the United States Dollar

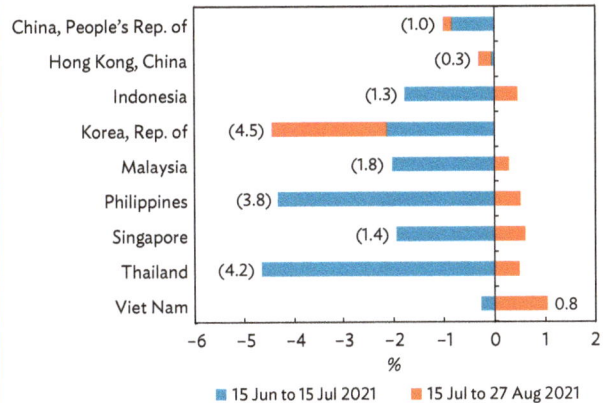

China, People's Rep. of (1.0)
Hong Kong, China (0.3)
Indonesia (1.3)
Korea, Rep. of (4.5)
Malaysia (1.8)
Philippines (3.8)
Singapore (1.4)
Thailand (4.2)
Viet Nam 0.8

%

■ 15 Jun to 15 Jul 2021   ■ 15 Jul to 27 Aug 2021

Notes:
1. Changes from 15 June to 15 July 2021 and from 15 July to 27 August 2021.
2. Figures on the chart refer to the net change between the two periods.
3. A positive (negative) value for the foreign exchange rate indicates the appreciation (depreciation) of the local currency against the United States dollar.
Source: *AsianBondsOnline* computations based on Bloomberg LP data.

Figure E.1: Credit Default Swap Spreads in Select Asian Markets (senior 5-year)

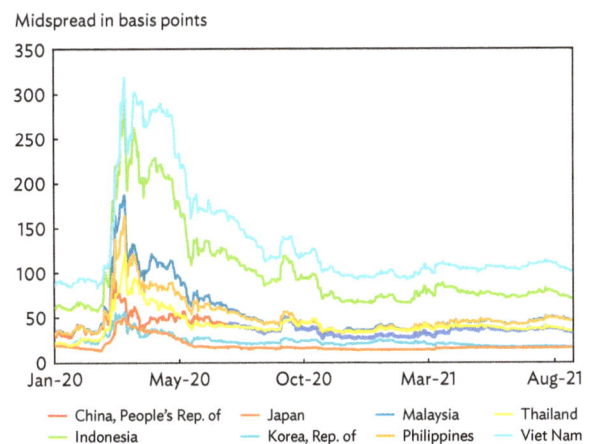

Midspread in basis points

— China, People's Rep. of   — Japan   — Malaysia   — Thailand
— Indonesia   — Korea, Rep. of   — Philippines   — Viet Nam

USD = United States dollar.
Notes:
1. Based on USD-denominated sovereign bonds.
2. Data coverage is from 1 January 2020 to 27 August 2021.
Source: Bloomberg LP.

one hand, reflected a broad strengthening of the US dollar that was driven by a strong economic rebound and the possibility of earlier-than-expected monetary tightening. On the other hand, there was fickle sentiment with regard to risky assets in the region as surging cases weighed on the economic recovery outlook. During the review period, the Korean won weakened the most among all emerging East Asian currencies, partly driven by foreign portfolio outflows in its equity market. The Thai baht also depreciated 4.2% as surging COVID-19 cases loomed over the recovery in the domestic economy, which is largely dependent on tourism and trade. The National Economic and Social Development Council expects tourist visitors in Thailand to reach only 0.15 million in 2021, down from earlier projections of 0.50 million. In 2019, Thailand recorded close to 40 million tourist arrivals.

As shown in Table A, risk premiums in the region remained largely stable with only marginal changes during the review period. Credit default swaps and sovereign stripped spreads trended slightly upward in June, as the Federal Reserve implied there might be a shift in its monetary stance and outbreaks of new COVID-19 cases emerged across the region (**Figures E.1** and **E.2**). Some improvements in credit default swaps were recorded in July and August as many markets released relatively better Q2 2021 GDP figures.

Fickle global investment sentiment was evident in capital flow patterns during the first half of 2021. As shown in

Figures F and **G**, capital outflows have been recorded in regional financial markets around global shocks. In late Q1 2021 and May, capital outflows were recorded in many regional bond and equity markets over concerns of rising US inflation and bond yields, as well as earlier-than-expected monetary normalization by the Federal Reserve. In June and July, capital outflows were observed in

Figure E.2: JP Morgan Emerging Markets Bond Index Sovereign Stripped Spreads

Basis points

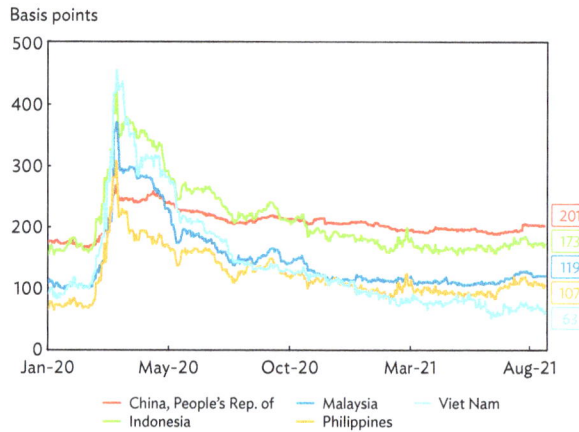

USD = United States dollar.
Notes:
1. Based on USD-denominated sovereign bonds.
2. Data coverage is from 1 January 2020 to 27 August 2021.
Source: Bloomberg LP.

Figure G: Capital Flows into Equity Markets in Emerging East Asia

USD billion

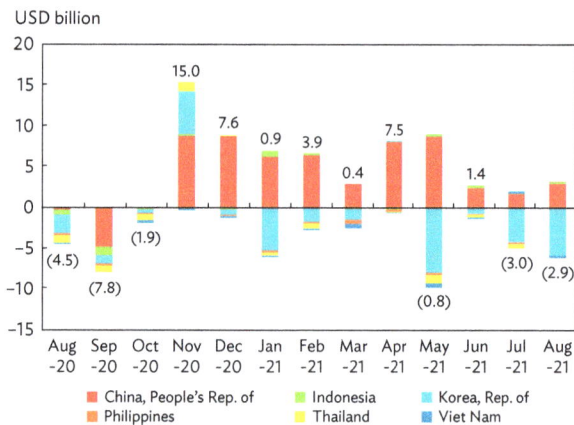

( ) = outflows, USD = United States dollar.
Notes:
1. Data coverage is from 1 August 2020 to 27 August 2021.
2. Figures refer to net inflows (net outflows) for each month.
Source: Institute of International Finance.

Figure F: Foreign Capital Flows in Local Currency Bond Markets in Emerging East Asia

USD billion

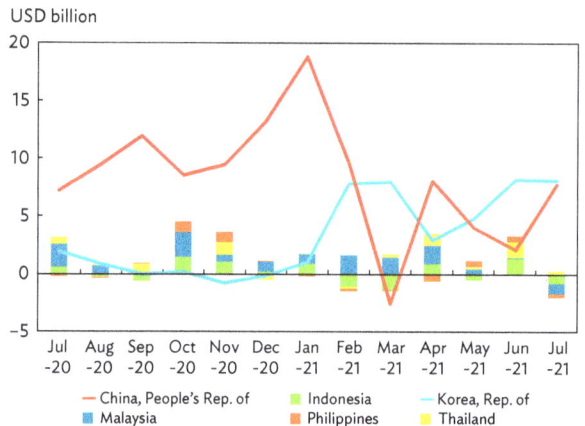

USD = United States dollar.
Notes:
1. The Republic of Korea and Thailand provided data on bond flows. For the PRC, Indonesia, Malaysia, and the Philippines, month-on-month changes in foreign holdings of LCY government bonds were used as a proxy for bond flows.
2. Data as of 31 July 2021.
3. Figures were computed based on 31 July 2021 exchange rates to avoid currency effects.
Sources: People's Republic of China (*Wind Information*); Indonesia (Directorate General of Budget Financing and Risk Management, Ministry of Finance); Republic of Korea (Financial Supervisory Service); Malaysia (Bank Negara Malaysia); Philippines (Bureau of the Treasury); and Thailand (Thai Bond Market Association).

Figure H: Foreign Holdings Share in Local Currency Government Bond Markets in Select Emerging East Asian Economies

Change in share (%)

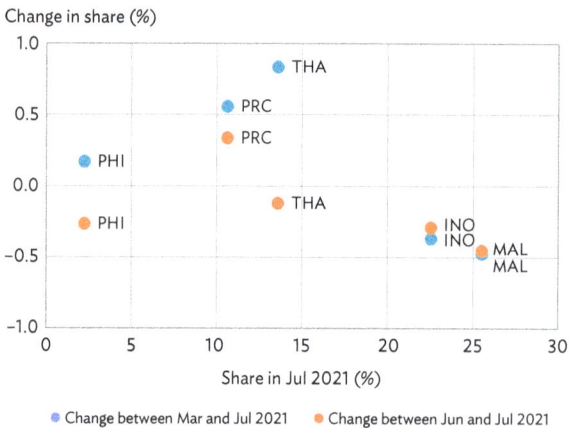

INO = Indonesia, MAL = Malaysia, PHI = Philippines, PRC = People's Republic of China, THA = Thailand.
Note: Data coverage is from March to July 2021.
Source: *AsianBondsOnline*.

many Association of Southeast Asian Nations (ASEAN) markets, tracking a strong US economic rebound as well as looming uncertainty over the regional economic recovery amid rising COVID-19 cases (**Figure H**). Between June and July, the share of foreign holdings fell in nearly all markets, except in the PRC.

During the recent period of uncertainty, the domestic investor base in emerging East Asian markets played an important role in supporting local currency (LCY) bond

markets (**Figure I**). During the pandemic, a number of markets have seen increased ownership of bonds by domestic financial institutions, particularly banks, highlighting the importance of further broadening the domestic investor base. The low bond yields amid

Figure I: Investor Profiles of Local Currency Government Bonds in Select Emerging East Asian Markets

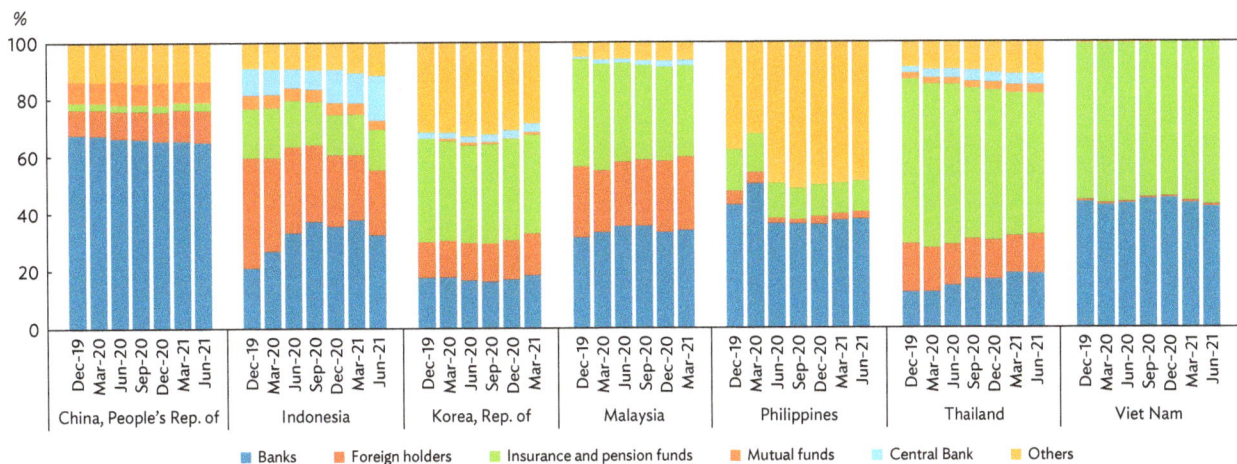

Notes:
1. Data coverage is from December 2019 to June 2021 except for the Republic of Korea and Malaysia (March 2021).
2. Others include central banks, governments, individuals, securities companies, custodians, private corporations, and all other investors not elsewhere classified.
Source: *AsianBondsOnline*.

expanding bond markets implied that the region's bond markets still have reasonable market capacity. Notably during the pandemic, a few emerging East Asian central banks conducted small-scale asset purchase programs to support LCY bond market functioning and facilitate monetary policy implementation. The central banks of Indonesia, the Republic of Korea, Malaysia, the Philippines, and Thailand each increased their respective holdings of LCY government bonds. **Box 2** discusses market capacity and LCY asset purchase programs in the region.

Risks to Outlook: Downside Risks Outweigh Upside Risks

The short-term economic outlook for the world and emerging East Asia is clearly positive. The global and regional economies are recovering strongly from the sharp pandemic-induced downturn of 2020, albeit at divergent speeds across subregions and economies. Despite the overall bright outlook, downside risks continue to outweigh upside risks, thanks largely to the persistent uncertainty surrounding the trajectory of the COVID-19 pandemic. Beyond the short-term, there is also a great deal of uncertainty about the contours of the societies and economies that will emerge as COVID-19 recedes. For example, will education and international travel be permanently affected? If so, in what ways?

There are also some upside risks related to COVID-19, especially in the short-term. In particular, global

cooperation may speed up the achievement of global herd immunity against the disease. As noted earlier, there is a stark divide between advanced economies and developing economies, with vaccination rates far higher in the former than in the latter. Advanced economies have more vaccines than they can use, while developing economies are suffering severe shortages. However, global herd immunity mandates that all economies, regardless of income level, be adequately vaccinated. If the advanced economies muster the political will to help increase the supply of vaccines to developing economies, they will not only help the world but also help themselves. If this were to happen, we can expect a big boost to global economic growth.

The more immediate risk pertaining to COVID-19 is tilted to the downside. In March, India suffered a massive new outbreak that had a substantial impact on private consumption and domestic demand. As a result, in July the Asian Development Bank downgraded its 2021 growth forecast for India from its April forecast. India has managed to contain the outbreak in recent months, primarily by ramping up the production and administration of vaccines, and its economic prospects are improving again. On the other hand, members of ASEAN have suffered major outbreaks since June, with many economies imposing quarantines and movement restrictions. The reduction of mobility has had a palpable impact on domestic demand and economic growth, which is why the Asian Development Bank downgraded the region's GDP growth forecast for 2021 from 4.4% to 4.0%.

Box 2: Market Capacity and Asset Purchasing Programs in Emerging East Asian Bond Markets

A number of governments in emerging East Asia are facing increased budget funding needs due to the COVID-19 pandemic.[a] Fiscal deficits have risen as a result of the combination of reduced tax revenues due to decreased economic activity and rising expenditures needed to support recovery and mitigate the impacts of the pandemic (**Figure B2.1**). In response, many regional governments, particularly members of the Association of Southeast Asian Nations, have tapped local currency (LCY) bond markets in search of financing, as evidenced by increased LCY government bond issuance in 2020 and the first half of 2021 compared to pre-pandemic levels (**Figure B2.2**).

Concerns over uncertainty in emerging East Asia's economic recovery amid the ongoing pandemic, a strong economic rebound and rising inflation in the United States (US), and the potential for earlier-than-expected changes in monetary stances in advanced economies (particularly by the US Federal Reserve) have led to intermittent foreign portfolio outflows from the region's equity and bond markets (**Figure B2.3**). While foreign investors can be fickle and their holdings dependent upon sudden changes in sentiment, emerging East Asia's domestic financial institutions, particularly commercial banks, have supported regional LCY bond markets during the pandemic (**Figure B2.4**).

To facilitate the functioning of LCY bond markets, some emerging East Asian central banks deployed modest asset

purchases program (i.e., "quantitative easing [QE]-like" programs) for the first time with policy rates well above zero (**Figure B2.5**). Regional central banks have implemented such asset purchase programs to improve

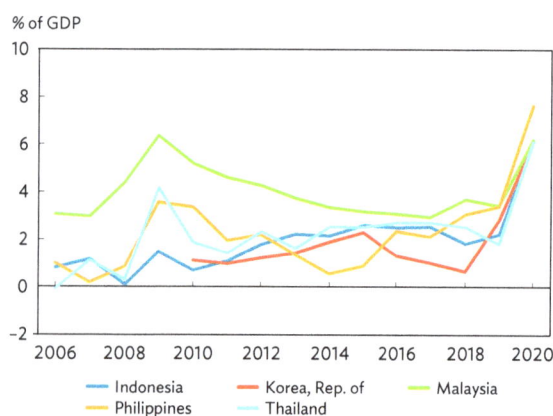

Figure B2.2: Quarterly Treasury Bond Issuance

ASEAN = Association of Southeast Asian Nations, USD = United States dollar.
Notes:
1. Data include Treasury bills and bonds and are computed based on the 30 June 2021 exchange rate.
2. ASEAN comprises Indonesia, Malaysia, the Philippines, Singapore, Thailand, and Viet Nam.
Source: AsianBondsOnline.

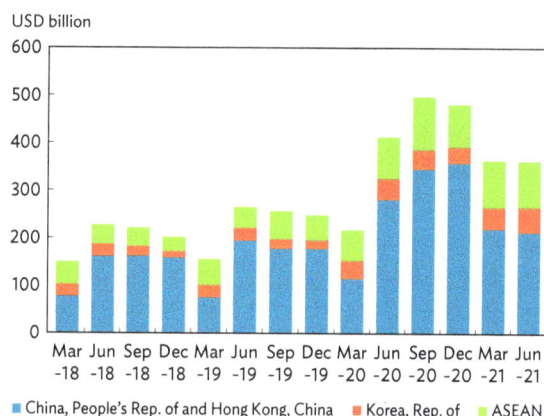

Figure B2.1: Fiscal Deficit in Select Emerging East Asian Markets

GDP = gross domestic product.
Sources: Asian Development Outlook Database; Haver Analytics (accessed 19 August 2021).

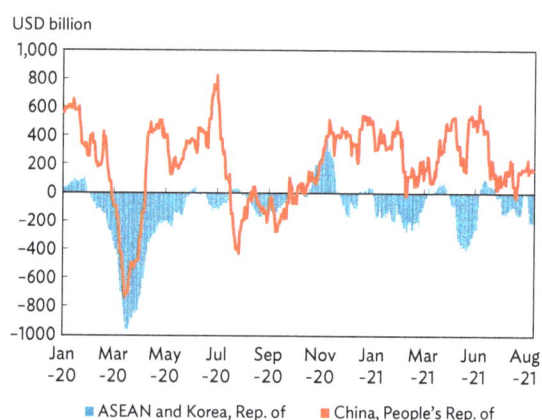

Figure B2.3: Foreign Portfolio Flows

ASEAN = Association of Southeast Asian Nations, USD = United States dollar.
Notes:
1. Data for ASEAN and the Republic of Korea includes Indonesia, the Republic of Korea, Malaysia, the Philippines, Thailand, and Viet Nam.
2. Figures are based on 28-day moving average.
Source: AsianBondsOnline computations based on data from the Institute of International Finance (accessed 23 August 2021).

[a] This box was written by Shu Tian (Economist) in the Economic Research and Regional Cooperation Department of the Asian Development Bank.

continued on next page

Box 2: Market Capacity and Asset Purchasing Programs in Emerging East Asian Bond Markets
continued

Figure B2.4: Contributions to Change in Local Currency Government Bond Holdings between December 2019 and June 2021

Percentage points

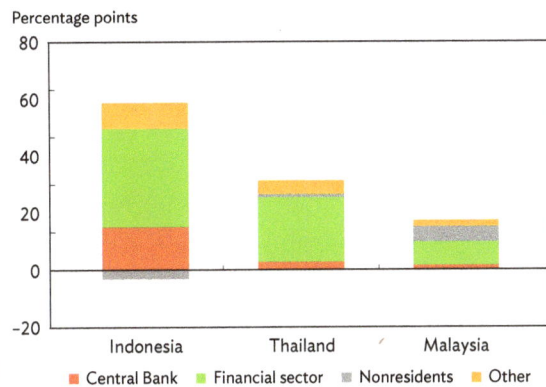

Central Bank   Financial sector   Nonresidents   Other

Note: For Malaysia, data are from December 2019 to March 2021.
Sources: Indonesia (Directorate General of Budget Financing and Risk Management, Ministry of Finance); Malaysia (Bank Negara Malaysia); and Thailand (Bank of Thailand).

Figure B2.5: Central Bank Local Currency Bond Purchase Programs in Emerging East Asia

% of GDP

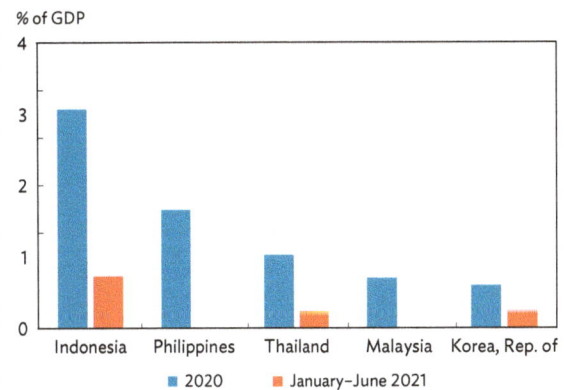

2020   January–June 2021

GDP = gross domestic product.
Notes:
1. Share to GDP is based on 2020 GDP.
2. For Indonesia, data for 2021 cover the period 1 January–15 June 2021.
3. Data for Malaysia and the Philippines for the period January to June 2021 are not available.
Sources: National sources and Haver Analytics (accessed 20 August 2021).

bond market liquidity and bolster private investor confidence. Some central banks, such as Bank Indonesia and the Bangko Sentral ng Pilipinas, are also aiming to temporarily ease their respective government's financing pressures.

These asset purchase programs, while not large in scale, have helped stabilize LCY bond markets and kept long-term bond yields low to facilitate the effectiveness of policy rate cuts. Amid market conditions that include adequate foreign exchange reserves, a manageable current account, fair currency valuation, and relatively low inflation risk, these asset purchase programs have been effective as additional tools to complement conventional monetary policy.

With support from domestic investor bases and central banks, interest rate movements in the region in 2020 and the first half of 2021 largely exhibited downward trends, suggesting that there is market capacity to absorb new bond issuances. In 2021, economic reopening and recovery in most regional markets should help narrow budget deficits and free up liquidity to support market capacity. Most regional economies are planning to reduce their budget deficits in 2021, as

evidenced by a decline in central bank asset purchases in the first half of 2021.[b]

While these asset purchases are relatively small in scale and function, regional authorities still need to be aware of possible associated risks. A key difference between QE in advanced markets and the asset purchase programs conducted in the region is that QE programs in advanced economies are in G3 currencies (US dollars, euros, or Japanese yen). This implies that there is always demand from global investors for such currencies that act as a "safe haven" and even enjoy increased demand during shocks and market turmoil. On the other hand, LCY asset purchase programs in emerging East Asia target largely domestic investors and these assets will have reduced demand when investment sentiment sours during periods of market turmoil.

Favorable market conditions in emerging East Asia—such as sufficient foreign reserves, robust current account performances, moderate inflation levels, and fair currency valuations—have all contributed to the successful functioning of asset purchase programs in the region. In the unlikely

[b] For example, the People's Republic of China aims to reduce its budget deficit from above 3.6% of GDP in 2020 to 3.2% in 2021, Indonesia is targeting a 5.7% budget-deficit-to-GDP ratio in 2021 versus an actual 6.1% ratio in 2020, and Viet Nam aims for a budget deficit of 4.0% of GDP in 2021 from an estimated 5.0%–5.6% in 2020. Singapore aims for a budget deficit of 2.1% of GDP in 2021 versus 13.9% in 2020 and is drawing upon its reserves to pay for pandemic support measures. Malaysia expects to maintain a budget deficit equivalent to 6.0% of GDP in 2021, similar to 2020. On the other hand, a few markets are raising their budget-deficit-to-GDP target level in 2021. For example, the Philippines has set a budget deficit target of 8.9% of GDP in 2021, up from 7.5% in 2020, and Thailand plans a budget deficit of 3.7% of GDP for fiscal year 2021, compared with 5.0% for fiscal year 2020.

continued on next page

Box 2: Market Capacity and Asset Purchasing Programs in Emerging East Asian Bond Markets
continued

case that some of these fundamental economic factors change in the future in a particular market, an asset purchase program might trigger inflation fears, capital outflows, and currency depreciation. While these potential risks have yet to materialize, especially given the small scale of these programs, market conditions should be continuously monitored to avoid a buildup of stress in the region's financial systems.

Transparency and communication with investors on these measures are needed to maintain market confidence and central bank credibility. Authorities must also maintain the ability to make policy adjustments and smoothly reverse these programs, if necessary, without causing big swings in either interest rates or the exchange rate.

The ups and downs in the growth trajectory of the Indian and ASEAN economies suggest that Asia and the Pacific has not yet reached a post-COVID-19 normal. Instead, the short-term economic outlook remains hostage to the vagaries of the pandemic. Greater uncertainty in the economic recovery requires more attention be given to monitoring financial stability, particularly with the rapid buildup of private debt before the pandemic. The Bank of Korea hiked the base rate on 26 August to curb debt expansion.

A potential tightening of global financial conditions, which remain relatively benign at the moment, cannot be completely ruled out. Early monetary policy normalization by the Federal Reserve could lead to discrepancies in monetary stances between the US and the region. This would weaken the attractiveness of regional assets, which could lead to capital outflows and put pressure on regional currencies. Currency stress would increase debt burdens on external debt, especially in regional markets with higher external debt exposure. However, the risk to emerging East Asia's financial stability from monetary tightening in advanced economies, especially the US, remains relatively limited. Above all, any shift in the Federal Reserve's monetary policy is likely to be gradual and measured rather than abrupt and unexpected. A clear sign of the Federal Reserve's cautious approach to normalization came at its 27–28 July meeting, when it kept the federal funds rate at between 0.0% and 0.25%. The decision to hold the rate steady largely reflected its assessment of the US economy, which is recovering at a healthy pace thanks to impressive vaccination progress and an aggregate USD3 trillion of fiscal stimulus in response to the pandemic. However, a strong US economic recovery may eventually push up US government bond yields, which would spillover to emerging East Asia and raise regional financing and

refinancing costs even in local currencies. Nevertheless, the seemingly strong domestic economy in the US is also subject to a lot of uncertainty, primarily due to the risk of renewed COVID-19 outbreaks. This explains why the Federal Reserve is prioritizing economic growth over inflationary pressures.

Equally important, emerging East Asian economies are recovering strongly, albeit at different speeds. They have strong fundamentals, including ample foreign exchange reserves; low inflation; and sound current account balances. Resilient economies and strong fundamentals place the region in good stead in the event of any possible turmoil that emanates from outside the region. To sum up, notwithstanding the positive short-term economic outlook, risks remain tilted to the downside. Furthermore, the overarching downside risk is still the heavy fog of uncertainty surrounding COVID-19.

As the pandemic calls for more financing resources, debt levels have risen in regional markets. **Box 3** discusses debt levels and ongoing debt expansions in the region. While the region's current debt levels are not overly concerning, there are still a few risks, which means that authorities need to conduct frequent assessments and monitoring. Moreover, long-term bonds account for the majority of LCY bonds outstanding in the region, particularly among members of ASEAN, which suggests that LCY bond markets are contributing to greater resilience via more long-term financing (**Figures J.1** and **J.2**).

The COVID-19 pandemic has raised awareness of social issues and related market risks arising during the pursuit of a resilient and inclusive recovery. This poses new challenges and opportunities for regional investors. **Box 4** discusses emerging social risks and related opportunities that investors face in the era of greater social awareness.

Box 3: Debt Buildup during the Pandemic in Emerging East Asia

During the decade after the global financial crisis (GFC), sustained low interest rates spurred a debt buildup in both the public and private sectors in global emerging markets.[a] With the onset of COVID-19, additional financing needed to fight the pandemic and interest rate cuts by major central banks have further pushed up debt levels in most economies around the world. While global monetary stances have largely remained accommodative, it is important to assess the current debt buildup situation in emerging East Asian economies and how concerning it could be, especially with possible early monetary policy normalization led by the United States (US) Federal Reserve.[b]

Debt expanded more rapidly during the pandemic compared to the global financial crisis.

Emerging East Asian markets collectively witnessed rapid debt expansions in both the public and private sectors in 2020. **Figure B3.1** shows that Singapore posted the largest increase in the region in 2020 in terms of government debt as a share of gross domestic product (GDP) at 24.7%, followed by Malaysia (10.3%) and the Philippines (10.1%), largely driven by the introduction of stimulus packages during the pandemic. The average increase in the public debt ratio in Association of Southeast Asian Nations (ASEAN) markets (excluding Singapore) in 2020 was 6.9%, which contrasts

with a 3.5% decrease during the global financial crisis (GFC) of 2008–2009 relative to the pre-GFC level of 2006. This reflects the different nature of the COVID-19 pandemic from the GFC, as increased financing demand in 2020 by governments was largely driven by the need to provide basic services such as health and education, as well as to tackle economic and social issues.

Nonfinancial private debt also collectively increased during the pandemic, but not necessarily as much as the nonfinancial private debt buildup during the GFC. Relatively higher-income emerging East Asian markets such as Hong Kong, China; Singapore, the People's Republic of China (PRC), the Republic of Korea, and Malaysia saw larger private debt increases than other ASEAN markets in 2020. Malaysia, the Philippines, and Hong Kong, China recorded larger private debt increases in response to the pandemic in 2020 than during the GFC. The average aggregate private debt increases in ASEAN (excluding Singapore) stood at 3.5% and 1.7% in 2020 and the GFC, respectively. Overall, while debt in both the public and private sectors has increased during the pandemic, the pandemic has driven government borrowing more significantly as fighting its impacts requires a lot of public resources.

Figure B3.2 shows the dynamics of debt levels in emerging East Asia. During the decade after the GFC from 2009 to

Figure B3.1: Change in Public and Private Debt during COVID-19 versus the GFC

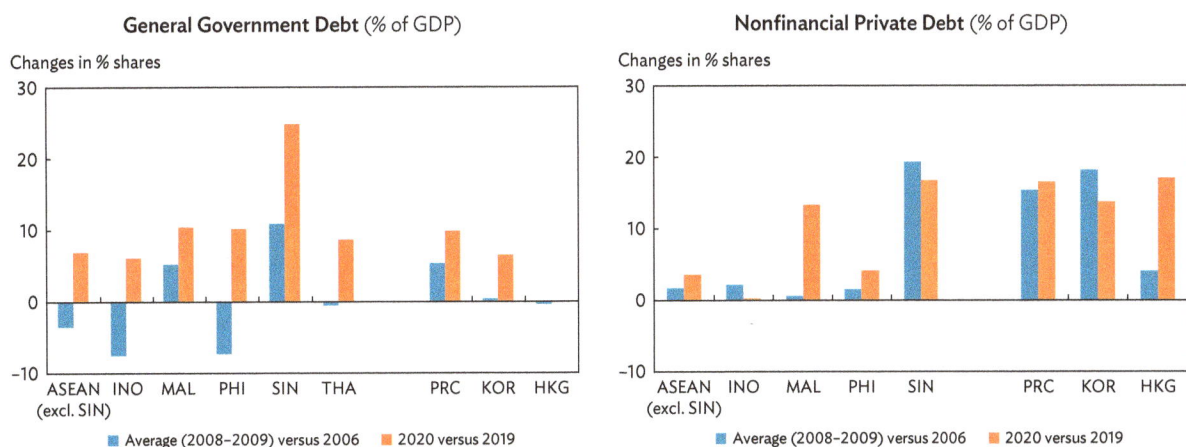

General Government Debt (% of GDP)

Nonfinancial Private Debt (% of GDP)

ASEAN = Association of Southeast Asian Nations; COVID-19 = coronavirus disease; excl. = excluding; GDP = gross domestic product; GFC = global financial crisis; HKG = Hong Kong, China; INO = Indonesia; KOR = Republic of Korea; MAL = Malaysia; PHI = Philippines; PRC= People's Republic of China; SIN = Singapore; THA = Thailand.
Note: Subregional figures for ASEAN are calculated using 2020 GDP (United States dollar equivalent).
Sources: International Monetary Fund. *World Economic Outlook, April 2021*. Washington, DC; Haver Analytics; CEIC Data Company (for public and private debt) (accessed 20 July 2021).

---

[a] This box was written by Shu Tian (economist) and Shiela Camingue-Romance (economics officer) in the Economic Research and Regional Cooperation Department. Helpful discussions and suggestions from Matteo Lanzafame (senior economist) and Irfan Qureshi (economist) are deeply appreciated.
[b] Emerging East Asia refers to members of the Association of Southeast Asian Nations plus the People's Republic of China; Hong Kong, China; and Republic of Korea.

continued on next page

Box 3: Debt Buildup during the Pandemic in Emerging East Asia   *continued*

Figure B3.2: Dynamics in Public and Private Debt in Emerging East Asia, 2005–2020

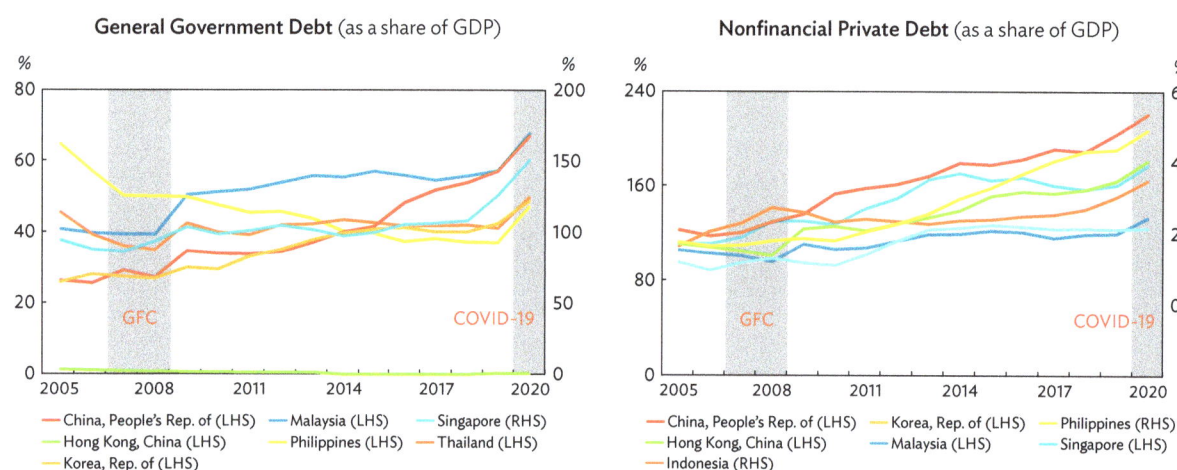

COVID-19 = coronavirus disease, GDP = gross domestic product, GFC = global financial crisis, LHS = right-hand side, RHS = right-hand side.
Sources: International Monetary Fund. *World Economic Outlook, April 2021.* Washington, DC; Haver Analytics; CEIC Data Company (for public and private debt) (accessed 20 July 2021).

2019, most emerging East Asian markets saw relatively stable and steady increases in public debt (as a share of GDP) except for the PRC and Singapore, which posted relatively rapid gains in public debt of 22.5% and 22.3%, respectively. In 2009, the weighted average of public debt in ASEAN and ASEAN excluding Singapore was 45.9% and 37.3%, respectively, which steadily increased to 49.4% and 37.9% by the end of 2019 and further to 59.5% and 45.8% in 2020 amid the introduction of fiscal stimulus packages and easy monetary policies to fight the pandemic.

Turning to the private sector, most emerging East Asian markets witnessed a gradual private debt buildup during the low interest rate era that followed the GFC. The PRC posted the fastest private debt expansion, from 137.0% in 2009 to 205.1% in 2019, partly driven by a relaxed borrowing environment fostered by the economic stimulus package worth about CNY4 trillion introduced in 2008-2009. Markets with relatively developed financial markets—such as Singapore; the Republic of Korea; the PRC; Hong Kong, China; and Malaysia—experienced relatively large gains in private debt, with an average increase of 16.0% in 2020, which continued the debt expansion that occurred in 2019 when average private debt increased 13.7% among these economies. This indicates that the 2020 expansion in private debt might not necessarily be solely driven by financing pandemic-related needs, as the pandemic also subdued economic activities and soured investment sentiment in the private sector.

The region's external debt has risen modestly and its maturity structure has improved during the pandemic.

In 2020, external debt as a share of GDP collectively rose in all emerging East Asian markets. **Figure B3.3** shows the level of external debt increase was much higher in Singapore and Hong Kong, China, given their roles as financial centers. The average external debt expansion in emerging East Asia (excluding Singapore and Hong Kong, China) was 2.4% in 2020, compared with 0.4% in 2019, indicating that regional economies tapped international debt markets to finance pandemic-related needs. However, compared to the 9.2% increase in public debt and 15.0% increase in private debt in 2020, regional markets (excluding Singapore and Hong Kong, China) largely relied on domestic markets to finance investment needs during the pandemic. During the decade following the GFC, external debt levels in ASEAN (excluding Singapore) remained largely stable (**Figure B3.4**). Average external debt levels in ASEAN (excluding Singapore) rose marginally from 36.2% in 2009 to 36.9% in 2019, which further increased to 41.8% in 2020. Overall, the rise in external debt in the region has been modest due in part to the development of local currency funding in domestic financial markets.

One important difference regarding external debt is the difference in maturity structure in 2020 compared to the GFC period. **Figure B3.5** shows the share of short-term

continued on next page

Box 3: Debt Buildup during the Pandemic in Emerging East Asia   *continued*

Figure B3.3: Changes in Gross External Debt in 2020

Changes in % shares

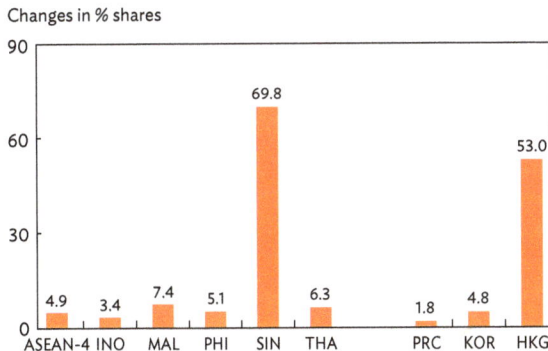

ASEAN = Association of Southeast Asian Nations; HKG = Hong Kong, China; INO = Indonesia; KOR = Republic of Korea; MAL = Malaysia; PHI = Philippines; PRC= People's Republic of China; SIN = Singapore; THA = Thailand.
Note: ASEAN-4 comprises Indonesia, Malaysia, the Philippines, and Thailand.
Source: *AsianBondsOnline* calculations using data from Haver Analytics (accessed 20 July 2021).

Figure B3.4: Dynamics in Gross External Debt in Emerging East Asia, 2005–2020

% of GDP   % of GDP

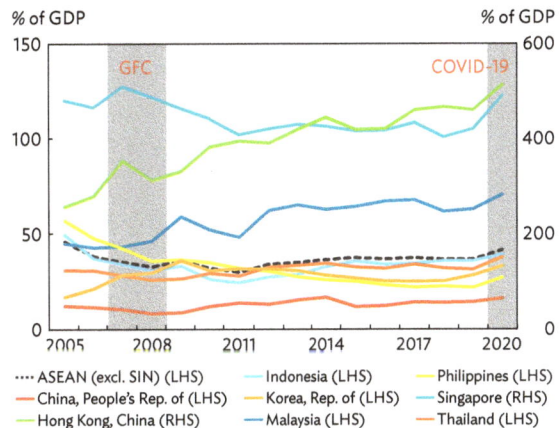

ASEAN = Association of Southeast Asian Nations, COVID-19 = coronavirus disease, excl. = excluding, GDP = gross domestic product, GFC = global financial crisis, LHS = left-hand side, RHS = right-hand side.
Note: Subregional figures for ASEAN are calculated using 2020 GDP (United States dollar equivalent).
Source: *AsianBondsOnline* calculations using data from Haver Analytics (accessed 20 July 2021).

Figure B3.5: Dynamics in the Share of Short-Term External Debt in Emerging East Asia, 2005–2020

% of total

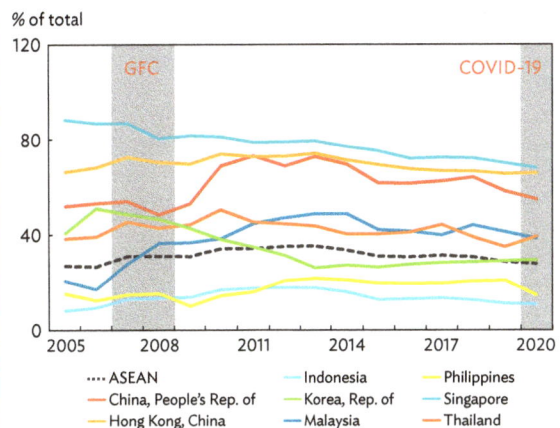

ASEAN = Association of Southeast Asian Nations, COVID-19 = coronavirus disease, GDP = gross domestic product, GFC = global financial crisis.
Note: Subregional figures for ASEAN are calculated using 2020 GDP (United States dollar equivalent).
Source: *AsianBondsOnline* calculations using data from Haver Analytics (accessed 20 July 2021).

external debt in total external debt rose in many regional markets during the GFC period before declining beginning in 2011. The average share of short-term external debt to total external debt in the region was 49.6% in 2006 and 61.8% in 2010 shortly after the GFC. It then gradually declined to 51.9% in 2019 and further fell to 49.2% in 2020. This indicates that while external debt levels rose during the pandemic, the increase was largely driven by long-term external debt, which provides relatively stable funding and will not trigger immediate liquidity issues. This was the opposite of what occurred during the GFC when the share of short-term external debt increased in most regional markets.

Overall, the buildup of debt in emerging East Asia amid the pandemic has not significantly exacerbated debt conditions in the region and is therefore not that concerning, especially with abundant liquidity in the market and continued accommodative monetary stances globally and regionally. The current low interest rates also enabled refinancing at a relatively low cost, particularly in markets with stronger fiscal positions and better capital market access. As shown in **Figure B3.6**, compared to the average 2008–2009 levels, both short- and long-term government bond yields were significantly lower in 2020 across the region, particularly for long-term funding.

continued on next page

Box 3: Debt Buildup during the Pandemic in Emerging East Asia *continued*

Figure B3.6: Government Bond Yield Changes in Emerging East Asia, 2008–2009 versus 2020

Basis points

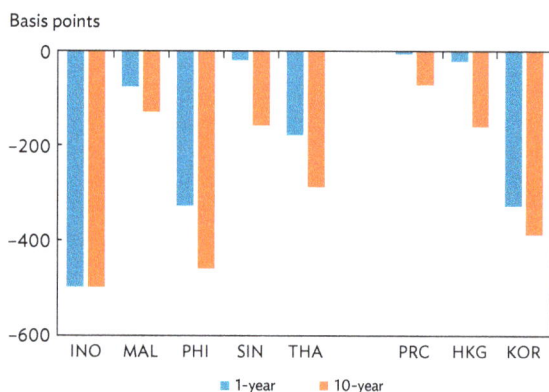

HKG = Hong Kong, China; INO = Indonesia; KOR = Republic of Korea; MAL = Malaysia; PHI = Philippines; PRC= People's Republic of China; SIN = Singapore; THA = Thailand.
Notes: The 2-year (2008–2009) and annual (2020) averages are based on end-of-month bond yields.
Source: *AsianBondsOnline* computations using Bloomberg (accessed 18 August 2021).

However, the current debt buildup still calls for continuous monitoring. A few risk factors are particularly relevant to regional policy makers. First, at the Federal Open Market Committee meeting in July 2021, the Federal Reserve implied that tapering would start either in late 2021 or early 2022. Combined with a possible earlier-than-expected rate hike in late 2022 or 2023, the discrepancies in monetary stances between the US and most emerging East Asian markets could cause capital outflows and currency stress in the region. This might increase debt burdens, especially in markets with higher levels of external debt. Second, the strong economic rebound and inflation situation in the US could push up its bond yields, which would spill over into emerging markets and thus increase the refinancing cost of debt, even for local currency debt. Third, uncertainty in the trajectory of the economic recovery due to the recent surge in COVID-19 cases could affect debt service capacity in the region, particularly in the private sector. In conclusion, emerging East Asian authorities still need to closely monitor financial conditions to maintain financial stability in the region.

Figure J.1: Maturity Profiles of Local Currency Government Bonds Outstanding in Emerging East Asia

% share to total

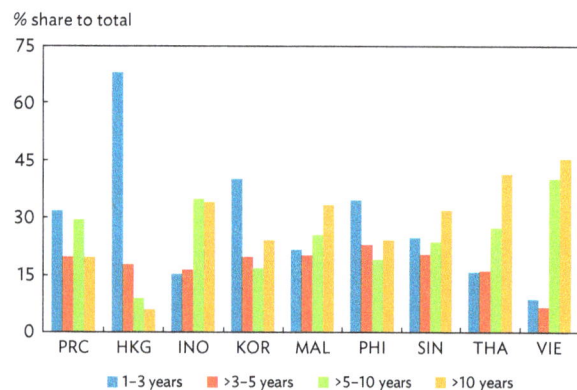

PRC = People's Republic of China; HKG = Hong Kong, China; INO = Indonesia; KOR = Republic of Korea; MAL = Malaysia; PHI = Philippines; SIN = Singapore; THA = Thailand; VIE = Viet Nam.
Notes:
1. Government bonds include Treasury bills and bonds.
2. Data as of the end of June 2021.
Source: *AsianBondsOnline*.

Figure J.2: Maturity Profiles of Local Currency Government Bond Issuance in Emerging East Asia

% share to total

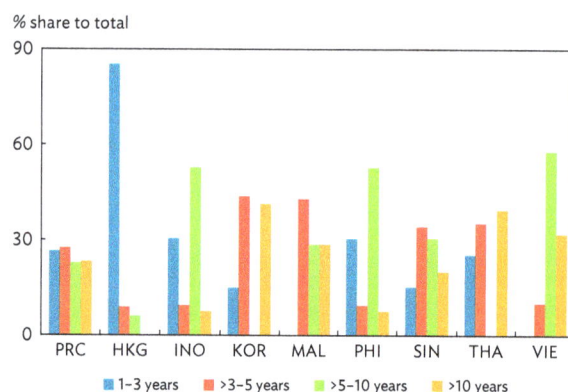

PRC = People's Republic of China; HKG = Hong Kong, China; INO = Indonesia; KOR = Republic of Korea; MAL = Malaysia; PHI = Philippines; SIN = Singapore; THA = Thailand; VIE = Viet Nam.
Notes:
1. Government bonds include Treasury bills and bonds.
2. Data are based on issuance for the second quarter of 2021.
Source: *AsianBondsOnline*.

Recent rapid developments in social bond markets globally and in the region have provided solutions to address some of these social risks. However, the social areas being addressed by the regional social bond market remain limited. **Box 5** discusses potential social issues that can be further addressed via social or sustainability bond financing.

Box 4: Opening the Pandora's Box of Social Risks—Consequences of Investors

The COVID-19 crisis has been a real turning point for social issues, in particular inequality.[a] It has clearly shown the tragic effects—from an economic and societal perspective—that systemic shocks can have on unequal, nonresilient societies.

Even prior to the pandemic, Moody's Investors Services estimated that USD8 trillion of the debt that it rates was subject to material social risks—that is, four times the amount exposed to climate change risks.[b] However, differently from climate change, there is no real consensus on which kind of social risks should be considered material for investing. Using a stakeholder-based framework, in this article we explore several social risks that have proven their materiality in specific contexts.

The materiality of social risks is expected to increase in the post-pandemic world for several reasons. Investors should thus start integrating social risks along their whole investment value chain—from analysis to engagement and voting—supported by their responsible asset managers.

"S" Is the New "E"

The issue of social inequality has been discussed for years but has never received as much media coverage as much as it has during the COVID-19 crisis. Indeed, while economic growth since the 1980s has led to a decrease in global income inequality due to improved economic conditions in certain developing countries, within-country inequality has increased in developed countries and some middle-income countries such as the People's Republic of China.[c]

In bringing some of these inequalities to the spotlight, the global pandemic has given investors significant opportunities to pursue the "S" pillar within environmental, social, and governance (ESG) investing. For example, in North American equity markets the social pillar (with a focus on employment conditions) had been lagging behind the environmental and governance pillars in terms of investment in previous years.

However, the social pillar outperformed the other two pillars in the first quarter of 2020.[d]

Assessing Material Social Risks through a Stakeholder-Based Approach

We consider social risks as being all risks emanating from social factors that can have a material impact on a company and its stakeholders. The "double materiality" concept is considered and expanded here; taking into account how social risks can affect a company's value is not sufficient since how a company either exacerbates or mitigates social issues can, in turn, become a risk that affects its value (**Figure B4**).

A notable example of how double materiality works is the probe around the OxyContin opioid painkillers produced by Purdue Pharma. The company—by enabling the supply of drugs without a legitimate medical purpose—greatly contributed to the dip in the United States' life expectancy in 2015 for the first time in a decade.[e] This complete lack of product responsibility led to a USD8.3 billion settlement with the Department of Justice and several other cases that are still under litigation.[f]

At a macroeconomic level of analysis, it is generally recognized that high levels of social inequality can have a negative impact on economic growth.[g] Research has shown that there seems to be a vicious circle between income inequality and financial instability.[h]

At a microeconomic level, material social risks can be analyzed through a stakeholder-based approach:

1. Employees

Labor and capital are considered the most important factors on which economic activity is based. However, the share of income distributed to labor, as opposed to capital, has decreased in most countries in recent decades.[i] Social

---

a   This box was written by Caroline Le Meaux, head of ESG research, engagement and voting, Amundi; and Sofia Santarsiero, business solutions and innovation analyst, Amundi. The content is based on a research paper by Amundi Asset Management. 2021. *Opening the Pandora's Box of Social Risks: Consequences for Investors*. https://research-center. amundi.com/article/shifts-narratives-7-opening-pandora-s-box-social-risks-consequences-investors.

b   *Moody's Investors Services*. 2019. Social Considerations Pose High Credit Risk for 14 Sectors, $8 Trillion Debt. 31 October.

c   Chancel, L. and T. Pikkety. 2021. *Global Income Inequality, 1820–2020*. 20 July. https://wid.world/news-article/global-income-inequality-1820-2020/.

d   Amundi Research. 2020. The Coronavirus and ESG Investing, The Emergence of the Social Pillar. *Amundi Insights Paper*. https://research-center.amundi.com/article/coronavirus-and-esg-investing-emergence-social-pillar.

e   Chatterjee, R. 2020. Life Expectancy Rose Slightly in 2018, as Drug Overdose Deaths Fell. *NPR*. 30 January. https://www.npr.org/sections/health-shots/2020/01/30/801016600/life-expectancy-rose-slightly-in-2018-as-drug-overdose-deaths-fell?t=1623089716621.

f   Sherman, N. Purdue Pharma to Plead Guilty in $8 bn Opioid Settlement. *BBC News*. 21 October. https://www.bbc.com/news/business-54636002.

g   Cingano, F. 2014. Trends in Income Inequality and its Impact on Economic Growth. *OECD Social, Employment and Migration Working Papers*. No. 163. http://dx.doi.org/10.1787/5jxrjncwxv6j-en.

h   Cihak, M. and R. Sahay. 2020. Finance and Inequality. *International Monetary Fund Staff Discussion Notes*. https://www.imf.org/en/Publications/Staff-Discussion-Notes/Issues/2020/01/16/Finance-and-Inequality-45129.

i   Amundi Research. 2020. The Day After #12—Changing Shares of Labour and Capital Incomes: What Implications for Investors? 21 October. https://research-center.amundi.com/article/day-after-12-changing-shares-labour-and-capital-incomes-what-implications-investors.

continued on next page

Box 4: Opening the Pandora's Box of Social Risks—Consequences of Investors   *continued*

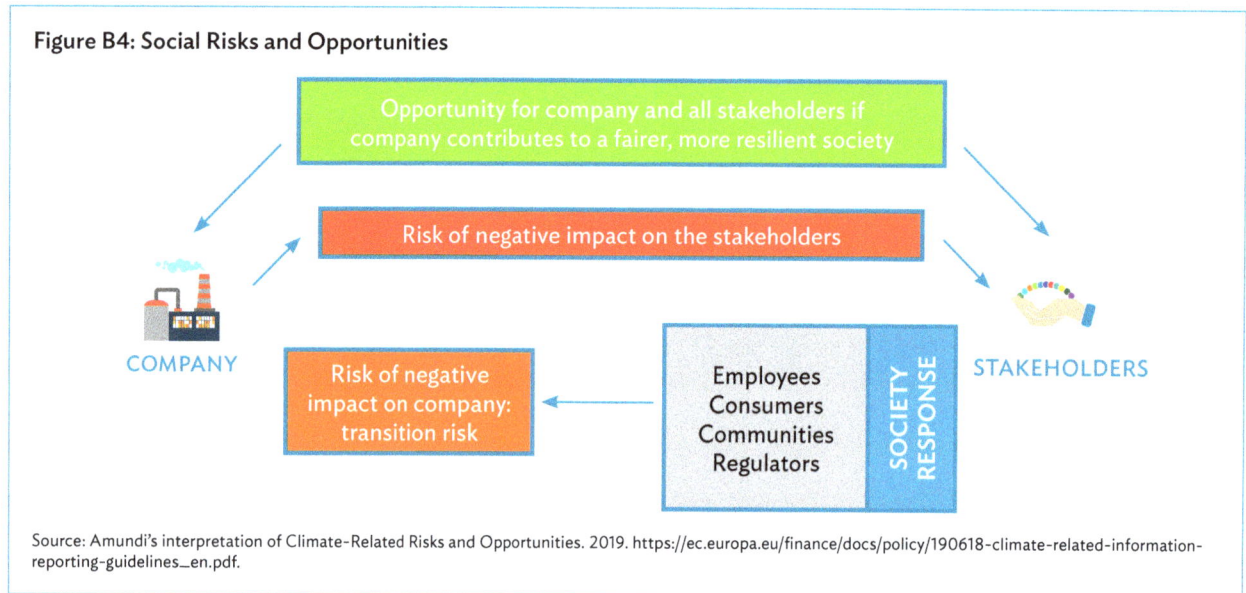

Figure B4: Social Risks and Opportunities

Opportunity for company and all stakeholders if company contributes to a fairer, more resilient society

Risk of negative impact on the stakeholders

COMPANY

Risk of negative impact on company: transition risk

Employees
Consumers
Communities
Regulators

SOCIETY RESPONSE

STAKEHOLDERS

Source: Amundi's interpretation of Climate-Related Risks and Opportunities. 2019. https://ec.europa.eu/finance/docs/policy/190618-climate-related-information-reporting-guidelines_en.pdf.

cohesion—in the form of employees' well-being, protection, and fair pay compared to C-level executives—has been identified as a key driver of financial performance.

2. Consumers

Consumers' impact on the future profitability of a company is immense, as they are capable of deciding whether they will continue to buy from that specific company or if they will turn to a direct competitor. For socially responsible companies, there is a higher likelihood that consumers will adopt pro-company behavior (e.g., purchases, loyalty, advocacy), leading to higher profitability and excess returns.[j]

3. Communities and Society

Companies that have invested resources in building positive relationships with the communities impacted by their operations have more financial value than their peers, all other elements being equal. These relationships can help ensure that operations and profitability are not heavily impacted by social unrest.

4. Regulatory Authorities

Regulatory bodies and governments are powerful key stakeholders that can profoundly impact a firm's operations,

business model, and profitability through policies and regulations. Companies that have not taken social-focused regulations into consideration—such as corporate tax reform or minimum wage increases—will experience worse financial results than their peers, as they would be more affected by an expected future wave of policies.

Incorporating Social Risks in the Investment Value Chain

From an investment perspective, investors should consider social risks in terms of the degrees of materiality outlined above. In terms of ESG analysis, asset owners, supported by asset managers and advisors, can identify the most material social factors influencing their portfolios. At Amundi, ESG analysis is performed based on 37 criteria, of which 19 are related to the social pillar. The generic criteria applied to all analyzed sectors include labor conditions and nondiscrimination, health and safety, client and supplier relations, product and societal responsibility, and local communities and human rights, thereby mirroring the stakeholder-based framework proposed.[k]

Investment solutions are also at investors' disposal to help in the process of integrating social risks. A first possibility would be to apply a filter excluding issuers with poor social practices from their portfolios. Asset owners can go one step further and invest in strategies and instruments, such as social

[j] Fornell, C., S. Mithas, F. Morgeson, and M.S. Krishnan. 2006. Customer Satisfaction and Stock Prices: High Returns, Low Risk. *Journal of Marketing*. 70 (1). https://www.researchgate.net/publication/228233854_Customer_Satisfaction_and_Stock_Prices_High_Returns_Low_Risk.
[k] Amundi. Documentation. https://www.amundi.com/int/ESG/Documentation.

continued on next page

Box 4: Opening the Pandora's Box of Social Risks—Consequences of Investors   *continued*

bonds, that directly encourage issuers to modify their business models toward higher social inclusivity and impact.

Within an ESG investment approach, ongoing engagement and consistent voting at annual general meetings are also crucial in terms of setting best practice and encouraging portfolio companies to develop and improve their social responsibility.

The COVID-19 crisis has opened the Pandora's box of social risks, which is unlikely to be closed again. On the bright side, firms with positive social practices are expected to provide attractive investment opportunities in the years to come. Whatever the case may be, we expect social risks to become increasingly material and a key development to watch.

Box 5: Social Bond Issues for Developing Asia

The COVID-19 pandemic has exacerbated a huge financing gap in the developing world as funds are needed to help economies, communities, and people weather the pandemic's impacts and build back better.[1] This has created an opportunity for social bonds to bridge the financing gap and address underlying social issues such as poverty and inequality.[a]

Social bond issuance set new records in 2020 and the first half of 2021, both globally and in Asia and the Pacific (**Figure B5.1**). Yet, the following questions remain: Does social bond financing actually address the region's social challenges? Which social impact areas should issuers prioritize? And finally,

should issuers and policy makers first address low-hanging fruit or instead focus on complex and challenging problems?

There has been a significant change in social bonds' impact areas in response to COVID-19, most notably a shift from a focus on affordable housing to more pandemic-related projects such as education and training (including unemployment support), and socioeconomic crisis alleviation (**Figure B5.2**).

Figure B5.1: Global Green and Social Bond Issuance, 2017–H1 2021 (USD-equivalent notional)

USD billion equivalent

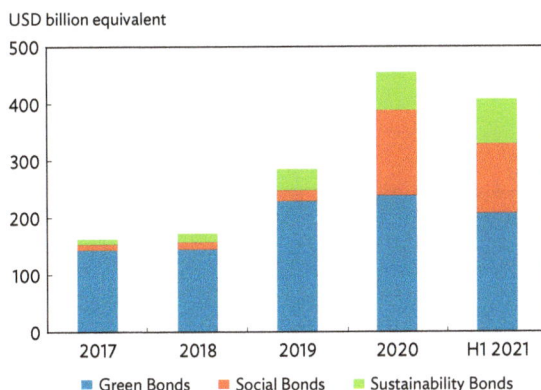

H1 = first half, USD = United States dollar.
Source: Author's calculations based on review of Bloomberg LP data, issuer social bond frameworks, and reviewer second opinions.

Figure B5.2: Global ICMA-Compliant Social Bond Issuance by Year and SBP Project Type, 2017–H1 2021 (USD-equivalent notional, estimated)

USD billion equivalent

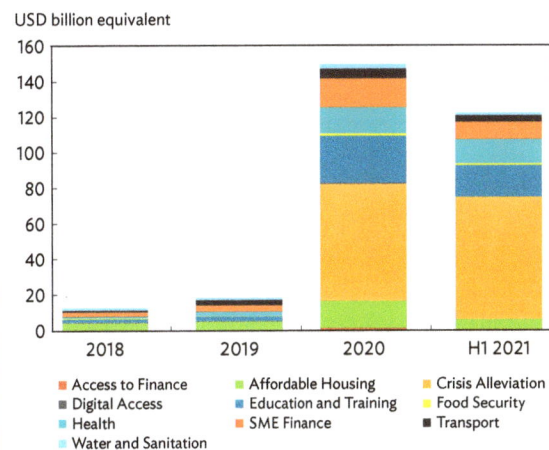

H1 = first half, ICMA = International Capital Market Association, SBP = Social Bond Principles, SMEs = small and medium-sized enterprises, USD = United States dollar.
Sources: Authors' calculations based on review of Bloomberg data, issuer social bond frameworks, and reviewer second opinions.

---

[a] This section was written by Jane Hughest (lead author), author of *Greed Gone Good: A Roadmap to Creating Social and Financial Value*, and Jason Mortimer, head of sustainable investment—fixed income and senior portfolio manager, Nomura Asset Management. The content is based on Asian Development Bank. 2021. Promoting Social Bonds for Impact Investments in Asia. https://www.adb.org/publications/social-bonds-impact-investments-asia.
[b] Social bonds are fixed-income instruments that raise funds for new and existing projects with positive social outcomes.

continued on next page

Box 5: Social Bond Issues for Developing Asia *continued*

Social Bonds in Response to COVID-19 Impacts in Developing Asia

Socioeconomic crisis alleviation. The pandemic has exposed the weaknesses, inequities, and shortages associated with health care in many developing economies and highlighted the need for increased investment. Health care investments funded via social bonds can both alleviate the impact of the COVID-19 crisis and improve services to prevent or mitigate such crises in the future.

The combination of rising expenditures to combat COVID-19's impacts and widening government budget deficits also makes a compelling case for the greater use of social bonds. By raising money from private investors to directly address social needs, social bonds can direct capital to the provision of health care and other services for vulnerable and underserved populations.

Food, water, and sanitation. One reason why COVID-19 and other diseases spread in developing economies is that billions of people lack adequate clean water for washing and sanitation, resulting from decades of underinvestment in water infrastructure. COVID-19 has also exposed weaknesses in global food systems by straining supplies, disrupting food chains, and increasing food insecurity for millions of people.

Small and medium-sized enterprises. SMEs account for more than 96% of all businesses in Asia and the Pacific, and more than two-thirds of the region's private sector workforce. However, even before the pandemic SMEs faced numerous obstacles, particularly a lack of access to finance. Providing support to SMEs to overcome the economic shock of the pandemic and associated lockdowns is a socioeconomic necessity with potentially large multiplier effects.

Education and gender equity. The pandemic has negatively impacted educational opportunities in developing economies, dramatically widening the educational deficit. Social bonds can channel funding toward building schools and hiring teachers. Promoting girls' education is one of the most effective ways to drive sustainable development, improve health, reduce conflict, and save lives. Social bonds can also help advance gender equity and empower women by improving working conditions for female employees, decreasing the digital divide between men and women, and providing capital for underfunded women-owned SMEs.

Social Impact Measurement: Supporting an Effective Social Bond Market

As issuance of green, social, and sustainability bonds explodes globally, investor concern is mounting about "greenwashing" and "social-washing," which is when issuers claim that the funds will be used for worthy environmental or social causes but the money ends up elsewhere. The International Capital Market Association recommends that issuers track and report qualitative performance indicators as well as quantitative metrics; and some national authorities are beginning to mandate environmental, social, and governance disclosures. Also, it is becoming more common for issuers to map their bonds' use of proceeds to individual Sustainable Development Goals.

Conclusions: Maximizing Impact in the COVID-19 Era and Beyond

It is challenging for policy makers, issuers, and investors to make investment decisions and plan resource allocation without clear and standardized impact measurement methods. Thankfully, impact measurement is improving and social bonds have proven to be valuable instruments for directing private capital to socioeconomic priorities. From resilience to SME support, gender equity to health care, social bonds are an essential tool for financing the work needed for developing Asia to build back better.

Bond Market Developments in the Second Quarter of 2021

Size and Composition

Emerging East Asia's local currency bond market expanded in the second quarter of 2021 to reach a size of USD21.1 trillion at the end of June.

The outstanding amount of local currency (LCY) bonds in emerging East Asia climbed to USD21.1 trillion at the end of June.[2] Overall growth quickened to 2.9% quarter-on-quarter (q-o-q) in the second quarter (Q2) of 2021 from 2.2% q-o-q in the first quarter (Q1) (**Figure 1a**). The faster expansion was driven primarily by higher growth in the government bond segment, as most governments in the region renewed bond issuance to support additional stimulus measures amid the resurgence of COVID-19 outbreaks.

All of the region's bond markets except for Hong Kong, China posted positive q-o-q growth rates in Q2 2021. Among those that recorded an expansion, the markets of Singapore and Viet Nam posted the fastest q-o-q growth in Q2 2021, while the markets of Indonesia and the Republic of Korea showed the weakest q-o-q growth. Compared with Q1 2021, the q-o-q growth rate accelerated in four of the region's nine markets.

On a year-on-year (y-o-y) basis, emerging East Asia's LCY bond market grew at a weaker pace of 13.6% in Q2 2021 versus 15.9% in Q1 2021 (**Figure 1b**). Five of the region's nine markets experienced a slowdown in y-o-y growth in Q2 2021 compared to the previous quarter. Nonetheless, all nine markets posted positive y-o-y growth in Q2 2021. Indonesia and Viet Nam posted the fastest y-o-y expansions, while Hong Kong, China and Thailand had the weakest y-o-y growth rates.

The bond market of the People's Republic of China (PRC) remained the largest in the region at the end of June with outstanding bonds of USD16.5 trillion. The PRC's share of the regional market inched up to 78.1% at the end of June from 78.0% at the end of March. Overall expansion in the PRC's bond market accelerated to 3.0% q-o-q in Q2 2021

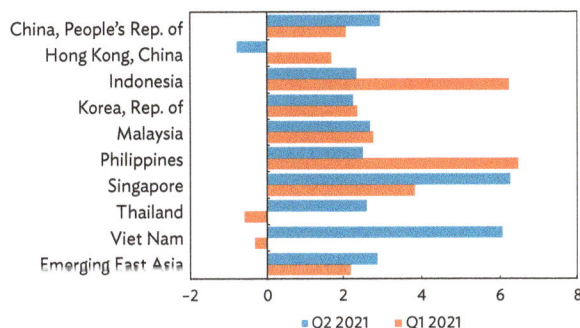

Figure 1a: Growth of Local Currency Bond Markets in the First and Second Quarters of 2021 (q-o-q, %)

q-o-q = quarter-on-quarter, Q1 = first quarter, Q2 = second quarter.
Notes:
1. For Singapore, corporate bonds outstanding are based on *AsianBondsOnline* estimates.
2. Calculated using data from national sources.
3. Growth rates are calculated from local currency base and do not include currency effects.
4. Emerging East Asia growth figures are based on 30 June 2021 currency exchange rates and do not include currency effects.
Sources: People's Republic of China (CEIC); Hong Kong, China (Hong Kong Monetary Authority); Indonesia (Bank Indonesia; Directorate General of Budget Financing and Risk Management, Ministry of Finance; and Indonesia Stock Exchange); Republic of Korea (KG Zeroin Corporation and The Bank of Korea); Malaysia (Bank Negara Malaysia); Philippines (Bureau of the Treasury and Bloomberg LP); Singapore (Monetary Authority of Singapore, Singapore Government Securities, and Bloomberg LP); Thailand (Bank of Thailand); and Viet Nam (Bloomberg LP and Vietnam Bond Market Association).

from 2.1% q-o-q in Q1 2021. Growth was mainly driven by strong issuance of Treasury and other government bonds, which expanded 35.8% q-o-q in Q2 2021, as the central and local governments resumed debt issuance to support domestic economic recovery. Growth in the PRC's corporate bond stock slowed to 2.3% q-o-q in Q2 2021 from 2.9% q-o-q in Q1 2021. On a y-o-y basis, the PRC's bond market expanded 14.4% in Q2 2021, down from 17.3% in the previous quarter.

The Republic of Korea's LCY bond market remained the second-largest in the region in Q2 2021, with its outstanding bonds reaching USD2.4 trillion at the end of June. Its share of the regional total was steady from Q1 2021 to Q2 2021 at 11.6%. Overall growth in the Republic of Korea's LCY bond market slowed to 2.3% q-o-q in Q2 2021 from 2.4% q-o-q in the previous

---

[2] Emerging East Asia comprises the People's Republic of China; Hong Kong, China; Indonesia; the Republic of Korea; Malaysia; the Philippines; Singapore; Thailand; and Viet Nam.

Figure 1b: Growth of Local Currency Bond Markets in the First and Second Quarters of 2021 (y-o-y, %)

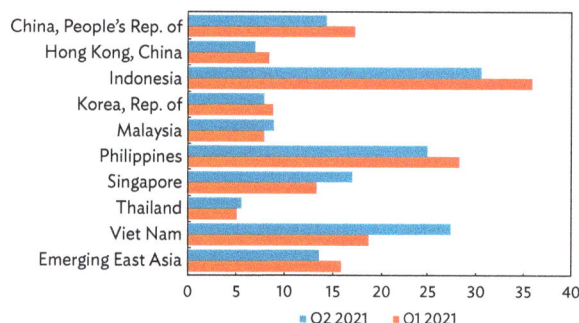

Q1 = first quarter, Q2 = second quarter, y-o-y = year-on-year.
Notes:
1. For Singapore, corporate bonds outstanding are based on *AsianBondsOnline* estimates.
2. Calculated using data from national sources.
3. Growth rates are calculated from local currency base and do not include currency effects.
4. Emerging East Asia growth figures are based on 30 June 2021 currency exchange rates and do not include currency effects.
Sources: People's Republic of China (CEIC); Hong Kong, China (Hong Kong Monetary Authority); Indonesia (Bank Indonesia; Directorate General of Budget Financing and Risk Management, Ministry of Finance; and Indonesia Stock Exchange); Republic of Korea (KG Zeroin Corporation and The Bank of Korea); Malaysia (Bank Negara Malaysia); Philippines (Bureau of the Treasury and Bloomberg LP); Singapore (Monetary Authority of Singapore, Singapore Government Securities, and Bloomberg LP); Thailand (Bank of Thailand); and Viet Nam (Bloomberg LP and Vietnam Bond Market Association).

quarter. Government bonds outstanding increased 3.2% q-o-q in Q2 2021, down from 4.0% q-o-q growth in Q1 2021. Growth in this market segment was driven mainly by an expansion in outstanding central government bonds, as the government continued to issue debt to frontload expenditures for 2021 and bolster domestic economic recovery. The stock of corporate bonds rose 1.6% q-o-q in Q2 2021, up from 1.2% q-o-q growth in the prior quarter. On a y-o-y basis, the Republic of Korea's bond market growth moderated to 7.9% in Q2 2021 from 8.9% in Q1 2021.

The size of the LCY bond market in Hong Kong, China stood at USD312.5 billion at the end of June. Total bonds outstanding contracted 0.8% q-o-q in Q2 2021, reversing the 1.7% q-o-q growth in the previous quarter. The negative growth was driven primarily by a contraction in the corporate bond segment, which shrank 3.7% q-o-q in Q2 2021 due to maturities and weak issuance during the review period. Growth in the outstanding stock of government bonds jumped to 2.4% q-o-q in Q2 2021 from 0.2% q-o-q in Q1 2021, boosted mainly by strong

growth in outstanding Hong Kong Special Administrative Region Bonds. Robust issuance, which included HKD20.0 billion of inflation-linked iBonds, contributed to this growth. On a y-o-y basis, the bond market of Hong Kong, China expanded 7.0% in Q2 2021, down from 8.4% in the previous quarter.

The aggregate amount of LCY bonds outstanding among member economies of the Association of Southeast Asian Nations (ASEAN) stood at USD1.9 trillion at the end of June.[3] Overall growth rose to 3.5% q-o-q in Q2 2021 from 3.0% q-o-q in Q1 2021. The total government bond stock reached USD1.3 trillion, while corporate bonds outstanding stood at USD0.5 trillion at the end of June. Thailand's LCY bond market remained the largest among all ASEAN members, while Singapore's bond market surpassed that of Malaysia in Q2 2021 to become the second-largest ASEAN market.

The outstanding amount of Thailand's LCY bonds totaled USD443.4 billion at the end of June. The bond market expanded 2.6% q-o-q in Q2 2021, reversing the 0.6% q-o-q drop in the previous quarter. Both the government and corporate segments rebounded in Q2 2021, contributing to the overall expansion. Government bonds outstanding rose 1.7% q-o-q in Q2 2021 versus a 0.8% q-o-q drop in the prior quarter. Strong issuance supported this growth, as the government issued debt during the review period to help support its fiscal deficit and fund relief measures amid a new wave of COVID-19 outbreaks. The stock of outstanding corporate bonds rose 5.1% q-o-q in Q2 2021, reversing the 0.1% q-o-q decline in Q1 2021. On an annual basis, growth in the Thai LCY bond market climbed to 5.6% in Q2 2021 from 5.1% in the previous quarter.

Singapore's LCY bonds outstanding reached USD412.5 billion at the end of June, with growth jumping to 6.3% q-o-q in Q2 2021 from 3.8% q-o-q in Q1 2021. Government bonds outstanding expanded 4.8% q-o-q in Q2 2021, as all components of the government bond market recorded an expansion, led by a 9.0% q-o-q rise in outstanding Monetary Authority of Singapore (MAS) bills and notes. The growth in MAS bills was spurred in part by the issuance of floating-rate notes tied to the Singapore overnight rate average in June, which was part of the MAS's ongoing move from the London Interbank Offered Rate to a benchmark alternative. Growth in the corporate

---

[3] LCY bond statistics for ASEAN include the markets of Indonesia, Malaysia, the Philippines, Singapore, Thailand, and Viet Nam.

bond segment surged 9.3% q-o-q in Q2 2021, following a contraction of 0.3% q-o-q in the previous quarter, driven by strong issuance as firms took advantage of the low-interest-rate environment. On a y-o-y basis, growth in Singapore's LCY bond market quickened to 17.1% in Q2 2021 from 13.4% in Q1 2021.

Malaysia's LCY bonds outstanding amounted to USD408.1 billion at the end of June. Overall growth inched down to 2.7% q-o-q in Q2 2021 from 2.8% q-o-q in Q1 2021. Growth in the government bond segment eased to 3.9% q-o-q in Q2 2021 from 4.3% q-o-q in the previous quarter. The expansion in government bonds stemmed primarily from strong growth in central government bonds, as outstanding central bank bills fell during the review period. Growth in corporate bonds outstanding rose to 1.3% q-o-q in Q2 2021 from 1.0% q-o-q in the prior quarter. On a y-o-y basis, Malaysia's LCY bond market growth climbed to 8.9% in Q2 2021 from 7.9% in Q1 2021.

Malaysia is home to the largest *sukuk* (Islamic bond) market in emerging East Asia, with a total of USD256.7 billion of *sukuk* outstanding at the end of June. *Sukuk* accounted for 62.9% of Malaysia's LCY bond market. At the end of June, the outstanding stock of government *sukuk* totaled USD105.7 billion, or 47.5% of Malaysia's government bond market. Outstanding corporate *sukuk* stood at USD151.0 billion, or 81.4% of the corporate bond market.

The outstanding amount of Indonesia's LCY bonds reached USD338.8 billion at the end of June, with growth moderating to 2.4% q-o-q in Q2 2021 from 6.2% q-o-q in the previous quarter. Expansion in the government bond segment drove overall growth, as the corporate bond segment contracted during the review period. The stock of outstanding government bonds rose 2.8% q-o-q in Q2 2021, driven by growth in the outstanding stock of central government bonds and Bank Indonesia instruments. The corporate bond market contracted 2.4% in Q2 2021, reversing the 1.7% q-o-q growth in the prior quarter, as issuance continued to decline amid the risk-off sentiment brought about by a new wave of COVID-19 outbreaks. On a y-o-y basis, Indonesia's LCY bond market growth eased to 30.6% in Q2 2021 from 36.0% in Q1 2021.

The Philippine LCY bond market reached a size of USD191.6 billion at the end of June. Overall growth

weakened to 2.5% q-o-q in Q2 2021 from 6.5% q-o-q in Q1 2021. The stock of outstanding government bonds expanded 3.9% q-o-q in Q2 2021 after rising 8.4% q-o-q in the prior quarter. Growth in outstanding Treasury bonds and Bangko Sentral ng Pilipinas securities contributed to the growth, as the government continued to issue debt to support the economy against the protracted impact of the pandemic. The contraction in the LCY corporate bond market steepened, declining 3.9% q-o-q in Q2 2021 after a 2.0% q-o-q drop in Q1 2021, as market sentiment remained subdued amid prolonged social distancing measures. On an annual basis, growth in the Philippine LCY bond market moderated to 25.1% y-o-y in Q2 2021 from 28.4% y-o-y in the previous quarter.

The LCY bond market in Viet Nam remained the smallest in emerging East Asia with an outstanding bond stock of USD76.5 billion at the end of June. Viet Nam's LCY bond market rebounded in Q2 2021, rising 6.1% q-o-q after a 0.3% q-o-q contraction in the prior quarter. The growth stemmed from the corporate bond segment, which expanded 36.6% q-o-q during the review period. The stock of outstanding government bonds continued to contract, declining 0.5% q-o-q in Q2 2021 after a 1.1% q-o-q drop in Q1 2021, due to a relatively high volume of maturities that outpaced robust issuance. On a y-o-y basis, Viet Nam's LCY bond market growth accelerated to 27.5% in Q2 2021 from 18.7% in Q1 2021.

At the end of March, government bonds continued to account for the majority of emerging East Asia's total LCY bond stock, representing a 62.1% share. In nominal terms, the outstanding amount of government bonds in the region climbed to USD13.1 trillion at the end of June (**Table 1**). Except for Viet Nam, all government bond markets in the region posted positive q-o-q growth in Q1 2021. The q-o-q growth of the region's government bond stock quickened to 3.3% q-o-q in Q2 2021 from 2.1% q-o-q in Q1 2021, as most governments raised debt to fund additional relief measures amid the resurgence of COVID-19 cases generated by the delta variant. On a y-o-y basis, growth in the region's LCY government bond market moderated to 15.9% in Q2 2021 from 18.0% in the previous quarter.

The PRC and the Republic of Korea maintained their positions as the first- and second-largest government bond markets in the region, respectively, with a combined

Table 1: Size and Composition of Local Currency Bond Markets

| | Q2 2020 | | Q1 2021 | | Q2 2021 | | Growth Rate (LCY-base %) | | | | Growth Rate (USD-base %) | | | |
| | Amount (USD billion) | % share | Amount (USD billion) | % share | Amount (USD billion) | % share | Q2 2020 | | Q2 2021 | | Q2 2020 | | Q2 2021 | |
							q-o-q	y-o-y	q-o-q	y-o-y	q-o-q	y-o-y	q-o-q	y-o-y
China, People's Rep. of														
Total	13,189	100.0	15,799	100.0	16,507	100.0	5.6	17.9	3.0	14.4	5.8	14.6	4.5	25.2
Government	8,332	63.2	10,102	63.9	10,591	64.2	5.4	15.1	3.3	16.2	5.6	11.9	4.8	27.1
Corporate	4,857	36.8	5,697	36.1	5,917	35.8	5.9	22.9	2.3	11.3	6.1	19.5	3.9	21.8
Hong Kong, China														
Total	293	100.0	315	100.0	313	100.0	0.6	(0.7)	(0.8)	7.0	0.6	0.04	(0.7)	6.8
Government	149	51.0	153	48.6	157	50.1	(1.1)	(0.7)	2.4	5.1	(1.1)	0.1	2.5	4.9
Corporate	144	49.0	162	51.4	156	49.9	2.4	(0.8)	(3.7)	8.9	2.4	(0.02)	(3.6)	8.7
Indonesia														
Total	264	100.0	330	100.0	339	100.0	6.6	14.9	2.4	30.6	21.9	13.7	2.5	28.5
Government	234	88.6	301	91.0	310	91.4	8.0	16.6	2.8	34.8	23.4	15.5	3.0	32.6
Corporate	30	11.4	30	9.0	29	8.6	(3.0)	3.0	(2.4)	(1.6)	10.9	2.0	(2.2)	(3.2)
Korea, Rep. of														
Total	2,123	100.0	2,382	100.0	2,447	100.0	3.1	9.5	2.3	7.9	4.5	5.2	2.8	15.3
Government	863	40.7	992	41.6	1,028	42.0	4.6	9.7	3.2	11.6	6.0	5.3	3.7	19.1
Corporate	1,260	59.3	1,390	58.4	1,419	58.0	2.1	9.4	1.6	5.4	3.5	5.0	2.1	12.6
Malaysia														
Total	363	100.0	398	100.0	408	100.0	1.8	4.5	2.7	8.9	2.6	0.7	2.6	12.5
Government	193	53.3	215	54.0	223	54.6	3.2	6.4	3.9	11.5	4.0	2.6	3.8	15.2
Corporate	169	46.7	183	46.0	185	45.4	0.2	2.4	1.3	6.0	1.0	(1.3)	1.2	9.5
Philippines														
Total	150	100.0	188	100.0	192	100.0	5.2	11.5	2.5	25.1	7.1	14.8	1.9	27.6
Government	119	79.0	155	82.7	160	83.8	6.8	11.6	3.9	32.7	8.7	14.9	3.3	35.4
Corporate	32	21.0	33	17.3	31	16.2	(0.4)	11.0	(3.9)	(3.6)	1.4	14.3	(4.5)	(1.6)
Singapore														
Total	340	100.0	388	100.0	412	100.0	2.9	12.4	6.3	17.1	5.0	9.2	6.2	21.2
Government	219	64.5	260	66.9	272	65.9	4.4	16.5	4.8	19.7	6.5	13.2	4.7	24.0
Corporate	121	35.5	129	33.1	141	34.1	0.3	5.7	9.3	12.3	2.4	2.6	9.2	16.3
Thailand														
Total	435	100.0	443	100.0	443	100.0	2.1	3.2	2.6	5.6	42.1	56.6	0.1	1.9
Government	315	72.4	325	73.3	322	72.7	4.1	4.4	1.7	6.1	39.3	51.4	(0.8)	2.4
Corporate	120	27.6	118	26.7	121	27.3	(2.6)	(0.03)	5.1	4.4	49.9	72.1	2.6	0.8
Viet Nam														
Total	59	100.0	72	100.0	76	100.0	(1.2)	11.7	6.1	27.5	0.7	12.2	6.3	28.5
Government	51	85.8	59	82.3	59	77.2	(7.6)	5.0	(0.5)	14.7	(5.9)	5.4	(0.2)	15.6
Corporate	8	14.2	13	17.7	17	22.8	70.3	81.8	36.6	104.5	73.6	82.6	36.9	106.2
Emerging East Asia														
Total	17,216	100.0	20,315	100.0	21,138	100.0	5.0	15.6	2.9	13.6	6.4	13.3	4.1	22.8
Government	10,475	60.8	12,561	61.8	13,122	62.1	5.1	13.9	3.3	15.9	6.6	11.9	4.5	25.3
Corporate	6,742	39.2	7,754	38.2	8,017	37.9	4.7	18.3	2.2	10.0	5.9	15.7	3.4	18.9
Japan														
Total	11,082	100.0	11,604	100.0	11,520	100.0	0.4	1.3	(0.4)	7.0	0.02	1.2	(0.7)	4.0
Government	10,288	92.8	10,793	93.0	10,691	92.8	0.4	1.0	(0.6)	7.0	0.1	0.9	(0.9)	3.9
Corporate	794	7.2	811	7.0	829	7.2	(0.1)	4.9	2.6	7.5	(0.4)	4.9	2.3	4.4

( ) = negative, LCY = local currency, q-o-q = quarter-on-quarter, Q1 = first quarter, Q2 = second quarter, USD = United States dollar, y-o-y = year-on-year.
Notes:
1. For Singapore, corporate bonds outstanding are based on *AsianBondsOnline* estimates.
2. Corporate bonds include issues by financial institutions.
3. Bloomberg LP end-of-period LCY–USD rates are used.
4. For LCY base, emerging East Asia growth figures based on 30 June 2021 currency exchange rates and do not include currency effects.
5. Emerging East Asia comprises the People's Republic of China; Hong Kong, China; Indonesia; the Republic of Korea; Malaysia; the Philippines; Singapore; Thailand; and Viet Nam.
Sources: People's Republic of China (CEIC); Hong Kong, China (Hong Kong Monetary Authority); Indonesia (Bank Indonesia; Directorate General of Budget Financing and Risk Management, Ministry of Finance; and Indonesia Stock Exchange); Republic of Korea (KG Zeroin Corporation and The Bank of Korea); Malaysia (Bank Negara Malaysia); Philippines (Bureau of the Treasury and Bloomberg LP); Singapore (Monetary Authority of Singapore, Singapore Government Securities, and Bloomberg LP); Thailand (Bank of Thailand); Viet Nam (Bloomberg LP and Vietnam Bond Market Association); and Japan (Japan Securities Dealers Association).

share of 88.5% of the region's total government bond stock at the end of June. ASEAN economies accounted for 10.3% of the region's government bonds outstanding. Among ASEAN economies, the largest government bond markets were those of Thailand, Indonesia, and Singapore.

LCY corporate bonds outstanding in emerging East Asia reached USD8.0 trillion at the end of June. On a q-o-q basis, growth in the region's corporate bond market dipped to 2.2% in Q1 2021 from 2.4% in the previous quarter. Compared with Q1 2021, growth in the corporate bond segment slowed in the PRC, while corporate bond markets contracted in Hong Kong, China; Indonesia; and the Philippines. On a y-o-y basis, growth in the region's LCY corporate bond stock moderated to 10.0% in Q2 2021 from 12.6% in Q1 2021.

The PRC and the Republic of Korea accounted for the majority of emerging East's Asia's corporate bond stock with a combined share of 91.5% at the end of June. ASEAN economies accounted for 6.5% of emerging East Asia's corporate bond stock. Within ASEAN, Malaysia had the largest corporate bond market at the end of June, followed by Singapore and Thailand.

The aggregate amount of LCY bonds outstanding in emerging East Asia was equivalent to 96.2% of the region's gross domestic product (GDP) at the end of June, which was barely changed from 96.4% at the end of March but up from 91.9% at the end of June 2020 (**Table 2**). Economies continued to borrow from the bond market to support growth as a resurgence of COVID-19 infections disrupted economic activities across the region. The GDP equivalent of government bonds was barely changed at 59.7% in Q2 2021 from 59.6% in Q1 2021, as well as for corporate bonds at 36.5% from 36.8% over the same period.

All markets in the region saw their bond market's share of GDP decline from Q1 2020 to Q2 2021 except for the Republic of Korea and Singapore, which both posted increases, and Thailand, where the share was practically unchanged. In Q2 2021, the Republic of Korea's bond market had the largest share of GDP in the region at 147.2%, followed by Malaysia (121.9%) and Singapore (112.8%). The rest of the markets in the region all had shares below 100%, with Viet Nam having the smallest share at 22.8%.

Table 2: Size and Composition of Local Currency Bond Markets (% of GDP)

	Q2 2020	Q1 2021	Q2 2021
China, People's Rep. of			
Total	94.8	97.7	97.5
Government	59.9	62.5	62.5
Corporate	34.9	35.2	34.9
Hong Kong, China			
Total	82.8	89.5	87.2
Government	42.2	43.4	43.7
Corporate	40.6	46.0	43.5
Indonesia			
Total	24.0	31.0	30.8
Government	21.2	28.2	28.1
Corporate	2.7	2.8	2.6
Korea, Rep. of			
Total	138.3	146.1	147.2
Government	56.2	60.8	61.9
Corporate	82.1	85.2	85.4
Malaysia			
Total	113.8	122.9	121.9
Government	60.7	66.3	66.5
Corporate	53.1	56.6	55.4
Philippines			
Total	39.8	51.1	50.6
Government	31.4	42.2	42.4
Corporate	8.4	8.8	8.2
Singapore			
Total	97.0	110.9	112.8
Government	62.5	74.1	74.4
Corporate	34.4	36.7	38.4
Thailand			
Total	82.9	88.7	88.8
Government	60.0	65.0	64.6
Corporate	22.9	23.6	24.3
Viet Nam			
Total	22.5	23.5	22.8
Government	19.3	19.3	17.6
Corporate	3.2	4.2	5.2
Emerging East Asia			
Total	91.9	96.4	96.2
Government	55.9	59.6	59.7
Corporate	36.0	36.8	36.5
Japan			
Total	219.1	239.4	235.0
Government	203.4	229.7	218.1
Corporate	15.7	16.7	16.9

GDP = gross domestic product, Q1 = first quarter, Q2 = second quarter.
Notes:
1. Data for GDP are from CEIC.
2. For Singapore, corporate bonds outstanding are based on *AsianBondsOnline* estimates.
Sources: People's Republic of China (CEIC); Hong Kong, China (Hong Kong Monetary Authority); Indonesia (Bank Indonesia; Directorate General of Budget Financing and Risk Management, Ministry of Finance; and Indonesia Stock Exchange); Republic of Korea (KG Zeroin Corporation and The Bank of Korea); Malaysia (Bank Negara Malaysia); Philippines (Bureau of the Treasury and Bloomberg LP); Singapore (Monetary Authority of Singapore, Singapore Government Securities, and Bloomberg LP); Thailand (Bank of Thailand); Viet Nam (Bloomberg LP and Vietnam Bond Market Association); and Japan (Japan Securities Dealers Association).

For government bonds, Singapore had the highest share of GDP in the region at 74.4% in Q2 2021, while Viet Nam had the lowest at 17.6%. For corporate bonds, the Republic of Korea had the highest share at 85.4%, while Indonesia had the smallest at 2.6%.

Foreign Investor Holdings

Movements in the shares of foreign investor holdings of local currency government bonds differed across emerging East Asian markets in Q2 2021.

The foreign investor holdings' share increased in the LCY bond markets of the PRC, the Philippines, and Thailand between Q1 2021 and Q2 2021, while it marginally declined in Indonesia (**Figure 2**). The shares in Malaysia and Viet Nam were almost unchanged over the same period. Differences in the stage of economic recovery and the associated risks among economies in the region largely influenced the portfolio management of foreign investors.

Foreign investors remained keen on PRC government bonds in Q2 2021, as denoted by the foreign holdings' share reaching 10.3% at the end of June from 10.1% at the end of March. The underlying appeal of PRC government bonds—yield premium, easy market access, and inclusion in global bond indexes—remained strong,

which prompted offshore investors to flock to the PRC's debt market. From the earliest data available in June 2014, when foreign holdings comprised only 2.0% of outstanding government bonds, this share had increased more than five times by the end of June 2021.

In the Philippines, foreign participants increased their exposure to government bonds, with the foreign holdings' share rising 0.2 percentage points in Q2 2021 to 2.5% at the end of June. This was in contrast to Q1 2021 when this share experienced a quarterly drop of 0.5 percentage point to 2.3%. The increase in foreign holdings in Q2 2021 was supported by fund inflows amid relatively few COVID-19 cases at that time, which in turn persuaded the government to hasten the reopening of the economy.

In Thailand, the foreign holdings' share of government bonds registered a quarterly increase in Q2 2021 to 13.7% at the end of June from 12.9% at the end of March, ending the downtrend in place since Q1 2019. Foreign investors took profits from government bonds in 2019 and since then had cut their exposure to the Thai market due to low returns. A turnaround was seen in Q2 2021, as Thai sovereign bonds' appeal to foreign investors was restored by the yield differential with United States (US) Treasuries favoring local bonds, expectations of the Thai baht's appreciation, and low inflationary pressures.

Foreign holdings of Indonesian government bonds continued to decline in Q2 2021, albeit only slightly to 22.8% at the end of June from 22.9% at the end of March. While there were fund flows into the market from overseas investors, these were not large enough to offset the outflows and reverse the declining trend. Concerns over Indonesia's economic recovery against the backdrop of rising COVID-19 cases negatively affected foreign sentiment.

The shares of foreign holdings in the government bond markets of Malaysia and Viet Nam barely changed in Q2 2021. In Malaysia, the share was 26.0% at the end of June, supported by continued inflows of foreign funds, albeit in an abated manner due to heightened risk aversion. Despite this, Malaysia's foreign holdings' share remained the highest among all emerging East Asian markets, having overtaken Indonesia's in Q1 2021. In Viet Nam, foreign participation in the government bond market registered a share of 0.8% in Q2 2021, the lowest in the region.

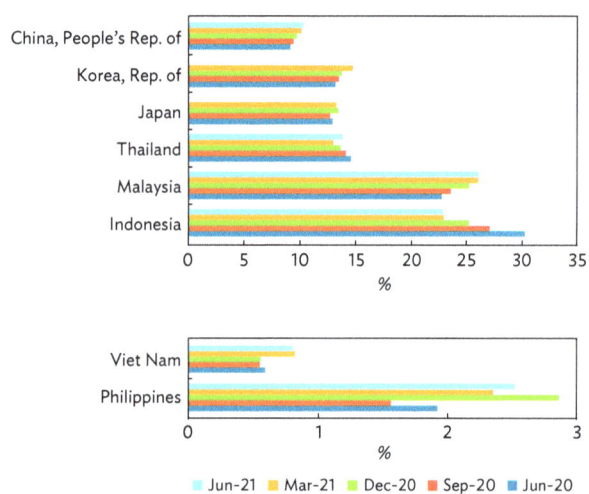

Figure 2: Foreign Holdings of Local Currency Government Bonds in Select Asian Markets (% of total)

Note: Data for Japan and the Republic of Korea are as of 31 March 2021.
Source: *AsianBondsOnline*.

In the Republic of Korea, the foreign holdings' share climbed to 14.6% of the government bond market at the end of March from 13.6% at the end of December 2020. The increase was backed by the entry of foreign funds into the market in Q1 2021, as investors reinvested capital after a large amount of maturities toward the end of 2020. The Republic of Korea's strong growth recovery and shorter timeframe toward monetary policy normalization prompted foreigners to increase their exposure to the Korean LCY bond market in pursuit of better returns.

Foreign Fund Flows into Bond Markets

Foreign buying of government bonds occurred in all emerging East Asian markets in Q2 2021.

LCY bond markets in emerging East Asia received total net inflows of USD36.8 billion in Q2 2021 (**Figure 3**). In contrast to previous quarters where at least one market experienced a foreign sell-off, all six markets in the region for which data are available drew in net foreign funds in Q2 2021. Investor sentiment toward emerging East Asian markets improved as the region's economic recovery

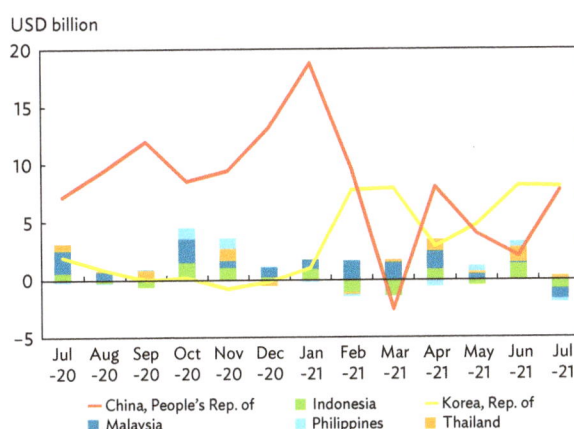

Figure 3: Foreign Capital Flows in Local Currency Bond Markets in Emerging East Asia

USD = United States dollar.
Notes:
1. The Republic of Korea and Thailand provided data on bond flows. For the People's Republic of China, Indonesia, Malaysia, and the Philippines, month-on-month changes in foreign holdings of LCY government bonds were used as a proxy for bond flows.
2. Data as of 31 July 2021.
3. Figures were computed based on 31 July 2021 exchange rates to avoid currency effects.
Sources: People's Republic of China (*Wind Information*); Indonesia (Directorate General of Budget Financing and Risk Management, Ministry of Finance); Republic of Korea (Financial Supervisory Service); Malaysia (Bank Negara Malaysia); Philippines (Bureau of the Treasury); and Thailand (Thai Bond Market Association).

was fairly gaining traction with progress being made in vaccination drives. Low inflation and yield gap against US Treasuries in favor of emerging East Asian markets also encouraged foreign fund flows into the region. However, foreign fund net inflows in Q2 2021 were lower compared to the USD44.6 billion of inflows in Q1 2021.

The resurgence of COVID-19 cases driven by the more transmissible delta variant remained a key risk that could derail the region's recovery and dampen investor confidence. Declining inflows in Q2 2021 compared to the previous 2 quarters were indicative of investor cautiousness. Investors may have been remanaging their portfolios, likely by directing capital toward the US given its better prospects for economic recovery and shorter time to policy normalization. In Q2 2021, the largest monthly inflows occurred in April (USD13.8 billion) before slowing in May (USD9.4 billion) and rebounding in June (USD13.5 billion).

In the PRC, foreign fund inflows amounted to USD14.1 billion in Q2 2021. Attractive returns generated demand for PRC government bonds as an important part of foreign investors' portfolios. The PRC's inclusion in major global bond indexes, such as the FTSE World Government Bond Index starting in October, also drove the influx of overseas funds into its government bond market. While the PRC's bond market continued to attract offshore funds, the inflows during Q2 2021 were nearly half that in Q1 2021. After experiencing net outflows in March as rising US Treasury yields dimmed PRC government bonds' appeal, foreign investors returned to the domestic market with a net USD8.0 billion of inflows in April. Inflows slowed in May (USD4.0 billion) and declined further in June (USD2.1 billion). The monthly numbers in Q2 2021 suggested the decreased momentum of fund inflows, which could have been due to disappointment among investors over an extension of the FTSE World Government Bond Index inclusion period to 3 years from 1 year. And while there remained a yield premium over developed economies, the difference has been narrowing.

The Republic of Korea drew in USD15.9 billion of foreign funds in Q2 2021, down from USD16.8 billion in Q1 2021. Although inflows into the Korean government bond market slowed during the quarter, they surpassed those into the PRC market, making the Republic of Korea emerging East Asia's largest recipient of foreign funds during Q2 2021. The government bond market sustained its investment appeal because of high yields and the strength of the Korean won, owing to the economy's resilient growth recovery and current account surplus. Expectations of a sooner hike in the Bank of Korea's policy rate also prompted foreign buying of Korean government bonds during the quarter. In Q2 2021, monthly inflows into the government bond market were highest in June (USD8.2 billion) and lowest in April (USD2.9 billion).

Foreign fund inflows into the Malaysian government bond market slowed to USD2.1 billion in Q2 2021 from USD3.9 billion in Q1 2021. While offshore investors remained net buyers of government bonds, their interest in the Malaysian market appeared to be faltering. In April, the bond market received a net USD1.6 billion of foreign funds, but this fell to USD0.5 billion in May and to USD0.1 billion in June. Reduced foreign investor appetite can be attributed to increased risk aversion generated by the rising number of COVID-19 infections that clouded the economic recovery.

Indonesia, the Philippines, and Thailand each saw improved foreign fund flows in Q2 2021 from the preceding quarter. In Indonesia, outflows in Q1 2021 were reversed in Q2 2021 when it attracted a net USD1.8 billion of inflows. Indonesia managed to draw in foreign capital despite a spike in COVID-19 cases that gave it the highest number of infections in the region. On a monthly basis, the Indonesian government bond market received net inflows in April (USD0.9 billion) and June (USD1.4 billion), which were partially countered by outflows in May of USD0.5 billion.

Foreign appetite for Philippine government bonds also recovered from the previous quarter as the market received a net USD0.3 billion of inflows in Q2 2021. The foreign selling streak in place since the start of the year continued through April, which saw USD0.6 billion in net outflows, the biggest fund withdrawal since May 2020. A rebound in foreign fund inflows occurred in May and June with USD0.5 billion each. The turnaround can be attributed to the continued reopening of the economy on the back of looser mobility restrictions as the reported number of COVID-19 infections were relatively low during these months.

In Thailand, foreign investors bought a net USD2.5 billion of Thai government bonds in Q2 2021, up from only USD0.1 billion in Q1 2021, which signaled restored investor confidence in the local bond market. The net

overseas buying was traced to attractive returns largely due to the expected appreciation of the Thai baht and a low inflation rate. Capital inflows amounted to USD1.0 billion in April, USD0.2 billion in May, and USD1.3 billion in June.

In July, emerging East Asia's government bond market recorded net foreign fund inflows of USD14.1 billion. Compared with the prior month, July's inflows were higher even when three out of the six markets for which data are available experienced a foreign sell-off. The PRC largely drove July's increase as foreign investors bought USD7.7 billion of its government bonds, nearly quadruple the amount in June. Other markets that saw net inflows in July were the Republic of Korea (USD8.1 billion) and Thailand (USD0.3 billion). On the other hand, net outflows were recorded in Indonesia (–USD0.8 billion), Malaysia (–USD0.9 billion), and the Philippines (–USD0.3 billion), all of which can be attributed to risk-off sentiment among foreign investors as the number of COVID-19 cases in those economies accelerated.

LCY Bond Issuance

LCY bond issuance in emerging East Asia rose to USD2.2 trillion in Q2 2021.

Q2 2021 saw more active issuance from emerging East Asia, as total LCY bond issuance reached USD2.2 trillion, up from USD2.0 trillion in Q1 2021 (**Table 3**). Overall growth quickened to 14.6% q-o-q, reversing the 1.6% q-o-q decline in Q1 2021. The high volume of issuance was driven largely by governments needing to support relief and recovery programs as the spread of COVID-19 variants in some markets continued to pummel economic growth. Issuance volume remained high relative to pre-COVID-19 levels, reflecting the region's resilience and capacity to fund vast amounts of spending through LCY borrowing.

All bond segments recorded faster q-o-q increases in issuance in Q2 2021. The issuance of central bank bonds and corporate bonds rebounded from declines in Q1 2021, while Treasury and other government bonds posted robust growth. Issuance accelerated in seven out of nine regional markets in Q2 2021, led by the PRC and the Republic of Korea, which are home to the two largest bond markets in emerging East Asia. The two markets that had less issuance in Q2 2021 were the Philippines and Hong Kong, China.

Table 3: Local-Currency–Denominated Bond Issuance (gross)

	Q2 2020		Q1 2021		Q2 2021		Growth Rate (LCY-base %) Q2 2021		Growth Rate (USD-base %) Q2 2021	
	Amount (USD billion)	% share	Amount (USD billion)	% share	Amount (USD billion)	% share	q-o-q	y-o-y	q-o-q	y-o-y
China, People's Rep. of										
Total	1,414	100.0	1,255	100.0	1,492	100.0	17.1	(3.6)	18.9	5.5
Government	736	52.1	575	45.8	793	53.1	35.8	(1.6)	37.8	7.7
Central Bank	0	0.0	0	0.0	0	0.0	–	–	–	–
Treasury and Other Govt.	736	52.1	575	45.8	793	53.1	35.8	(1.6)	37.8	7.7
Corporate	678	47.9	680	54.2	699	46.9	1.3	(5.8)	2.8	3.1
Hong Kong, China										
Total	138	100.0	143	100.0	140	100.0	(2.2)	2.1	(2.1)	1.9
Government	107	77.9	105	73.5	110	78.5	4.5	2.9	4.6	2.7
Central Bank	106	77.1	105	73.3	106	75.9	1.4	0.5	1.5	0.3
Treasury and Other Govt.	1	0.8	0.3	0.2	4	2.6	944.4	243.9	945.7	243.3
Corporate	30	22.1	38	26.5	30	21.5	(20.8)	(0.8)	(20.7)	(1.0)
Indonesia										
Total	30	100.0	34	100.0	39	100.0	12.0	30.9	12.2	28.7
Government	29	97.9	33	95.9	37	96.6	12.9	29.2	13.1	27.1
Central Bank	8	26.4	12	34.5	21	55.3	79.7	174.0	80.0	169.6
Treasury and Other Govt.	21	71.5	21	61.4	16	41.3	(24.6)	(24.3)	(24.5)	(25.5)
Corporate	0.6	2.1	1	4.1	1	3.4	(8.5)	108.3	(8.3)	104.9
Korea, Rep. of										
Total	208	100.0	205	100.0	235	100.0	14.2	5.8	14.7	13.0
Government	96	46.4	91	44.3	101	43.2	11.1	(1.5)	11.7	5.2
Central Bank	33	16.0	29	14.3	31	13.3	6.4	(12.2)	6.9	(6.2)
Treasury and Other Govt.	63	30.3	62	30.1	70	29.9	13.4	4.2	14.0	11.3
Corporate	112	53.6	114	55.7	134	56.8	16.6	12.2	17.2	19.8
Malaysia										
Total	22	100.0	24	100.0	24	100.0	1.0	7.4	0.9	11.0
Government	14	63.7	14	56.9	13	55.3	(1.8)	(6.7)	(1.8)	(3.6)
Central Bank	0.2	1.1	0	0.0	0	0.0	–	(100.0)	–	(100.0)
Treasury and Other Govt.	14	62.6	14	56.9	13	55.3	(1.8)	(5.1)	(1.8)	(1.9)
Corporate	8	36.3	10	43.1	11	44.7	4.7	32.1	4.6	36.4
Philippines										
Total	14	100.0	44	100.0	42	100.0	(4.0)	195.4	(4.5)	201.5
Government	13	96.0	43	97.3	41	97.7	(3.5)	200.6	(4.0)	206.8
Central Bank	0	0.0	23	51.2	26	60.8	14.0	–	13.4	–
Treasury and Other Govt.	13	96.0	20	46.0	16	36.9	(23.0)	13.6	(23.4)	15.9
Corporate	0.6	4.0	1	2.7	1	2.3	(20.2)	70.6	(20.6)	74.1
Singapore										
Total	136	100.0	169	100.0	194	100.0	15.3	38.4	15.3	43.4
Government	131	96.8	166	98.4	185	95.4	11.8	36.4	11.8	41.3
Central Bank	106	78.2	142	84.2	155	80.0	9.6	41.7	9.5	46.7
Treasury and Other Govt.	25	18.6	24	14.2	30	15.4	25.2	14.5	25.1	18.6
Corporate	4	3.2	3	1.6	9	4.6	228.3	98.9	228.1	106.0
Thailand										
Total	79	100.0	63	100.0	69	100.0	11.4	(9.5)	8.7	(12.7)
Government	71	89.6	54	85.1	54	78.4	2.6	(20.8)	0.1	(23.6)
Central Bank	59	75.2	34	53.1	35	51.0	7.0	(38.6)	4.4	(40.8)
Treasury and Other Govt.	11	14.4	20	32.0	19	27.4	(4.7)	72.6	(7.1)	66.6
Corporate	8	10.4	9	14.9	15	21.6	61.9	87.4	57.9	80.8

continued on next page

Table 3 *continued*

	Q2 2020		Q1 2021		Q2 2021		Growth Rate (LCY-base %)		Growth Rate (USD-base %)	
	Amount (USD billion)	% share	Amount (USD billion)	% share	Amount (USD billion)	% share	Q2 2021		Q2 2021	
							q-o-q	y-o-y	q-o-q	y-o-y
Viet Nam										
Total	6	100.0	3	100.0	9	100.0	271.1	57.1	272.0	58.4
Government	2	39.6	2	67.8	4	47.7	160.9	89.2	161.6	90.8
Central Bank	0	0.0	0	0.0	0	0.0	–	–	–	–
Treasury and Other Govt.	2	39.6	2	67.8	4	47.7	160.9	89.2	161.6	90.8
Corporate	4	60.4	0.8	32.2	5	52.3	503.0	36.0	504.5	37.1
Emerging East Asia										
Total	2,046	100.0	1,940	100.0	2,245	100.0	14.6	2.2	15.7	9.7
Government	1,201	58.7	1,082	55.8	1,340	59.7	23.0	4.8	23.8	11.6
Central Bank	313	15.3	344	17.7	375	16.7	9.3	18.5	9.0	19.9
Treasury and Other Govt.	888	43.4	738	38.1	965	43.0	29.3	0.3	30.7	8.7
Corporate	845	41.3	858	44.2	905	40.3	4.2	(1.3)	5.5	7.0
Japan										
Total	406	100.0	664	100.0	505	100.0	(23.7)	28.0	(24.0)	24.3
Government	370	91.1	640	96.4	462	91.5	(27.6)	28.5	(27.8)	24.8
Central Bank	20	5.0	0	0.0	10	1.9	–	(51.8)	–	(53.2)
Treasury and Other Govt.	350	86.1	640	96.4	452	89.6	(29.1)	33.2	(29.3)	29.4
Corporate	36	8.9	24	3.6	43	8.5	79.7	22.3	79.1	18.8

( ) = negative, – = not applicable, LCY = local currency, q-o-q = quarter-on-quarter, Q1 = first quarter, Q2 = second quarter, USD = United States dollar, y-o-y = year-on-year.
Notes:
1. Corporate bonds include issues by financial institutions.
2. Bloomberg LP end-of-period LCY–USD rates are used.
3. For LCY base, emerging East Asia growth figures are based on 30 June 2021 currency exchange rates and do not include currency effects.
Sources: People's Republic of China (CEIC); Hong Kong, China (Hong Kong Monetary Authority); Indonesia (Bank Indonesia; Directorate General of Budget Financing and Risk Management, Ministry of Finance; and Indonesia Stock Exchange); Republic of Korea (KG Zeroin Corporation and); Malaysia (Bank Negara Malaysia); Philippines (Bureau of the Treasury and Bloomberg LP); Singapore (Singapore Government Securities and Bloomberg LP); Thailand (Bank of Thailand and ThaiBMA); Viet Nam (Bloomberg LP, Hanoi Stock Exchange, and Vietnam Bond Market Association); and Japan (Japan Securities Dealers Association).

Although positive, the region's growth in bond issuance slipped to 2.2% y-o-y in Q2 2021 from 8.6% y-o-y in Q1 2021, with most regional markets posting a growth moderation or decline. On the other hand, the Philippines and Singapore saw faster y-o-y increases in issuance while the Republic of Korea and Viet Nam recorded positive y-o-y growth in Q2 2021 compared to Q1 2021.

Much of the issuance was dominated by government bonds, which accounted for 59.7% of the regional total in Q2 2021. This represented an uptick from the 55.7% share recorded in the previous quarter as corporate bond issuance remained muted. Total issuance of government bonds reached USD1,340.1 billion in Q2 2021, as growth swelled to 23.0% q-o-q from a marginal hike of 0.3% q-o-q in Q1 2021. On a y-o-y basis, government bond issuance eased to 4.8% in Q2 2021 from 10.8% in the preceding quarter.

Treasury securities and other government bonds accounted for 72.0% of the government bond issuance total during Q2 2021. This was up from the 68.5% share

recorded in Q1 2021. Growth in Treasury and other government bond issuance accelerated to 29.3% q-o-q in Q2 2021 from only 0.5% q-o-q in Q1 2021, due largely to the resurgence of issuance by the PRC; Hong Kong, China; Singapore; and Viet Nam. All four markets recorded contractions in issuance of Treasury and other government bonds in Q1 2021. On the other hand, issuance declined in Indonesia, Malaysia, the Philippines, and Thailand during the quarter compared with Q1 2021. While remaining positive, growth in Treasury and other government bonds in the Republic of Korea moderated in Q2 2021 from Q1 2021.

Regional issuance of central bank instruments rebounded in Q2 2021 on growth of 9.3% q-o-q, compared with a decline of 0.4% q-o-q in Q1 2021, to reach USD375.2 billion. The higher issuance volume during the quarter was fueled by increased issuance from the MAS as well as the Hong Kong Monetary Authority, Bank Indonesia, the Bank of Korea, and Bank of Thailand. On the other hand, the Bangko Sentral ng Pilipinas tapered its issuance, while Bank Negara Malaysia and the

State Bank of Vietnam have yet to resume issuance of central bank instruments. On a y-o-y basis, central bank issuance rose 18.5% in Q2 2021 versus 7.0% in Q1 2021.

Corporate bond issuance in emerging East Asia also recovered, with growth rising to 4.2% q-o-q in Q2 2021 following a decline of 3.9% q-o-q in Q1 2021. Growth was buoyed by higher bond sales in six markets in Q2 2021 compared with the previous quarter. Only the markets of Indonesia; the Philippines; and Hong Kong, China saw q-o-q declines in the issuance of corporate bonds in Q2 2021. On an annual basis, corporate bond sales in the region contracted 1.3% y-o-y in Q2 2021 versus a 5.9% y-o-y hike in the preceding quarter.

Total bond issuance in the PRC reached USD1,491.8 billion in Q2 2021, with growth rebounding strongly to 17.1% q-o-q from a contraction of 2.6% q-o-q in the prior quarter. The rapid growth in issuance in the PRC was largely due to increased sales of government bonds, which rose 35.8% q-o-q in Q2 2021 to USD792.8 billion after a 2.2% q-o-q decline in Q1 2021. The uptick in government bond issuance was largely due to increased issuance in local government bonds. Owing to the PRC's economic recovery and, correspondingly, improved revenue collection, Treasury bond issuance fell 4.5% q-o-q. Risk control measures also led to a 9.6% q-o-q decline in policy bank bond issuance. Compared with the same period in 2020, the PRC's LCY bond issuance declined 3.6% y-o-y in Q2 2021, a turnaround from the 8.0% y-o-y expansion in Q1 2021.

Much of the growth in government bond issuance stemmed from local government bonds, with issuance rising 173.5% q-o-q. The exponential increase was due to a low base effect, as local government bond issuance was curtailed in Q1 2021 due to a delay in the granting of local government bond quotas. Local governments subsequently issued more in Q2 2021 to make up for the shortfall and meet their respective quotas. However, the Government of the PRC remained focused on risk control as the aggregate local government bond issuance quota of CNY3.65 trillion for 2021 was less than the 2020 quota of CNY6.75 trillion. Furthermore, local government bond issuance for the first half of 2021 fell 4.2% y-o-y. On a y-o-y basis, total government bond issuance fell 1.6% in Q2 2021.

In contrast, corporate bonds grew 1.3% q-o-q in Q2 2021 to reach USD699.0 billion, after contracting

3.0% q-o-q in the prior quarter, as the improved economic outlook encouraged issuance. However, the PRC's risk control strategy dampened sentiments, as Q2 2021 issuance was down 5.8% y-o-y. The PRC also tightened restrictions on the issuance of debt by local government financing vehicles.

In the Republic of Korea, total bond sales tallied USD235.1 billion in Q2 2021, as growth surged to 14.2% q-o-q from only 1.6% q-o-q in Q1 2021. Corporate bond issuance contributed to much of the growth, rising 16.6% q-o-q in Q2 2021 and reversing the 9.9% q-o-q decline in the previous quarter as corporates took advantage of the low-interest-rate environment. Government bonds also contributed to the overall issuance growth as Treasury and other government bonds expanded 13.4% q-o-q in Q2 2021 in line with the government's frontloading policy. Central bank issuance was also up 6.4% q-o-q in Q2 2021. On an annual basis, LCY bond issuance in the Republic of Korea grew 5.8% y-o-y in Q2 2021 after declining 3.6% y-o-y in the preceding quarter.

LCY bond issuance in Hong Kong, China totaled USD140.2 billion in Q2 2021, a further contraction of 2.2% q-o-q following a 2.0% q-o-q decline in Q1 2021. The q-o-q contraction was due to reduced issuance of corporate bonds during the quarter in contrast to Q1 2021 when the government bond segment dragged down the overall issuance growth. Corporate bond sales slumped 20.8% q-o-q in Q2 2021 after rising 9.6% q-o-q in Q1 2021. On the other hand, government bonds posted growth of 4.5% q-o-q, buoyed by a tenfold increase in the issuance of Hong Kong Special Administrative Region Bonds. In June, the Hong Kong Monetary Authority issued a HKD20.0 billion inflation-linked retail bond, or iBond, the eighth of a series since the first issuance in 2011. Issuance of Exchange Fund Bills and Exchange Fund Notes rose a modest 1.4% q-o-q. On an annual basis, growth in issuance of LCY bonds in Hong Kong, China moderated to 2.1% y-o-y in Q2 2021 from 5.9% in Q1 2021.

Collectively, LCY bond issuance of ASEAN member economies reached USD377.7 billion in Q2 2021, representing a 16.8% share of emerging East Asia's issuance total. This, however, was a decline from the 17.1% share logged in Q1 2021 due to robust issuance in both the PRC and the Republic of Korea in Q2 2021. Overall bond issuance growth in ASEAN markets soared to 12.6% q-o-q in Q2 2021 from a marginal hike of

0.4% q-o-q in Q1 2021. All ASEAN member economies posted higher bond sales during the quarter vis-à-vis Q1 2021 except for the Philippines. The most active issuers were in Singapore, Thailand, and the Philippines, which accounted for 51.4%, 18.2%, and 11.2%, respectively, of the ASEAN issuance total in Q2 2021. On an annual basis, ASEAN issuance grew 30.7% y-o-y in Q2 2021, up from 21.7% y-o-y in Q1 2021.

Total LCY bond issuance in Singapore reached USD194.3 billion in Q2 2021 on growth of 15.3% q-o-q. This was stronger than the previous quarter's 4.7% q-o-q gain. Both government and corporate bond issuance growth accelerated on a q-o-q basis, but the larger gain was for corporate bonds. Corporate bond issuance grew 228.3% q-o-q in Q2 2021 after declining 17.9% q-o-q in Q1 2021, as companies issued longer-term maturities to lock in lower interest rates. Government bonds also contributed to the growth, with issuance rising 11.8% q-o-q in Q2 2021, up from a 5.1% q-o-q hike in the prior quarter. Issuance of Singapore Government Securities bills and bonds rose 25.2% q-o-q, after declining 3.9% q-o-q in the prior quarter, as the government reopened more tenors. Central bank issuance had a strong showing in Q2 2021, rising 9.6% q-o-q as the government continued to promote the use of MAS floating-rate notes, which use the Singapore overnight rate average for benchmark pricing. On a y-o-y basis, growth in LCY bond sales in Singapore accelerated to 38.4% in Q2 2021 from 27.5% in Q1 2021.

In Thailand, LCY bond issuance grew 11.4% q-o-q in Q2 2021 to USD68.9 billion after declining 11.1% q-o-q in Q1 2021. While both government bond and corporate bond issuance was stronger than in the previous quarter, market growth was largely driven by corporate bond issuance, which rose 61.9% q-o-q in Q2 2021 versus 6.4% q-o-q in the previous quarter. Thailand's government bond issuance grew 2.6% q-o-q to USD54.0 billion after falling 13.6% q-o-q in Q1 2021. Growth in government bonds was solely due to gains in central bank issuance, which rose 7.0% q-o-q in Q2 2021 after declining 29.0% q-o-q in Q1 2021. In March, the Bank of Thailand started issuing a floating-rate bond that is linked to the Thai Overnight Repurchase Rate. In contrast, Treasury bonds and other government bonds issuance fell 4.7% q-o-q, reversing the 34.5% q-o-q hike in the preceding quarter. On a y-o-y basis, LCY bond issuance in Thailand contracted 9.5% in Q2 2021 versus a 16.3% decline in Q1 2021.

LCY bond issuance in the Philippines fell 4.0% q-o-q in Q2 2021 to USD42.1 billion, a reversal from the 53.5% q-o-q gain in Q1 2021. Both government bond and corporate bond issuance posted q-o-q declines. The Government of the Philippines' bond issuance fell 3.5% q-o-q to USD41.2 billion due to a 23.0% q-o-q decline in Treasury and other government bonds from a high base in Q1 2021 that was driven by the issuance of a USD9.3 billion Retail Treasury Bond in March. A 14.0% q-o-q rise in central bank issuance partially offset the decline in Treasury and other government bond issuance. Philippine corporate bond issuance declined 20.2% q-o-q to USD1.0 billion in Q2 2021, following a 0.2% decline in Q1 2021, as the reimposition of movement restrictions in March led to negative sentiment among corporates. On an annual basis, Philippine LCY bond issuance surged 195.4% y-o-y in Q2 2021 after a gain of 147.4% y-o-y in Q1 2021.

LCY bond issuance in Indonesia reached USD38.6 billion in Q2 2021, as growth rebounded to 12.0% q-o-q from a 24.6% q-o-q contraction in Q1 2021. Government bonds rose 12.9% q-o-q, driven solely by an increase in the issuance of Sukuk Bank Indonesia. Central bank issuance during the quarter was limited to Sukuk Bank Indonesia as the central bank ceased issuance of Sertifikat Bank Indonesia in April (the last issuance was in March). The government also tapered its issuance of Treasury bills and bonds due to excess funds from borrowing in 2020 and improved revenue collection in the first half of 2021. Issuance of Treasury instruments declined 24.6% q-o-q in Q2 2021 after falling 30.9% q-o-q in Q1 2021. Corporate bonds further contracted by 8.5% q-o-q in Q2 2021 from a 4.4% q-o-q decline in the prior quarter. On a y-o-y basis, LCY bond issuance growth in Indonesia moderated to 30.9% in Q2 2021 from 61.0% in Q1 2021.

Malaysia's LCY bond issuance was relatively stable in Q2 2021, with bond issuance rising 1.0% q-o-q to USD24.4 billion in Q2 2021 after an 11.7% q-o-q gain in Q1 2021. The sole driver of growth came from corporate bonds, with issuance rising 4.7% q-o-q in Q2 2021. Malaysia's government bond issuance declined marginally by 1.8% q-o-q in Q2 2021 after rising 81.0% q-o-q in Q1 2021. The Government of Malaysia kept the overall issuance of government bonds stable to fund pandemic measures due to the reimposition of Movement Control Orders in response to the rise in COVID-19 cases. On an annual basis, bond issuance growth in Malaysia eased to 7.4% y-o-y in Q2 2021 from 8.2% y-o-y in Q1 2021.

Viet Nam's LCY bond issuance totaled USD9.3 billion in Q2 2021, gaining 271.1% q-o-q after declining 66.2% q-o-q in Q1 2021. This was due to both government and corporate bond segments posting triple-digit growth rates, albeit from a low base. Government bond issuance rose 160.9% q-o-q from a decline of 68.7% q-o-q in Q1 2021. Viet Nam did not issue any central bank bills in Q2 2021, with all the issuances stemming from Treasury bonds and other government bonds. Corporate bond issuance rose 503.0% q-o-q to USD4.9 billion in Q2 2021 after a 59.2% q-o-q decline in the previous quarter. On an annual basis, issuance rose 57.1% y-o-y in Q2 2021 after declining 68.3% y-o-y in Q1 2021.

Cross-Border Bond Issuance

Emerging East Asia's cross-border bond issuance reached USD7.5 billion in Q2 2021.

Emerging East Asia's cross-border bond issuance registered a 32.8% q-o-q increase in Q2 2021 to reach USD7.5 billion, up from USD5.6 billion in the previous quarter. Institutions from five economies issued cross-border bonds in Q2 2021, led by firms from Hong Kong, China who together accounted for 74.2% of the regional total (**Figure 4**). Other economies with cross-border bond issuance in Q2 2021 were the PRC, the Republic of Korea, Malaysia, and Singapore. Monthly issuance volumes amounted to USD2.3 billion, USD1.5 billion, and USD3.8 billion for the months of April, May, and June, respectively. On an annual basis, total intraregional bond issuance increased 25.8% y-o-y.

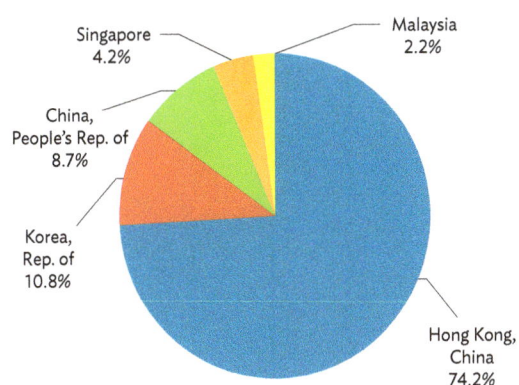

Figure 4: Origin Economies of Intra-Emerging East Asian Bond Issuance in the Second Quarter of 2021

Source: *AsianBondsOnline* calculations based on Bloomberg LP data.

Hong Kong, China accounted for most intraregional bond issuance in emerging East Asia in Q2 2021, reaching an aggregate volume of USD5.6 billion. This was a 44.1% q-o-q increase from the USD3.9 billion raised in Q1 2021 and a 41.9% y-o-y rise from the same period in 2020. The growth can be attributed to the increased attractiveness of issuing dim sum bonds for companies in Hong Kong, China, which has been driven by the strengthening of the Chinese yuan. A total of 23 firms issued cross-border bonds in Q2 2021, which were all denominated in Chinese yuan except for one that was in Singapore dollars. Financial companies led the issuance of intraregional bonds, comprising almost half of the total volume. China Everbright and China Mengniu Dairy were the two largest issuers from Hong Kong, China in Q2 2021 at USD619.5 million each. China Everbright, also had the single-largest issuance with a 3-year bond, while Mengniu Dairy issued multi-tenor short-term bonds. Another notable cross-border bond issuance during the quarter was from government-owned Hong Kong Mortgage Corporation, which raised USD494 million via a multitranche bond. Real estate developer Henderson Land also issued USD418.1 million worth of 2-year and 3-year bonds.

In Q2 2021, the Republic of Korea registered the second-largest cross-border bond issuance volume in the region. The total amount raised reached USD809.7 million, a 49.9% q-o-q increase from USD540.1 million in Q1 2021 and a 55.7% y-o-y increase from USD520.2 million in Q2 2020. Cross-border bond issuances in the Republic of Korea were denominated in Chinese yuan, Hong Kong dollars, and Indonesian rupiah. Four banks issued intraregional bonds, led by the Export–Import Bank of Korea with aggregate issuance of USD323.9 million via 2-year and 3-year bonds. State-owned Korea Development Bank issued USD129.2 million worth of 1-year and 2-year bonds. Other banks include Hana Bank (USD116.6 million) and Kookmin Bank (USD85.2 million). The only nonbank that issued cross-border bonds in the Republic of Korea in Q2 2021 was energy and petrochemical firm Hanhwa Solutions, which raised USD154.9 million via a 3-year bond.

Best Path Global was the sole issuer of intraregional bonds in the PRC in Q2 2021, raising USD648.8 million worth of 1-year HKD-denominated bonds, which was also the region's single-largest issuance during the quarter.

In Singapore, three institutions raised funds in Q2 2021 through the issuance of cross-border bonds totaling USD313 million. China Construction Bank Corporation of Singapore raised USD309.7 million worth of 2-year CNY-denominated bonds, DBS Bank issued USD3.0 million of HKD-denominated bonds, and Nomura International Fund raised USD0.3 million via issuance of 5-year CNY-denominated bonds.

In Malaysia, only two institutions issued intraregional bonds in Q2 2021 with an aggregate amount of USD163.7 million denominated in Chinese yuan and Hong Kong dollars. This included Malayan Banking (USD85.1 million) and CIMB Bank (USD78.6 million).

In Q2 2021, the top 13 issuers of intraregional bonds in emerging East Asia (four issuers shared the 10th spot) had an aggregate issuance volume of USD5.5 billion and comprised 73.5% of the regional total. Ten of the firms were from Hong Kong, China with a total issuance volume of USD4.2 billion. This included China Everbright, Mengniu Dairy, and Hong Kong Mortgage Corporation. The region's top issuer in Q2 2021 was Best Path Global from the PRC. Other firms that were included in the list were from the Republic of Korea and Singapore.

The Chinese yuan remained the predominant currency of cross-border bond issuance in emerging East Asia in Q2 2021 with a total volume of USD5.9 billion and a share of 78.7% of the regional total (**Figure 5**). The continued increase in the issuance of bonds denominated in Chinese yuan was mainly driven by the appreciation of the currency and expectations of its further strengthening. Firms that issued in Chinese yuan came from Hong Kong, China; the Republic of Korea; Malaysia; and Singapore. Other issuance currencies were the Hong Kong dollar (USD1.1 billion, 14.4%), Singapore dollar (USD371.6 million, 5%), and the Indonesian rupiah (USD146.5 million, 2.0%).

G3 Currency Issuance

Issuance of G3 currency bonds in emerging East Asia in January–July totaled USD246.7 billion.

The total amount of G3 currency bond issuance in emerging East Asia was USD246.7 billion in January–July, an expansion of 13.4% y-o-y from the USD217.5 billion recorded during the same period in 2020 (**Table 4**).[4] The growth was due to an increased volume of G3 issuances in most of the region's economies compared to the prior year. Taking advantage of a low-yield environment, some issuers fast-tracked their funding strategies, cautiously expecting that rates might increase in the near future. Sustainable bond issuance increased on a y-o-y basis during the first half of 2021, and this trend was expected to continue during the second half of the year.

Out of the total issuance of G3 currency bonds in the first 7 months of 2021, 93.5% was denominated in US dollars, 5.8% in euros, and 0.7% in Japanese yen. During the review period, USD230.7 billion worth of bonds in US dollars was issued in emerging East Asia, increasing 13.5% y-o-y from a year earlier, spurred by high levels of issuance from the Republic of Korea and Hong Kong, China. A total of USD14.3 billion worth of EUR-denominated bonds was issued in January–July, an increase of 17.1% y-o-y, driven by well-received fund-raising efforts in the PRC, Indonesia, the Philippines, and Singapore. Bond issuance in Japanese yen amounted to USD1.7 billion, a contraction of 17.4% y-o-y as JPY-denominated bond issuance in Hong Kong, China and Indonesia dropped, and Malaysia decided not to issue any such bonds during the review period.

Figure 5: Currency Shares of Intra-Emerging East Asian Bond Issuance in the Second Quarter of 2021

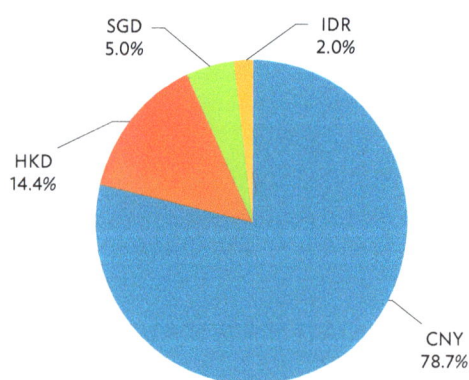

CNY = Chinese yuan, HKD = Hong Kong dollar, IDR = Indonesian rupiah, SGD = Singapore dollar.
Source: *AsianBondsOnline* calculations based on Bloomberg LP data.

---

[4] G3 currency bonds are denominated in either euros, Japanese yen, or US dollars. For the discussion on G3 currency issuance, emerging East Asia comprises Cambodia; the People's Republic of China; Hong Kong, China; Indonesia; the Republic of Korea; Malaysia; the Philippines; Singapore; Thailand; and Viet Nam.

Table 4: G3 Currency Bond Issuance

2020			January–July 2021		
Issuer	Amount (USD billion)	Issue Date	Issuer	Amount (USD billion)	Issue Date
Cambodia	**0.4**		**Cambodia**	**0.0**	
China, People's Rep. of	**232.3**		**China, People's Rep. of**	**134.8**	
Industrial and Commercial Bank of China 3.58% Perpetual	2.9	23-Sep-20	China Development Bank 0.380% 2022	2.0	10-Jun-21
Bank of China 3.60% Perpetual	2.8	4-Mar-20	Prosus 3.061% 2031	1.9	13-Jul-21
Bank of Communications 3.80% Perpetual	2.8	18-Nov-20	Tencent Holdings 3.840% 2051	1.8	22-Apr-21
Others	223.8		Others	129.2	
Hong Kong, China	**34.8**		**Hong Kong, China**	**28.8**	
AIA Group 3.200% 2040	1.8	16-Sep-20	NWD Finance BVI 4.125% Perpetual	1.2	10-Jun-21
MTR Corporation 1.625% 2030	1.2	19-Aug-20	Hong Kong (Sovereign) 1.375% 2031	1.0	2-Feb-21
AIA Group 3.375% 2030	1.0	7-Apr-20	Bank of Communications (Hong Kong) 2.304% 2031	1.0	8-Jul-21
Others	30.9		Others	25.6	
Indonesia	**27.9**		**Indonesia**	**20.4**	
Indonesia (Sovereign) 3.85% 2030	1.7	15-Apr-20	Indonesia (Sovereign) 3.05% 2051	2.0	12-Jan-21
Indonesia (Sovereign) 4.20% 2050	1.7	15-Apr-20	Perusahaan Penerbit SBSN Indonesia III 1.50% 2026	1.2	9-Jun-21
Indonesia (Sovereign) 0.90% 2027	1.2	14-Jan-20	Indonesia (Sovereign) 1.85% 2031	1.3	12-Jan-21
Others	23.4		Others	15.9	
Korea, Rep. of	**30.0**		**Korea, Rep. of**	**30.2**	
Korea Housing Finance Corporation 0.010% 2025	1.2	5-Feb-20	Korea Housing Finance Corporation 0.010% 2026	1.2	29-Jun-21
Korea Development Bank 1.250% 2025	1.0	3-Jun-20	Naver 1.500% 2026	1.1	29-Mar-21
Export–Import Bank of Korea 0.829% 2025	0.9	27-Apr-20	SK Hynix 2.375% 2031	1.0	19-Jan-21
Others	26.9		Others	26.9	
Malaysia	**17.2**		**Malaysia**	**12.1**	
Petronas Capital 4.55% 2050	2.8	21-Apr-20	Petronas Capital 3.404% 2061	1.8	28-Apr-21
Petronas Capital 3.50% 2030	2.3	21-Apr-20	Petronas Capital 2.480% 2032	1.3	28-Apr-21
Others	12.2		Others	9.1	
Philippines	**15.5**		**Philippines**	**7.4**	
Philippines (Sovereign) 2.65% 2045	1.5	10-Dec-20	Philippines (Sovereign) 3.20% 2046	2.3	6-Jul-21
Philippines (Sovereign) 2.95% 2045	1.4	5-May-20	Philippines (Sovereign) 1.75% 2041	0.9	28-Apr-21
Others	12.6		Others	4.2	
Singapore	**14.7**		**Singapore**	**9.6**	
United Overseas Bank 0.010% 2027	1.2	1-Dec-20	BOC Aviation 1.625% 2024	1.0	29-Apr-21
Oversea-Chinese Banking Corporation 1.832% 2030	1.0	10-Sep-20	United Overseas Bank 0.100% 2029	0.9	25-May-21
Others	12.5		Others	7.7	
Thailand	**5.3**		**Thailand**	**2.3**	
Bangkok Bank in Hong Kong, China 5.0% Perpetual	0.8	23-Sep-20	GC Treasury 2.98% 2031	0.7	18-Mar-21
PTT Treasury 3.7% 2070	0.7	16-Jul-20	Krung Thai Bank 4.40% Perpetual	0.6	25-Mar-21
Others	3.8		Others	1.0	
Viet Nam	**0.1**		**Viet Nam**	**1.0**	
Emerging East Asia Total	**378.1**		**Emerging East Asia Total**	**246.7**	
Memo Items:			Memo Items:		
India	**14.3**		**India**	**15.6**	
Vedanta Holdings Mauritius II 13.00% 2023	1.4	21-Aug-20	Vedanta Resources 8.95% 2025	1.2	11-Mar-21
Others	12.9		Others	14.4	
Sri Lanka	**0.4**		**Sri Lanka**	**0.8**	
Sri Lanka (Sovereign) 6.57% 2021	0.1	30-Jul-20	Sri Lanka (Sovereign) 7.95% 2024	0.2	3-May-21
Others	**0.3**		**Others**	**0.6**	

USD = United States dollar.
Notes:
1. Data exclude certificates of deposit.
2. G3 currency bonds are bonds denominated in either euros, Japanese yen, or US dollars.
3. Bloomberg LP end-of-period rates are used.
4. Emerging East Asia comprises Cambodia; the People's Republic of China; Hong Kong, China; Indonesia; the Republic of Korea; Malaysia; the Philippines; Singapore; Thailand; and Viet Nam.
5. Figures after the issuer name reflect the coupon rate and year of maturity of the bond.
Source: *AsianBondsOnline* calculations based on Bloomberg LP data.

More than half of the region's G3 currency bond issuance came from the PRC, where entities issued a combined USD134.8 billion in January–July. The Republic of Korea followed with USD30.2 billion and Hong Kong, China with USD28.8 billion. For the first 7 months of 2021, y-o-y growth in G3 currency bond issuance was posted in the Republic of Korea (63.0%); Hong Kong, China (59.3%); Singapore (34.3%); the PRC (9.4%); and Malaysia (3.9%). Issuance of G3 currency bonds declined in Thailand (–36.8%), the Philippines (–33.5%), and Indonesia (–14.0%). Cambodia had no issuance of G3 currency bonds during the review period after issuing USD-denominated bonds in January–July 2020. On the other hand, Viet Nam resumed issuance of G3 currency bonds in January–July 2021 after not issuing any during the same period in 2020.

Entities from the PRC accounted for 54.6% of all G3 currency bond issuance in emerging East Asia in January–July 2021: USD128.3 billion was issued in US dollars and USD6.5 billion equivalent was issued in euros. In July, technology company Prosus issued a USD1.9 billion 10-year callable bond denominated in US dollars. It also had a dual-tranche issuance of EUR-denominated bonds with tenors of 8 years and 12 years totaling USD2.2 billion. Proceeds from the issuances will be used to finance the company's offer to buy back some of its existing bonds and for general corporate purposes. Also in July, Sunac China Holdings sold a USD-denominated 3.25-year callable bond worth USD400.0 million. The property developer's issuance took advantage of the People's Bank of China's decision to cut the reserve requirement ratio by 50 basis points. Proceeds from the issuance will be used to refinance the company's existing debts.

The Republic of Korea had a 12.2% share of all G3 currency bond issuance during the review period, comprising USD28.4 billion in US dollars and the equivalent of USD1.9 billion in euros. In May and June, the Export–Import Bank of Korea increased its stock of USD-denominated bonds via issuances with tenors ranging from 3 years to 30 years. Part of the export credit agency's issuance was a USD2.0 billion bond with three tranches (3 years, 6 years, and 20 years) issued in June, the proceeds of which will be used for general corporate purposes. In May, the

Korea Development Bank increased its stock of USD-denominated bonds with an issuance of a 4-year bond worth USD200.0 million.

An 11.7% share of G3 currency bonds issued in January–July 2021 came from Hong Kong, China. In terms of currency, USD28.5 billion was issued in US dollars, while JPY-denominated bonds amounted to USD0.2 billion and EUR-denominated bonds totaled USD0.1 billion. In May and July, Graphex Group, a renewable energy company, issued two 2-year convertible bonds denominated in US dollars. Each issuance had a coupon rate of 5.5% and was worth USD500.0 million. In July, Seaspan, an owner and operator of container ships, issued a USD750.0 million 8-year callable bond with a 5.5% periodic distribution rate denominated in US dollars. Proceeds from the issuance will be used to finance projects that fall under the company's Blue Transition Bond Framework, which promotes Seaspan's sustainability efforts.

ASEAN member economies' issuance of G3 currency bonds in January–July 2021 fell 8.4% y-o-y.[5] The ASEAN region's G3 currency bond issuance total was USD52.9 billion, down from USD57.7 billion in January–July 2020 due to reduced issuance from most member economies. As a percentage of emerging East Asia's total G3 currency bond issuance, ASEAN issuance in the first 7 months of 2021 was 21.4% versus a 26.5% share during the same period in the prior year. In spite of a drop in its G3 issuance, Indonesia led all ASEAN members in having the largest G3 issuance during the review period. This was followed by Malaysia, Singapore, the Philippines, Thailand, and Viet Nam.

Indonesia issued USD17.7 billion of USD-denominated bonds in January–July 2021, the equivalent of USD1.8 billion in euros, and USD0.9 billion in Japanese yen, which cumulatively accounted for 8.3% of total G3 issuance in emerging East Asia during the review period. In May, the Government of Indonesia issued the equivalent of USD900.0 million in samurai bonds in six tranches with tenors ranging from 3 years to 20 years. Proceeds from the issuance will be used to fund the government's expanded budget deficit caused by expenditures related to COVID-19. In July, the government had a dual-currency issuance (euros and US dollars), with the USD-denominated bond totaling USD600.0 million

---

[5] For the discussion on G3 currency issuance, data for ASEAN include Cambodia, Indonesia, Malaysia, the Philippines, Singapore, Thailand, and Viet Nam.

and the EUR-denominated bond having about the same equivalent amount. Both were callable bonds. The EUR-denominated bond and the USD-denominated bond had tenors of 8 years and 10 years, respectively. Proceeds from the offering will be used for general budgetary purposes and the funding of COVID-19 relief efforts. In June, Indonesian government's special purpose vehicle Perusahaan Penerbit SBSN Indonesia III issued USD-denominated bonds worth USD3.0 billion in three tranches (5 years, 10 years, and 30 years). Funds raised from the issuance will be used for general purposes, with the 30-year tranche to be used for eligible green projects as outlined in Indonesia's Green Bond and Green Sukuk Framework.

G3 currency bond issuance by Malaysia was 4.9% of emerging East Asia's total during the first 7 months of 2021 with bonds amounting to USD12.1 billion, all of which was denominated in US dollars. May saw Dua Capital issuing a dual-tranche callable bond worth USD1.0 billion. The special purpose vehicle issued the 5-year and 10-year bonds for Khazanah Nasional under the *wakalah* principle wherein the Islamic bonds are backed by an investor and an agent's agreement, and the bondholders are eligible to profits based on the agreement of the two parties. Proceeds raised from the offering will be used for the activities of Khazanah that are Shariah-compliant. Toward the end of June, RHB Bank offered a 5-year bond worth USD500.0 million and with a coupon rate of 1.658%. The issuance was from the bank's USD5.0 billion medium-term note program.

Singapore had a 3.9% share of total G3 currency bond issuance in emerging East Asia during the January–July period, involving USD8.0 billion in US dollars, USD1.5 billion worth of bonds in euros, and the equivalent of USD0.1 billion in Japanese yen. United Overseas Bank issued a EUR-denominated bond in May and a USD-denominated bond in June. The bond denominated in euros amounted to around USD900.0 million and had a tenor of 8 years, while the US dollar issuance was a 5-year bond worth USD150.0 million. The EUR-denominated bond was the first covered bond in Singapore in 2021 and had the longest tenor for a covered bond by a bank in Singapore. GLP, an investment management firm, issued two USD-denominated perpetual securities totaling USD1.2 billion during the last 2 months of the Q2 2021. Both issuances were drawn from GLP's EUR-denominated medium-term note program. Notable among the two issuances was the

USD850.0 million bond issued in May, which is the largest USD-denominated green subordinated perpetual bond offered globally to date. Proceeds from the green issuance will be used to finance eligible green projects based on GLP's Green Finance Framework.

The Philippines accounted for a 3.0% share of total issuance of G3 currency bonds in emerging East Asia during the first 7 months of 2021. Its issuances comprised bonds denominated in US dollars amounting to USD4.5 billion, EUR-denominated bonds worth USD2.5 billion, and USD0.5 billion of bonds in Japanese yen. In July, the Government of the Philippines raised USD3.0 billion from a dual-tranche Dollar Global Bond with tenors of 10.5 years and 25 years. Proceeds from the offering will be used for general purposes, which include budgetary support. In June, SMC Global Power issued a USD600.0 million perpetual bond with a coupon rate of 5.45%. Funds raised from the USD-denominated issuance by the power company will be used mainly for investment in a combined-cycle power plant.

Thailand's share of all G3 currency bonds issued in the region during the review period was 0.9%, with issuance solely in US dollars totaling USD2.3 billion. In July, Minor International, a hospitality, restaurant, and lifestyle company, issued a USD300.0 million perpetual bond with a periodic distribution rate of 2.7%. Proceeds raised from the offering will be used by the company to fund a tender offer for its existing perpetual bond callable on 4 December.

In January–July 2021, 0.4% of all G3 currency issuance in emerging East Asia was from entities in Viet Nam, with a combined USD1.0 billion worth of USD-denominated bonds. In May, property developer BIM Land raised USD200.0 million from a 5-year callable bond. The issuance was the first green bond offering by the company, and the capital raised from it will be used to fund the company's eligible green projects. In July, another real estate developer, Novaland, issued a USD300.0 million 5-year convertible bond. Proceeds from the offering will be used to expand its landbank, fund its project developments, and improve the company's debt profile.

Monthly G3 currency bond issuance in emerging East Asia from July 2020 to July 2021 is presented in **Figure 6**. After a high volume of issuance in April, issuance activities temporarily fell across all economies in the region in May

Figure 6: G3 Currency Bond Issuance in Emerging East Asia

USD billion

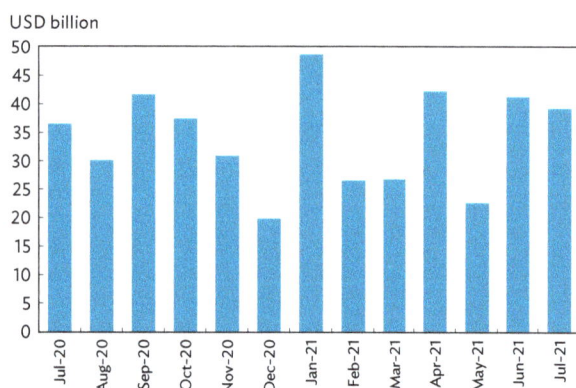

USD = United States dollar.
Notes:
1. Emerging East Asia comprises Cambodia; the People's Republic of China; Hong Kong, China; Indonesia; the Republic of Korea; the Lao People's Democratic Republic; Malaysia; the Philippines; Singapore; Thailand; and Viet Nam.
2. G3 currency bonds are bonds denominated in either euros, Japanese yen, or US dollars.
3. Figures were computed based on 31 July 2021 currency exchange rates and do not include currency effects.
Source: *AsianBondsOnline* calculations based on Bloomberg LP data.

as news of the more contagious delta variant spread around the world, forcing governments to reinstate border closures and movement restrictions. The region's offerings of G3 currency bonds recovered in June and July, spurred by increased issuance from both the PRC and Hong Kong, China.

Emerging East Asia's local currency government bond yields mostly fell on the back of a worsening global economic outlook driven by rising COVID-19 cases amid the emergence of variants.

Rising COVID-19 cases in some parts of the region led some markets to impose quarantine restrictions, threatening to derail the economic growth trajectory for 2021. Individual market impacts were influenced by government responses as well as the pace of their ongoing vaccination campaigns.

A softening economic outlook has affected not only developing economies but also advanced economies. While the US Federal Reserve has shifted to a more hawkish stance, with its updated forecasts for June showing an expected 50 basis points (bps) rise in its federal funds target range in 2023 and its recent

27–28 July monetary policy statement indicating that substantial progress had been made in economic gains, some economic data have indicated a potential slowdown.

The University of Michigan's consumer sentiment index fell 11 points to 70.3 in August on concerns over rising COVID-19 cases. Consumer price inflation was steady at 5.4% in July and June. US yields at the longer-end exhibited a decline over global growth concerns and risk aversion.

While the Federal Reserve shifted to a more hawkish stance, the European Central Bank (ECB) has turned more dovish. While monetary policy was left unchanged during its 22 July meeting, it revised its forward guidance. The ECB is moving toward a symmetric 2.0% inflation target from a previous "near to 2.0%" inflation target. The move will allow the ECB to tolerate inflation running above the 2.0% target in the short-term. The Bank of Japan also largely left its monetary policy unchanged at its 18 June meeting but extended the end of its purchase program of commercial paper and corporate bonds from September 2021 to March 2022.

In emerging East Asia, the largest decline in 2-year yields was seen in the PRC between 15 June and 15 August (**Figure 7a**). This occurred despite the PRC's economic recovery as there are concerns that the PRC's growth momentum might slow. Sentiment was also further driven by a reserve requirement ratio cut of 50 bps by the People's Bank of China in July, suggesting a shift in the PRC's monetary stance.

The Republic of Korea was the only market that saw significant upward movement in its 2-year yield, led by expectations of a rate hike by the Bank of Korea due to rising inflationary pressures. On the other hand, 2-year yield movements for markets such as Malaysia, Thailand, and Viet Nam were roughly stable (**Figure 7b**).

In contrast to its 2-year yield movement, the Republic of Korea's 10-year yield trended downward, tracking global yield trends amid the worsening global outlook (**Figure 8a**). The 10-year yield also fell in the PRC; Hong Kong, China; Singapore; Thailand; and Viet Nam but was relatively stable in Indonesia and Malaysia (**Figure 8b**). In August, 10-year yields spiked in most regional bond markets, tracking US yields and buoyed by a strong recovery in Q2 2021 GDP.

Figure 7a: 2-Year Local Currency Government Bond Yields

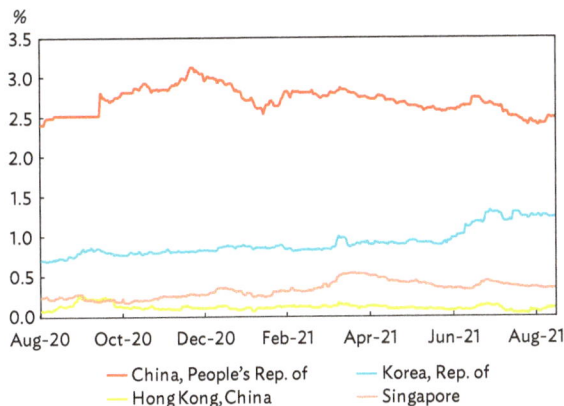

Note: Data coverage is from 1 August 2020 to 15 August 2021.
Source: Based on data from Bloomberg LP.

Figure 7b: 2-Year Local Currency Government Bond Yields

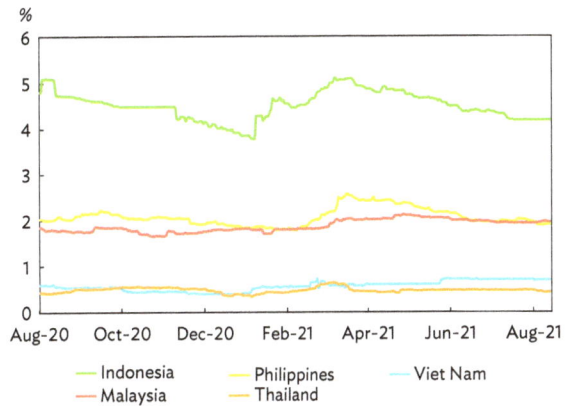

Note: Data coverage is from 1 August 2020 to 15 August 2021.
Source: Based on data from Bloomberg LP.

Figure 8a: 10-Year Local Currency Government Bond Yields

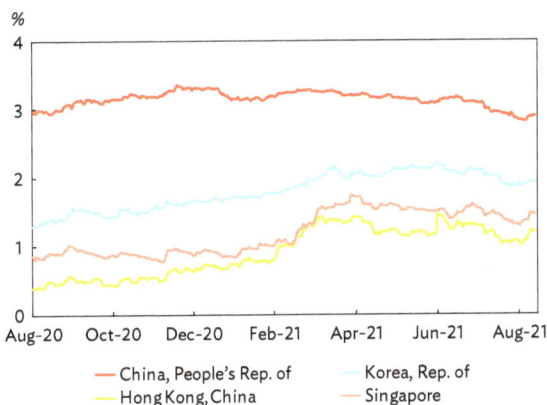

Note: Data coverage is from 1 August 2020 to 15 August 2021.
Source: Based on data from Bloomberg LP.

Figure 8b: 10-Year Local Currency Government Bond Yields

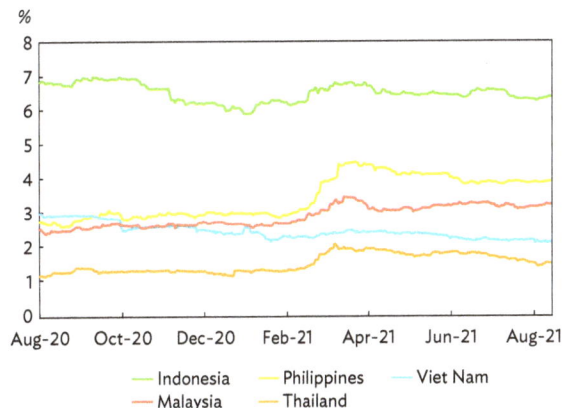

Note: Data coverage is from 1 August 2020 to 15 August 2021.
Source: Based on data from Bloomberg LP.

Similarly, yield curves shifted downward in most emerging East Asian LCY government bond markets between 15 June and 15 August (**Figure 9**). The largest shift was in the PRC's yield curve, which fell an average of 23 bps, with all tenors declining. This was largely due the previously mentioned reserve requirement ratio cut. Viet Nam was the only other market in the region that showed a decline in all tenors, due to strong financial liquidity and a negative economic outlook amid rising COVID-19 cases. The worsening global economic outlook led to yields falling for most tenors in Hong Kong, China; the Philippines; and Thailand. In Indonesia, Malaysia, and the Republic of Korea were yield

curve movements mixed. Singapore's yield curve was mostly unchanged.

In Indonesia, yields fell for maturities of 10 years or less due to continued bond purchases by Bank Indonesia, slower growth expectations over mobility restrictions, and rising risk aversion. In contrast, yields at the longer-end rose due to reduced demand for longer-dated securities from investors, particularly foreign investors. In the Republic of Korea, there was a rise at the shorter-end of the curve driven by expectations of a rate hike by the Bank of Korea, while yields at the longer-end followed declining global yield trends. Subsequently, on 26 August,

Figure 9: Benchmark Yield Curves—Local Currency Government Bonds

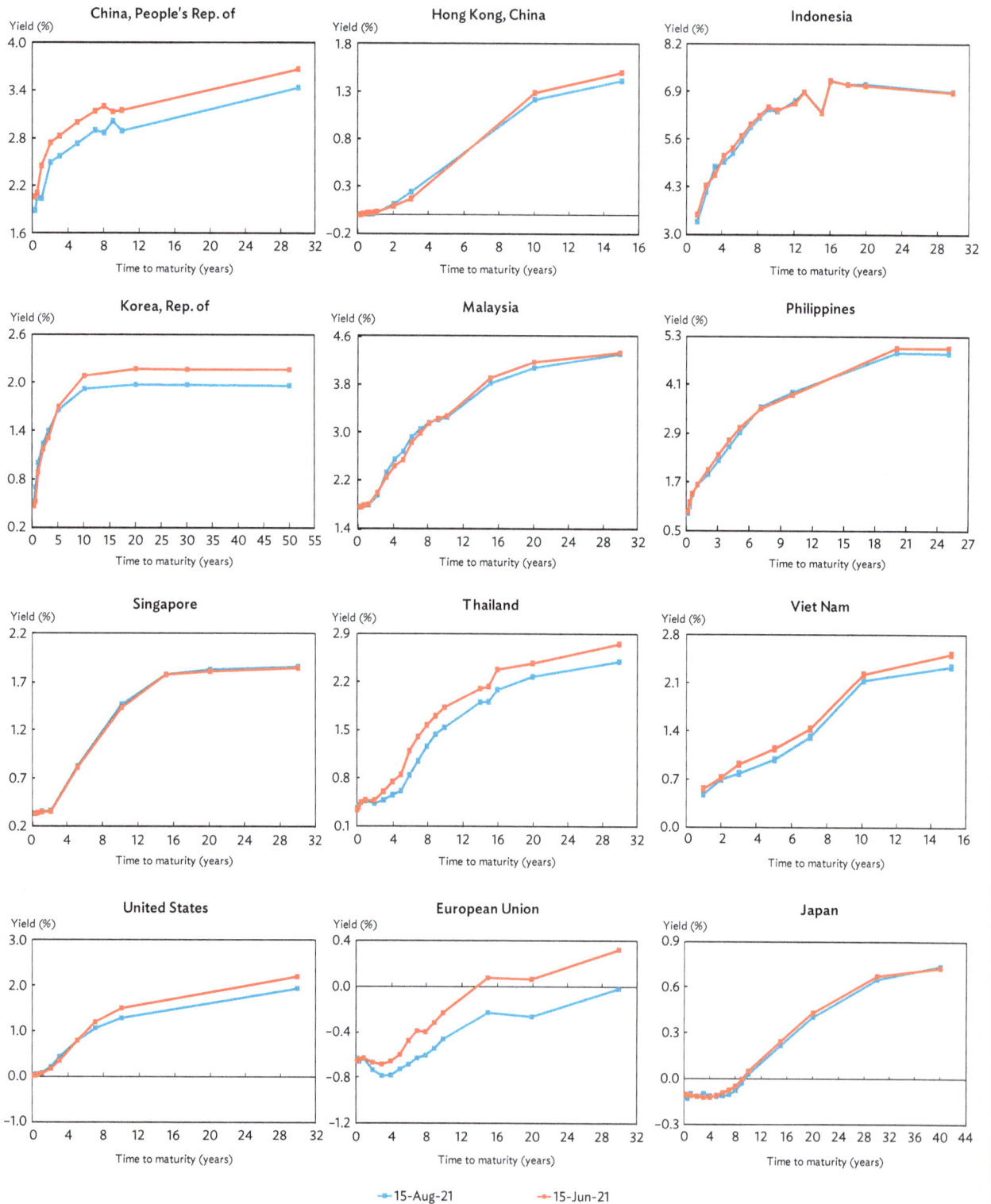

Sources: Based on data from Bloomberg LP and Thai Bond Market Association.

Figure 10: Yield Spreads between 2-Year and 10-Year Government Bonds

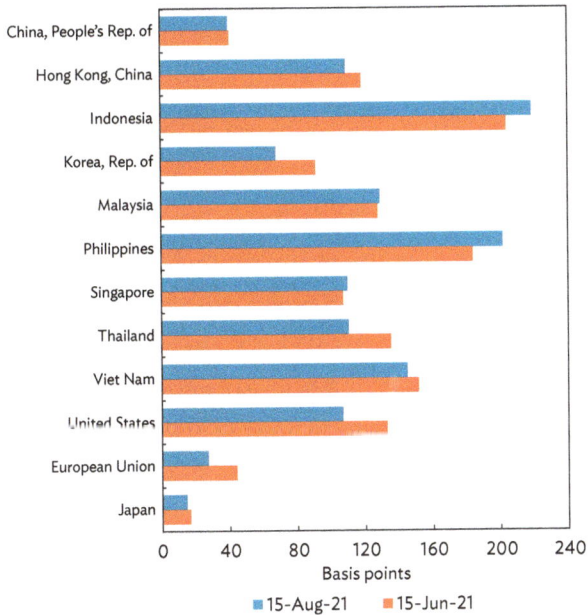

Basis points

■ 15-Aug-21 ■ 15-Jun-21

Source: *AsianBondsOnline* computations based on Bloomberg LP data.

PRC; Hong Kong, China; the Republic of Korea; Thailand; and Viet Nam (**Figure 10**).

All emerging East Asian economies posted positive GDP growth rates in Q2 2021, with nearly all posting either accelerated growth or a rebound from negative GDP growth in Q1 2021. The exceptions were the PRC and Hong Kong, China, which exhibited a slowdown in their respective growth momentums, with the PRC posting Q2 2021 growth of 7.9% y-o-y (from 18.3% y-o-y) and Hong Kong, China reporting 7.6% y-o-y growth (from 8.0% y-o-y). The following economies posted a rebound in y-o-y growth in Q2 2021 following a contraction in Q1 2021: Indonesia (7.1% from –0.7%), Malaysia (16.1% from –0.5%), the Philippines (11.8% from –3.9%), and Thailand (7.5% from –2.6%). The following economies recorded an acceleration in y-o-y growth between Q1 2021 and Q2 2021: the Republic of Korea (6.0% from 1.9%), Singapore (14.7% from 1.5%), and Viet Nam (6.6% from 4.7%).

After emerging East Asia posted a strong GDP performance in Q2 2021, inflation largely trended upward in July. The exceptions were Thailand (**Figure 11a**), and the PRC, Malaysia, and the Philippines (**Figure 11b**). A steep increase in inflation was noted in Hong Kong, China in July. The accelerated inflation in Hong Kong, China was mainly due to a low base in the previous year. Inflationary pressures prompted the Bank of Korea to raise its policy rate in August (**Table 5**).

the Bank of Korea raised by 25 bps the 7-day reverse repo rate to 0.75%.

Most emerging East Asian markets experienced a flattening of the yield curve, consistent with the more pessimistic economic outlook. The 2-year versus 10-year yield spread fell between 15 June and 15 August in the

Figure 11a: Headline Inflation Rates

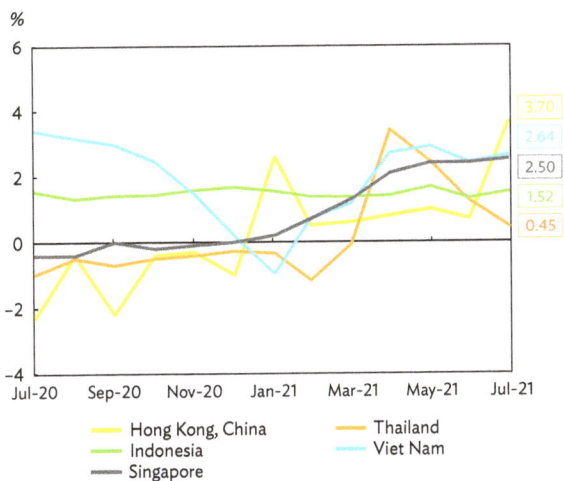

Hong Kong, China
Indonesia
Singapore
Thailand
Viet Nam

Note: Data coverage is from July 2020 to July 2021.
Source: Based on data from Bloomberg LP.

Figure 11b: Headline Inflation Rates

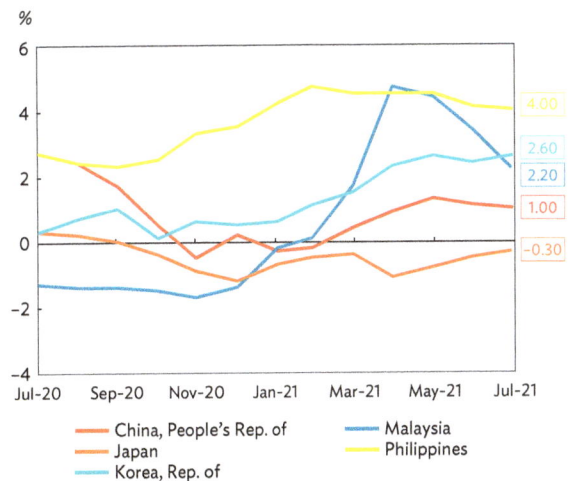

China, People's Rep. of
Japan
Korea, Rep. of
Malaysia
Philippines

Note: Data coverage is from July 2020 to July 2021.
Source: Based on data from Bloomberg LP.

Table 5: Policy Rate Changes

Economy	Policy Rate 1-Sep-2020 (%)	Rate Change (%)												Policy Rate 27-Aug-2021 (%)	Change in Policy Rates (basis points)
		Sep-2020	Oct-2020	Nov-2020	Dec-2020	Jan-2021	Feb-2021	Mar-2021	Apr-2021	May-2021	Jun-2021	Jul-2021	Aug-2021		
United States	0.25													0.25	0
Euro Area	(0.50)													(0.50)	0
Japan	(0.10)													(0.10)	0
China, People's Rep. of	2.95													2.95	0
Indonesia	4.00			↓0.25			↓0.25							3.50	↓ 50
Korea, Rep. of	0.50												↑0.25	0.75	↑ 25
Malaysia	1.75													1.75	0
Philippines	2.25			↓0.25										2.00	↓ 25
Thailand	0.50													0.50	0
Viet Nam	4.50	↓0.50												4.00	↓ 50

( ) = negative.
Notes:
1.   Data coverage is from 1 September 2020 to 27 August 2021.
2.   For the People's Republic of China, data used in the chart are for the 1-year medium-term lending facility rate. While the 1-year benchmark lending rate is the official policy rate of the People's Bank of China, market players use the 1-year medium-term lending facility rate as a guide for the monetary policy direction of the People's Bank of China.
Sources: Various central bank websites.

However, the need to ensure a durable economic recovery left the remaining central banks in the region largely maintaining their accommodative monetary policy stances. In the PRC, while the People's Bank of China has yet to adjust policy rates, it reduced the reserve requirement ratio in July.

AAA-rated corporate spreads fell in the PRC and Malaysia but rose in the Republic of Korea and Thailand.

The spread between AAA-rated yields and government yields fell in the PRC, following a rise in corporate defaults that led to increased demand for better-rated securities, and in Malaysia (**Figure 12a**). The spread rose in the Republic of Korea and Thailand.

The rise in corporate bond defaults led to a worsening spread for lower-rated corporates in the PRC (**Figure 12b**). The spread fell in Malaysia but was roughly unchanged in the Republic of Korea and Thailand.

Figure 12a: Credit Spreads—Local Currency Corporates Rated AAA versus Government Bonds

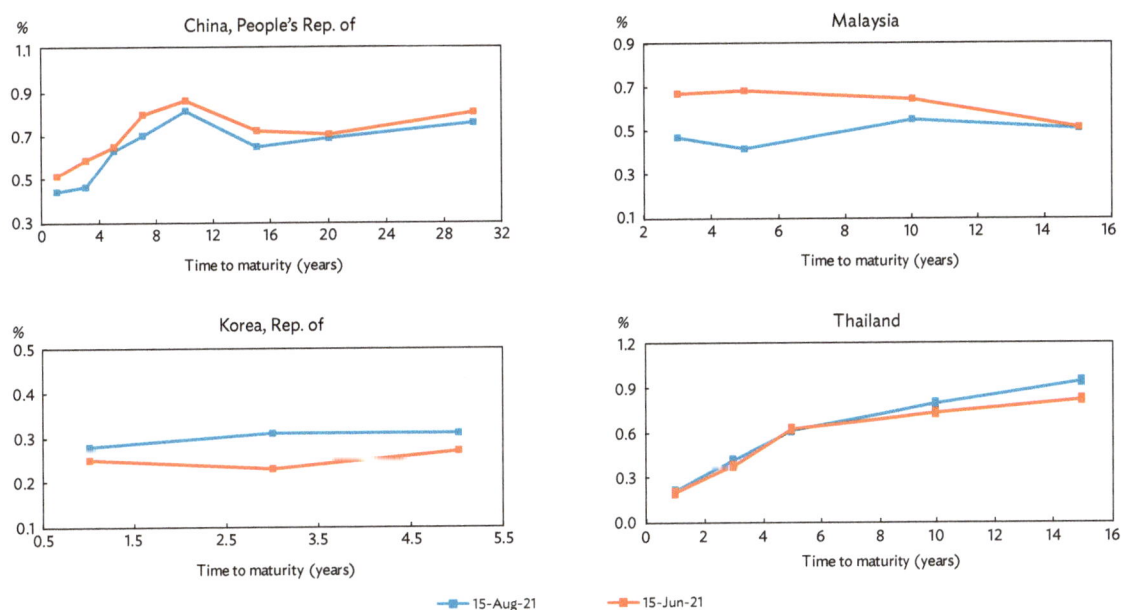

Notes:
1. Credit spreads are obtained by subtracting government yields from corporate indicative yields.
2. For the Republic of Korea, data on corporate bond yields are as of 15 June and 13 August 2021.
3. For Malaysia, data on corporate bonds yields are as of 14 June and 13 August 2021.
Sources: People's Republic of China (Bloomberg LP); Republic of Korea (KG Zeroin Corporation); Malaysia (Fully Automated System for Issuing/Tendering Bank Negara Malaysia); and Thailand (Bloomberg LP).

Figure 12b: Credit Spreads—Lower-Rated Local Currency Corporates versus AAA

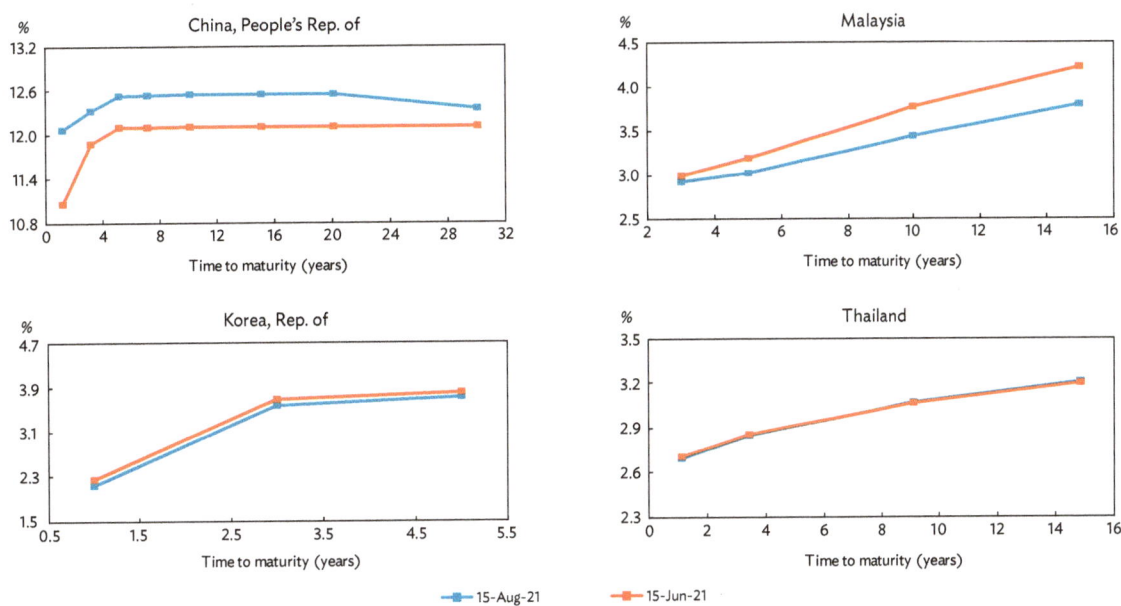

Notes:
1. Credit spreads are obtained by subtracting government yields from corporate indicative yields.
2. For the Republic of Korea, data on corporate bond yields are as of 15 June and 13 August 2021.
3. For Malaysia, data on corporate bonds yields are as of 14 June and 13 August 2021.
Sources: People's Republic of China (Bloomberg LP); Republic of Korea (KG Zeroin Corporation); Malaysia (Fully Automated System for Issuing/Tendering Bank Negara Malaysia); and Thailand (Bloomberg LP).

Recent Developments in ASEAN+3 Sustainable Bond Markets

Sustainable bond markets in ASEAN+3 maintained their growth trajectory in the second quarter (Q2) of 2021.[6] Total bonds outstanding rose 13.1% quarter-on-quarter (q-o-q) in Q2 2021, which was almost similar to the growth of 13.3% q-o-q in the previous quarter, to reach a total of USD345.2 billion at the end of June (**Figure 13**). On a year-on-year (y-o-y) basis, market growth accelerated, with sustainable bonds gaining 53.5% in Q2 2021 versus 45.1% in the first quarter (Q1) of 2021. ASEAN+3 markets continued to be a significant source of sustainable bonds, comprising 19.0% of the global outstanding stock at the end of Q2 2021.

Sustainable bond markets in ASEAN+3 remained dominated by green bonds, which totaled USD249.0 billion and accounted for 72.1% of the region's sustainable bonds outstanding at the end of June. Demand for green bonds was relatively stable in Q2 2021, with green bonds outstanding growing 9.6% q-o-q and 33.5% y-o-y versus 10.3% q-o-q and 27.3% y-o-y in Q1 2021. ASEAN member economies comprised 5.6% of the region's outstanding stock of green bonds at the end of June, while the PRC accounted for a majority share of 69.2% (**Figure 14**).

While green bonds enjoyed solid demand in Q2 2021, interest in social and sustainability bonds grew at an even more rapid pace. Social bonds outstanding grew 19.2% q-o-q and 121.7% y-o-y to USD42.9 billion at the end of June, accounting for 12.4% of ASEAN+3's outstanding sustainable bond total. Sustainability bonds were the fastest-growing sustainable bond category in Q2 2021, posting growth of 27.0% q-o-q and 180.9% y-o-y. At the end of June, sustainability bonds comprised 15.4% of the outstanding stock of ASEAN+3 sustainable bonds. The Republic of Korea accounted for the largest share of social bonds and sustainability bonds outstanding in ASEAN+3 with shares of 62.4% and 41.8%, respectively, followed by Japan with shares of 35.5% and 31.0%.

In Q2 2021, sustainable bond issuance slowed compared with the previous quarter, falling to USD49.7 billion from USD52.1 billion in Q1 2021 (**Figure 15**). The slower growth was mostly due to a decline in the issuance of green bonds to USD30.7 billion in Q2 2021 from USD35.1 billion in Q1 2021. Nonetheless, there is a strong momentum in sustainable bond issuance in the region. Total issuance of sustainable bonds in the first 6 months of the year reached USD101.8 billion, surpassing the 2020 full-year issuance of USD94.5 billion (**Figure 16**). The strong issuance in the first half of 2021 was fueled by active issuance of green bonds and sustainability bonds.

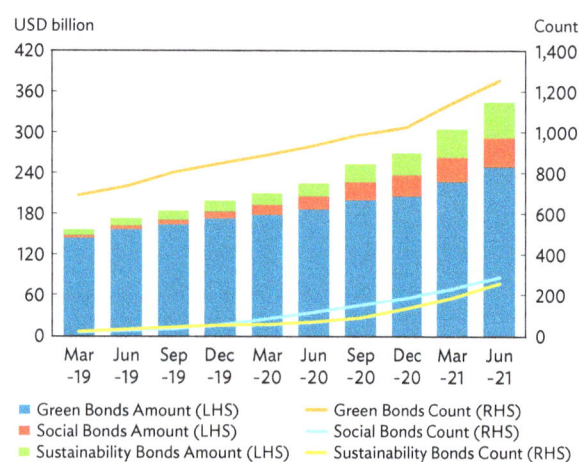

Figure 13: Outstanding Amount of Green, Social, and Sustainability Bonds in ASEAN+3 Markets

ASEAN = Association of Southeast Asian Nations, LHS = left-hand side, RHS = right-hand side, USD = United States dollar.
Notes:
1. ASEAN includes the markets of Indonesia, Malaysia, the Philippines, Singapore, and Thailand.
2. ASEAN+3 includes ASEAN members plus the People's Republic of China; Hong Kong, China; Japan; and the Republic of Korea.
Source: *AsianBondsOnline* computations based on Bloomberg LP data.

---

[6] For the discussion on sustainable bonds, ASEAN+3 includes Association of Southeast Asian Nations (ASEAN) members Indonesia, Malaysia, the Philippines, Singapore, and Thailand, plus the People's Republic of China; Hong Kong, China; Japan; and the Republic of Korea.

Figure 14: Outstanding Green, Social, and Sustainability Bonds in ASEAN+3 by Economy (share of total)

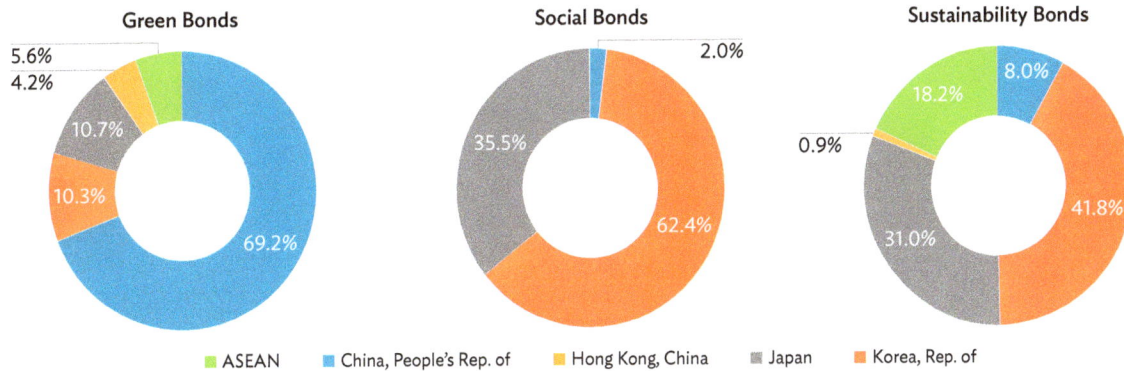

Green Bonds

5.6%
4.2%
10.7%
10.3%
69.2%

Social Bonds

2.0%
35.5%
62.4%

Sustainability Bonds

8.0%
18.2%
0.9%
31.0%
41.8%

■ ASEAN   ■ China, People's Rep. of   ■ Hong Kong, China   ■ Japan   ■ Korea, Rep. of

ASEAN = Association of Southeast Asian Nations.
Notes:
1. Data as of 30 June 2021.
2. ASEAN includes the markets of Indonesia, Malaysia, the Philippines, Singapore, and Thailand.
3. ASEAN+3 includes ASEAN members plus the People's Republic of China; Hong Kong, China; Japan; and the Republic of Korea.
4. For social bonds, ASEAN share for 30 June 2021 is 0.04%.
Source: *AsianBondsOnline* computations based on Bloomberg LP data.

Figure 15: Quarterly Issuance of Green, Social, and Sustainability Bonds in ASEAN+3

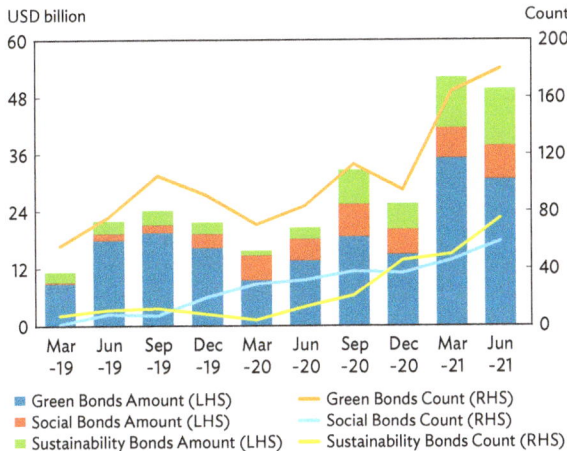

USD billion / Count

■ Green Bonds Amount (LHS)   ── Green Bonds Count (RHS)
■ Social Bonds Amount (LHS)   ── Social Bonds Count (RHS)
■ Sustainability Bonds Amount (LHS)   ── Sustainability Bonds Count (RHS)

ASEAN = Association of Southeast Asian Nations, LHS = left-hand side, RHS = right-hand side, USD = United States dollar.
Notes:
1. ASEAN includes the markets of Indonesia, Malaysia, the Philippines, Singapore, and Thailand.
2. ASEAN+3 includes ASEAN members plus the People's Republic of China; Hong Kong, China; Japan; and the Republic of Korea.
Source: *AsianBondsOnline* computations based on Bloomberg LP data.

Figure 16: Issuance Volume of Green, Social, and Sustainability Bonds in ASEAN+3

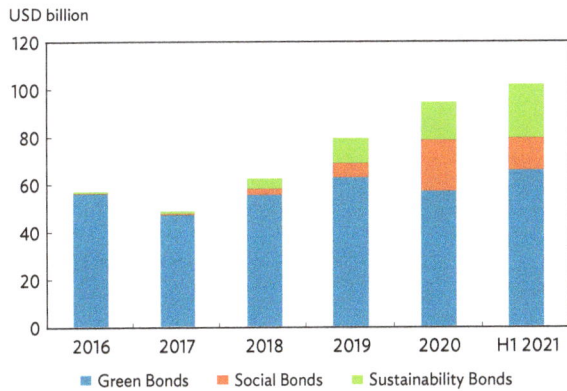

USD billion

■ Green Bonds   ■ Social Bonds   ■ Sustainability Bonds

ASEAN = Association of Southeast Asian Nations, H1 = first half,
USD = United States dollar.
Notes:
1. ASEAN includes the markets of Indonesia, Malaysia, the Philippines, Singapore, and Thailand.
2. ASEAN+3 includes ASEAN members plus the People's Republic of China; Hong Kong, China; Japan; and the Republic of Korea.
Source: *AsianBondsOnline* computations based on Bloomberg LP data.

Corporates are the dominant issuers in the ASEAN+3 sustainable bond market, accounting for 80.8% of sustainable bonds outstanding in the region at the end of June (**Figure 17**). Government issuers accounted for a 10.1% share, while government-linked corporates accounted for 9.2%. By bond category, corporates are by far the largest issuers in the green bond market,

accounting for an 88.1% share of the total at the end of June. At the same time, the share of green bonds issued by governments and government-linked corporates increased to 8.4% and 3.4%, respectively, at the end of June. from 6.7% and 2.9% at the end of December 2020. The shares of corporates rose in both the social and sustainability bond markets from the end of 2020 to Q2 2021, with the corporate sector accounting for

Figure 17: Outstanding Green, Social, and Sustainability Bonds in ASEAN+3 by Type of Bond

USD billion

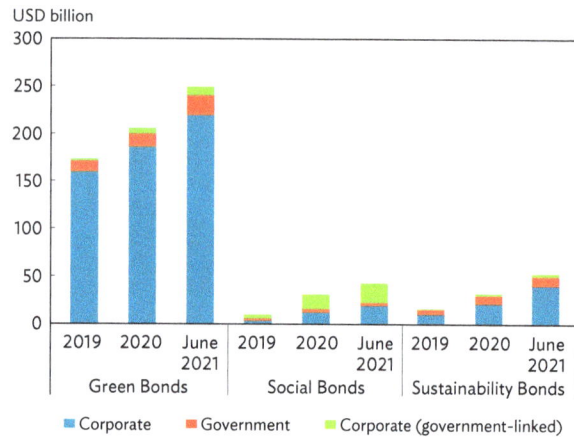

USD = United States dollar.
Notes: Corporate denotes bonds issued by private sector corporations. Government bonds include bonds issued by sovereigns, regional governments, and local governments. Corporate (government-linked) denotes corporations with government affiliations.
Source: AsianBondsOnline computation based on Bloomberg LP data.

44.4% of social bonds and 75.5% of sustainability bonds outstanding at the end of June, up from 39.0% and 65.9%, respectively, at the end of December 2020.

By sector, financials continued to be the most dominant issuer of sustainable bonds. The green bond market has a relatively more diversified issuer base compared to social and sustainability bonds. Financials account for 36.1% of outstanding green bonds, 63.8% of social bonds, and 47.2% of sustainability bonds (**Figure 18**). By currency, green bonds and social bonds outstanding at the end of June were mostly denominated in a domestic currency versus a foreign currency, with LCY-denominated issuances comprising 65.5% and 78.4% of the market, respectively (**Figure 19**). On the other hand, sustainability bonds outstanding were mostly (58.3%) denominated in a foreign currency at the end of June.

Figure 18: Outstanding Green, Social, and Sustainability Bonds in ASEAN+3 by Sector of Issuer (share of total)

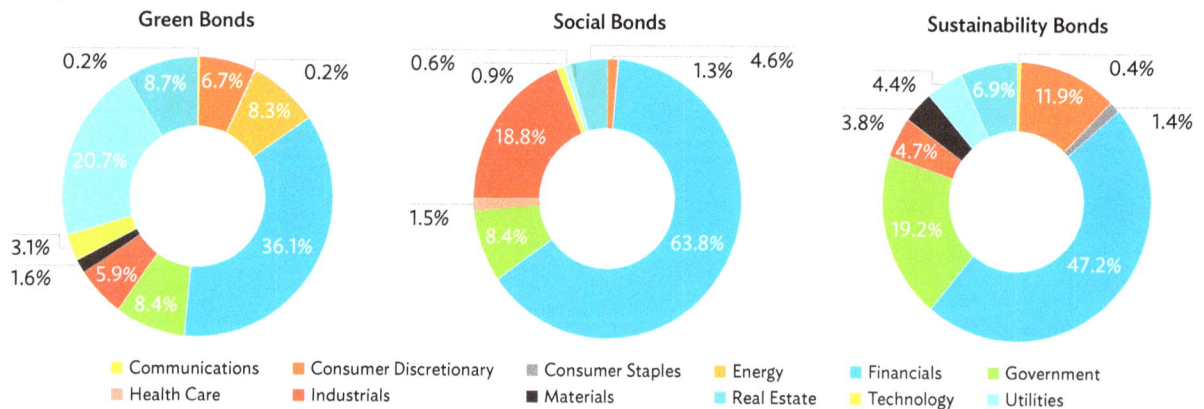

ASEAN = Association of Southeast Asian Nations.
Notes:
1. Data as of 30 June 2021.
2. ASEAN includes the markets of Indonesia, Malaysia, the Philippines, Singapore, and Thailand.
3. ASEAN+3 includes ASEAN members plus the People's Republic of China; Hong Kong, China; Japan; and the Republic of Korea.
Source: AsianBondsOnline computations based on Bloomberg LP data.

Figure 19: Outstanding Green, Social, and Sustainability Bonds in ASEAN+3 by Type of Currency (share of total)

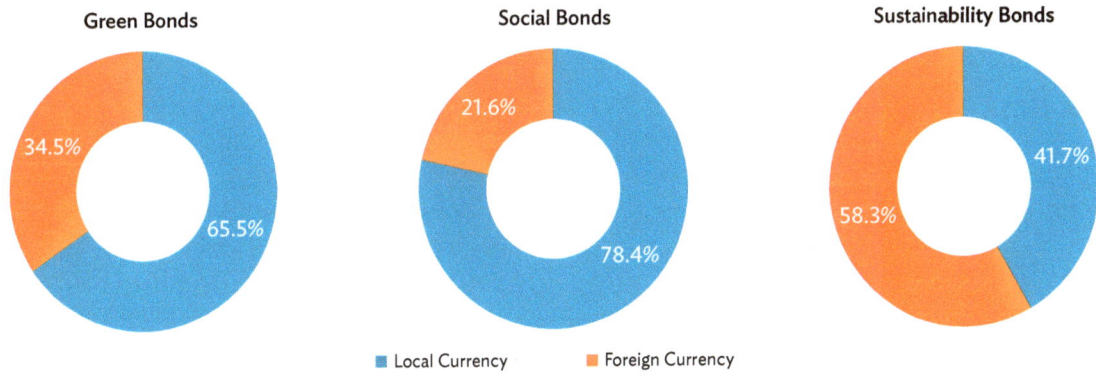

Green Bonds

Social Bonds

Sustainability Bonds

■ Local Currency   ■ Foreign Currency

ASEAN = Association of Southeast Asian Nations.
Notes:
1. Data as of 30 June 2021.
2. ASEAN includes the markets of Indonesia, Malaysia, the Philippines, Singapore, and Thailand.
3. ASEAN+3 includes ASEAN members plus the People's Republic of China; Hong Kong, China; Japan; and the Republic of Korea.
Source: *AsianBondsOnline* computations based on Bloomberg LP data.

Policy and Regulatory Developments

People's Republic of China

People's Bank of China Reduces Reserve Requirement Ratios

Effective 15 July, the People's Bank of China (PBOC) reduced the reserve requirement ratio of financial institutions by 50 basis points (excluding institutions with an existing 5% reserve requirement ratio). The PBOC estimated that the move would reduce the weighted average reserve requirement ratios of financial institutions to 8.9%. The PBOC's stated goal was to reduce borrowing costs and support the economy.

Hong Kong, China

Hong Kong Monetary Authority Holds Countercyclical Capital Buffer at 1.0%

On 5 August, the Hong Kong Monetary Authority announced that the countercyclical buffer (CCyB) would remain unchanged at 1.0%. The Hong Kong Monetary Authority noted that while there have been initial signs of recovery, the economy continued to face uncertainties driven by the global pandemic. Thus, holding the CCyB steady and monitoring the economic situation for a few more quarters was deemed more appropriate. The CCyB is an integral part of the Basel III regulatory capital framework designed to increase the resilience of the banking sector during periods of excess credit growth. A lower CCyB releases additional liquidity into the banking system by raising banks' lending capacity to support the economy.

Indonesia

Bank Indonesia Broadens Local Currency Settlement Framework with Bank Negara Malaysia and the Ministry of Finance, Japan

Effective 2 August, Bank Indonesia and Bank Negara Malaysia expanded their local currency settlement framework to encourage the use of Indonesian rupiah and Malaysian ringgit for the settlement of trade and direct investment transactions between Indonesia and Malaysia. The new policies in the expanded settlement framework are as follows: (i) inclusion of direct investments, income, and transfers as eligible transactions; (ii) inclusion of individuals as eligible participants; and (iii) simplified documentary requirements for tapping the framework. Both central banks also appointed additional banks to facilitate the local currency settlement framework.

Effective 5 August, Bank Indonesia and the Ministry of Finance, Japan relaxed some policies related to their existing Indonesian rupiah and Japanese yen settlement framework. This move was made to further support trade and investment activities between Indonesia and Japan. The policies that were relaxed include the (i) use of cross-currency swap and domestic nondeliverable forward transactions as hedging tools, (ii) removal of underlying documents for transactions of up to USD500,000 from the previous USD25,000, and (iii) expansion of eligible criteria for hedging transactions and extension of hedging maturities to more than 1 year.

Republic of Korea

National Assembly Passes Second Supplementary Budget

On 24 July, the National Assembly passed the second supplementary budget for 2021 worth KRW34.9 trillion, which was KRW1.9 trillion higher than the proposed amount. This was the sixth supplementary budget related to the government's response to the pandemic since 2020: KRW14.9 trillion was allotted for pandemic relief packages, KRW12.6 trillion for local economic support and subsidies to local governments, KRW4.9 trillion for vaccine purchases and disease prevention efforts, and KRW2.5 trillion for employment support and low-income household aid. The supplementary budget brought the overall budget for 2021 to KRW604.9 trillion from an original amount of KRW558.0 trillion. The new 2021 budget is expected to produce a fiscal deficit equal to 4.4% of GDP and cumulative government debt equal to 47.2% of GDP.

The Bank of Korea Announces Changes to Monetary Stabilization Bonds Issuance System

On 2 August, the Bank of Korea announced changes to the issuance system of Monetary Stabilization Bonds (MSBs) to enhance liquidity management efficiency. Regular auctions of 182-day MSBs will be suspended given the introduction of 3-year MSBs. Meanwhile, the issuance of 1-year, 2-year, and 3-year MSBs will be held once a month. Issuance of 91-day MSBs—at auctions to be held once a week—will be slightly expanded to around KRW1 trillion. Finally, the issuance of 1-year and 2-year MSBs will be significantly reduced due to the issuance of 3-year MSBs. The new system will be implemented effective 1 September.

Malaysia

Bank Negara Malaysia Revises Reference Rate Framework

On 11 August, Bank Negara Malaysia released its revised Reference Rate Framework, effective 1 August 2022. In the revised version, all financial institutions will use a common rate, the standardized base rate, as the reference rate for new issuances of floating-rate notes and refinancing of existing loans in Malaysia. This replaces the current use of a base rate that differs across financial institutions. Furthermore, the standardized base rate will be linked to the overnight policy rate. The revision allows consumers to understand better the changes in their loan repayments. This will also facilitate the transmission of the policy rate to the broader economy.

Philippines

Bureau of the Treasury Plans to Borrow PHP685 Billion in the Third Quarter of 2021

The Bureau of the Treasury planned to borrow PHP235 billion from the domestic debt market in July, comprising PHP60 billion of Treasury bills and PHP175 billion of Treasury bonds. Less borrowing was set for August at PHP200 billion: PHP60 billion of Treasury bills and PHP140 billion of Treasury bonds. In September, the borrowing plan was set to PHP250 billion, comprising PHP75 billion of Treasury bills and PHP175 billion of Treasury bonds. The borrowing program in Q3 2021,

totaling PHP685 billion, upsized the offer volume for longer-tenor securities, as the Bureau of the Treasury tried to extend its maturity profile amid strong market liquidity and low interest rates.

Bangko Sentral ng Pilipinas Eases Foreign Exchange Regulations

On 10 August, the Bangko Sentral ng Pilipinas (BSP) amended the foreign exchange (FX) regulations to allow access to FX without prior BSP approval in select trade and nontrade current account transactions. According to the BSP, the amendment will promote ease of use of FX resources of the banking system and further simplify procedures and documentary requirements for FX transactions. These transactions include (i) the sale of FX by banks without prior BSP approval involving payments for e-commerce; living allowance and medical expenses of dependents abroad; and importation of goods with services covered by engineering, procurement, and construction contracts among others; (ii) FX derivatives transactions to be entered into by nonbank government entities; and (iii) use of peso receipts relating to trade transactions to fund the peso deposit accounts of nonresidents. The reform took effect 15 banking days after its publication.

Singapore

Monetary Authority of Singapore to Issue Infrastructure Bonds in October

Monetary Authority of Singapore announced on 3 August that it would issue infrastructure bonds called Singapore Government Securities (Infrastructure) beginning 1 October. The first issuance of this kind will be a 30-year benchmark bond and the maiden issuance under the Significant Infrastructure Government Loan Act, which was passed by Singapore's Parliament on 10 May to fund major long-term infrastructure projects.

Thailand

Cabinet Approves Emergency Decree for Additional THB500 Billion of Borrowing

In June, Thailand's House of Representatives approved an executive decree authorizing the Ministry of Finance to borrow up to an additional THB500 billion for relief measures in response to the impacts of COVID-19. Up to THB30 billion will be allocated for the Ministry of Public Health. The rest of the loan amount was earmarked for assistance to individuals (THB300 billion) and businesses (THB170 billion) affected by the pandemic.

Viet Nam

Hanoi Stock Exchange Launches 10-Year Government Bond Futures

On 28 June, the Hanoi Stock Exchange launched the 10-year government bond futures, which will be traded on the exchange's derivatives market. The base asset of the derivatives product is a 10-year government bond issued by the State Treasury of Viet Nam amounting to VND100,000 and with an annual interest rate of 5.0%. According to the Hanoi Stock Exchange, the new bond futures product aims to diversify derivatives securities in the market and provide more risk prevention tools for long-term government bonds. The 10-year government bond futures is the third derivatives product in the Vietnamese bond market, following the VN30 Index and 5-year government bond futures.

Market Summaries

People's Republic of China

Yield Movements

The entire yield curve of the People's Republic of China's (PRC) local currency (LCY) bond market shifted downward between 15 June and 15 August (**Figure 1**). The largest decline was for the 1-year tenor, which declined 41 basis points (bps), while the smallest declines were for the 6-month tenor (6 bps) and 9-year tenor (12 bps). All other tenors fell between 17 bps and 33 bps during the review period. The 2-year versus 10-year yield spread was barely changed between 15 June and 15 August, falling marginally from 41 bps to 40 bps.

The PRC's yield curve continues to decline despite continued economic growth. The decline was largely due to concerns that the PRC's growth momentum would slow due to headwinds in the global economy, owing once again to rising COVID-19 cases. The PRC's gross domestic product (GDP) grew 7.9% year-on-year (y-o-y) in the second quarter (Q2) of 2021 after gaining 18.3% y-o-y in the first quarter (Q1). While all major sectors posted slower growth, the largest decline was in the secondary sector, where growth fell to 7.5% y-o-y in Q2 2021 from 24.4% y-o-y in Q1 2021. The next largest decline was in the tertiary sector, which grew 8.3% y-o-y after expanding 15.6% y-o-y in the previous quarter. The growth rate in the primary sector was more stable, with a growth rate of 7.6% y-o-y versus 8.1% y-o-y during the same review period.

Other more recent economic indicators also indicate a potential slowdown in momentum. The PRC's industrial production grew 6.4% y-o-y in July, falling from the 8.3% y-o-y expansion posted in June. The PRC's manufacturing Purchasing Managers Index dipped to 50.4 in July from 50.9 in June, while inflation also seems to have leveled off. The PRC reported consumer price inflation of 1.0% y-o-y in July versus 1.1% y-o-y in June and 1.3% y-o-y in May. Producer prices recorded a 9.0% y-o-y gain in July, compared with 8.8% y-o-y in June and 9.0% y-o-y in May.

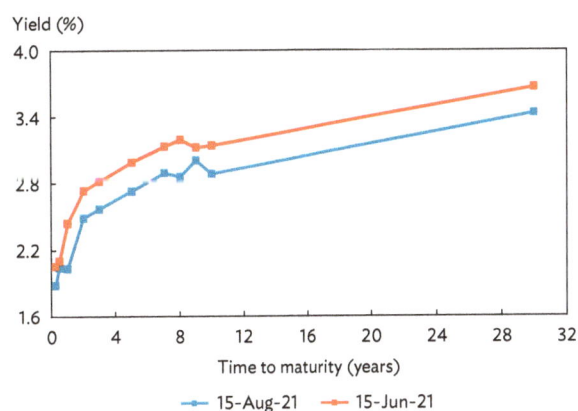

Figure 1: The People's Republic of China's Benchmark Yield Curve—Local Currency Government Bonds

Source: Based on data from Bloomberg LP.

Market sentiment was influenced by statements from the State Council on 7 July suggesting a shift toward policy easing via monetary tools such as reserve requirement ratio cuts to help support the economy, particularly smaller businesses. On 9 July, the People's Bank of China (PBOC) announced a 50-bps cut to its reserve requirement ratio, fueling market speculation that a cut in interest rates such as the 1-year loan prime rate would be next. However, the PBOC has so far left unchanged its benchmark interest rates.

Size and Composition

Growth in the PRC's outstanding LCY bonds accelerated to 3.0% quarter-on-quarter (q-o-q) in Q2 2021 from 2.1% q-o-q in Q1 2021, reaching a size of CNY106.6 trillion (USD16.5 trillion) (**Table 1**). On a y-o-y basis, the growth rate for Q2 2021 was slightly lower at 14.4% versus 17.3% in the previous quarter. The faster q-o-q growth for Q2 2021 was largely due to an increase in local government bonds.

Table 1: Size and Composition of the Local Currency Bond Market in the People's Republic of China

| | Outstanding Amount (billion) | | | | | | Growth Rates (%) | | | |
| | Q2 2020 | | Q1 2021 | | Q2 2021 | | Q2 2020 | | Q2 2021 | |
	CNY	USD	CNY	USD	CNY	USD	q-o-q	y-o-y	q-o-q	y-o-y
Total	91,285	13,189	103,528	15,799	106,590	16,507	5.6	17.9	3.0	14.4
Government	58,867	8,332	66,198	10,102	68,384	10,591	5.4	15.1	3.3	16.2
Treasury Bonds and Other Government Bonds	17,775	2,516	21,032	3,210	21,548	3,337	5.5	15.0	2.5	21.2
Central Bank Bonds	15	2	15	2	15	2	(18.9)	0.0	0.0	0.0
Policy Bank Bonds	16,662	2,358	18,382	2,805	18,658	2,890	4.2	9.5	1.5	12.0
Local Government Bonds	24,415	3,456	26,769	4,085	28,163	4,362	6.2	19.3	5.2	15.4
Corporate	34,320	4,857	37,329	5,697	38,207	5,917	5.9	22.9	2.3	11.3

CNY = Chinese yuan, q-o-q = quarter-on-quarter, Q1 = first quarter, Q2 = second quarter, USD = United States dollar, y-o-y = year-on-year.
Notes:
1. Calculated using data from national sources.
2. Treasury bonds include savings bonds and local government bonds.
3. Bloomberg LP end-of-period local currency–USD rates are used.
4. Growth rates are calculated from local currency base and do not include currency effects.
Sources: CEIC and Bloomberg LP.

Government bonds. The PRC's government bonds outstanding rose 3.3% q-o-q in Q2 2021 to CNY68.4 trillion after gaining 1.6% q-o-q in Q1 2021. The faster growth was largely due to an increase in local government bonds outstanding as local governments sought to utilize their bond quotas.

Issuance of Treasury bonds declined 4.5% q-o-q, but fewer maturities during the quarter led to Treasury bonds and other government bonds outstanding rising 2.5% q-o-q to CNY21.5 trillion. The larger increase was partly due to a low base effect resulting from the PRC's focus on risk control, which led to only a 0.5% q-o-q increase in Treasury and other government bonds outstanding in Q1 2021. This was visible in the decline in the y-o-y growth rate in Treasury and other government bonds from 24.8% in Q2 2020 to 21.2% in Q2 2021. Similarly, policy bank bond issuance fell 9.6% q-o-q in Q2 2021, resulting in policy bank bonds outstanding rising 1.5% q-o-q to CNY18.7 trillion after gaining 1.9% q-o-q in the previous quarter.

On the other hand, there was a rise in the issuance of local government bonds, which rose 173.5% q-o-q in Q2 2021, resulting in a 5.2% q-o-q increase in local government bonds outstanding to CNY28.2 trillion at the end of June. This was due to a low base effect as local government issuance was down in Q1 2021 due to a delay in the release of local government bond quotas. Despite this, the overall quota for local bonds outstanding in 2021 was reduced to CNY3.65 trillion from CNY3.75 trillion in 2020. Overall, local government issuance for the first half of 2021 was down 4.2% from the same period in 2020.

On a y-o-y basis, local government bonds outstanding grew 15.4%, up from 16.4% in Q1 2021.

Corporate bonds. Corporate bonds outstanding in the PRC rose 2.3% q-o-q in Q2 2021, which was down from Q1 2021's 2.9% q-o-q growth on dampened sentiment due to government efforts to rein in credit risk and rising corporate defaults this year. The PRC has also tempered issuance of debt by local government financing vehicles. While corporate bond issuance in the PRC grew 1.3% q-o-q to USD699 billion in Q2 2021 after a decline of 3.0% q-o-q in Q1 2021, corporate bond issuance was down 5.8% y-o-y.

The value of commercial paper outstanding fell 2.8% q-o-q and 19.3% y-o-y in Q2 2021 to CNY2.3 trillion at the end of June, as companies preferred to lock in lower rates with longer-dated debt (**Table 2**). Concerns regarding credit risk and rising defaults also led most major corporate bond sectors to post q-o-q declines or weak growth rates. Enterprise bonds declined 1.4% q-o-q, while medium-term notes rose 1.0% q-o-q. Listed corporate bonds and financial bonds rose 3.6% q-o-q and 3.8% q-o-q, respectively.

Most major corporate bond segments showed a q-o-q increase in issuance, excluding commercial paper, which declined 20.3% q-o-q (**Figure 2**). However, versus the same period a year earlier, issuance of nearly all major categories of corporate bonds exhibited a decline, excluding asset-backed securities, enterprise bonds, and listed corporate bonds.

Table 2: Corporate Bonds Outstanding in Key Categories

	Amount (CNY billion)			Growth Rate (%)			
				Q2 2020		Q2 2021	
	Q2 2020	Q1 2021	Q2 2021	q-o-q	y-o-y	q-o-q	y-o-y
Financial Bonds	6,803	7,746	8,038	1.4	34.9	3.8	18.2
Enterprise Bonds	3,771	3,860	3,808	1.0	(1.4)	(1.4)	1.0
Listed Corporate Bonds	8,996	10,603	10,986	1.4	3.6	3.6	22.1
Commercial Paper	2,825	2,344	2,279	1.3	(2.8)	(2.8)	(19.3)
Medium-Term Notes	7,300	7,382	7,457	1.3	1.0	1.0	2.1
Asset-Backed Securities	2,406	2,942	3,075	1.4	4.5	4.5	27.8

( ) = negative, CNY = Chinese yuan, q-o-q = quarter-on-quarter, Q1 = first quarter, Q2 = second quarter, y-o-y = year-on-year.
Source: CEIC.

Figure 2: Corporate Bond Issuance in Key Sectors

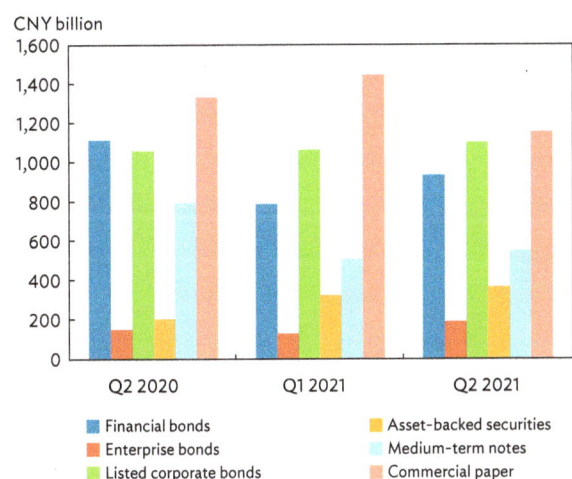

CNY = Chinese yuan, Q1 = first quarter, Q2 = second quarter.
Source: ChinaBond.

The top 30 issuers' share of total LCY corporate bonds outstanding fell to 28.5% in Q2 2021 from 28.7% in Q1 2021 (**Table 3**). By the end of June, the bonds outstanding of the top 30 issuers reached CNY10.9 trillion. Of the top 30, the 10 largest issuers accounted for an aggregate CNY7.1 trillion. China Railway remained the largest issuer, accounting for 24.3% of the total bonds outstanding of the top 30 issuers.

Table 4 lists the largest corporate bond issuances in Q2 2021. Of the five top issuances, four were from financial institutions that sought to increase their liquidity and funding during the quarter. To help raise funds, the Bank of Communications and the Industrial and Commercial Bank issued perpetual bonds.

Investor Profile

Government bonds. Commercial banks remained the dominant investor in the PRC's government bond market in Q2 2021, albeit with a declining share of the total (**Figure 3**). Banks are the most significant holders of local government bonds by far, holding a share of 87.0% in Q2 2021, down slightly from 87.9% in Q2 2020.

Banks are also significant holders of Treasury bonds, holding 65.0% of the total stock at the end of Q2 2021, down somewhat from 66.5% at the end of Q2 2020. Banks also held 55.5% of policy bank bonds at the end of June 2021, down from 57.3% in June 2020.

Foreign investors saw their share of government bond holdings increase the most. Their share of Treasury bonds increased to 11.1% in Q2 2021, up from 9.5% in Q2 2020, while the foreign holdings' share of policy bank bonds also rose to 5.5% from 3.8% in the same review period.

Liquidity

The volume of interest rate swaps rose 6.1% q-o-q in Q2 2021 after a 0.4% q-o-q gain in the previous quarter, reflecting increased demand (**Table 5**).

Table 3: Top 30 Issuers of Local Currency Corporate Bonds in the People's Republic of China

	Issuers	Outstanding Amount		State-Owned	Listed Company	Type of Industry
		LCY Bonds (CNY billion)	LCY Bonds (USD billion)			
1.	China Railway	2,648.5	410.17	Yes	No	Transportation
2.	Industrial and Commercial Bank of China	711.4	110.17	Yes	Yes	Banking
3.	Bank of China	658.1	101.92	Yes	Yes	Banking
4.	Agricultural Bank of China	650.3	100.71	Yes	Yes	Banking
5.	Bank of Communications	544.5	84.33	No	Yes	Banking
6.	Shanghai Pudong Development Bank	485.9	75.25	Yes	Yes	Banking
7.	Shanghai Pudong Development Bank	433.5	67.14	No	Yes	Banking
8.	China Construction Bank	388.1	60.10	Yes	Yes	Banking
9.	China Citic Bank	315.0	48.78	No	Yes	Banking
10.	China Securities Finance	302.5	46.85	Yes	No	Finance
11.	State Grid Corporation of China	296.5	45.92	Yes	No	Public Utilities
12.	China Minsheng Bank	290.0	44.91	No	Yes	Banking
13.	Industrial Bank	286.3	44.33	No	Yes	Banking
14.	China National Petroleum	274.9	42.58	Yes	No	Energy
15.	State Power Investment	253.3	39.22	Yes	No	Power
16.	China Merchants Bank	229.2	35.50	No	Yes	Banking
17.	China Everbright Bank	215.9	33.44	No	Yes	Banking
18.	Ping An Bank	185.0	28.65	No	Yes	Banking
19.	Huaxia Bank	180.0	27.88	No	Yes	Banking
20.	China Southern Power Grid	177.5	27.49	Yes	No	Public Utilities
21.	CITIC Securities	164.3	25.45	Yes	Yes	Brokerage
22.	Postal Savings Back of China	160.0	24.78	Yes	Yes	Banking
23.	Shaanxi Coal and Chemical Industry Group	156.0	24.16	Yes	Yes	Coal
24.	China Merchants Securities	150.9	23.37	No	No	Brokerage
25.	Tianjin Infrastructure Investment Group	147.4	22.83	Yes	No	Capital Goods
26.	Huatai Securities	141.7	21.94	No	Yes	Brokerage
27.	China Datang	115.7	17.91	Yes	No	Power
28.	China Three Gorges	115.0	17.81	Yes	No	Power
29.	GF Securities	113.9	17.64	No	Yes	Brokerage
30.	China Bohai Bank	113.0	17.49	No	No	Banking
	Total Top 30 LCY Corporate Issuers	**10,904.2**	**1,688.7**			
	Total LCY Corporate Bonds	**38,206.6**	**5,917.0**			
	Top 30 as % of Total LCY Corporate Bonds	**28.5%**	**28.5%**			

CNY = Chinese yuan, LCY = local currency, USD = United States dollar.
Notes:
1. Data as of 30 June 2021.
2. State-owned firms are defined as those in which the government has more than a 50% ownership stake.
Source: *AsianBondsOnline* calculations based on Bloomberg LP data.

Table 4: Notable Local Currency Corporate Bond Issuances in the Second Quarter of 2021

Corporate Issuers	Coupon Rate (%)	Issued Amount (CNY billion)
China Securities Finance[a]		
1-year bond	3.90	20.0
1-year bond	3.88	20.0
1-year bond	3.85	20.0
1-year bond	3.93	20.0
1-year bond	3.87	20.0
Bank of Communications		
1-year bond	3.40	40.0
Perpetual bond	4.06	41.5
Industrial and Commercial Bank		
Perpetual Bond	4.04	70.0
China Everbright Bank[a]		
1-year bond	2.82	3.0
1-year bond	2.02	8.0
1-year bond	2.86	4.0
1-year bond	2.84	3.0
1-year bond	2.80	2.5
1-year bond	2.98	6.0
2-year bond	2.88	3.0
2-year bond	2.93	5.0
2-year bond	3.09	3.0
2-year bond	3.13	6.0
2-year bond	3.23	4.5
2-year bond	3.20	4.5
China State Railway Group[a]		
10-year bond	3.54	5.0
10-year bond	3.54	5.0
10-year bond	3.54	5.0
20-year bond	3.80	5.0
20-year bond	3.84	5.0
20-year bond	3.80	5.0
20-year bond	3.80	5.0

CNY = Chinese yuan.
[a] Multiple issuance of the same tenor indicates issuance on different dates.
Source: Based on data from Bloomberg LP.

Policy, Institutional, and Regulatory Developments

People's Bank of China Reduces Reserve Requirement Ratios

Effective 15 July, the PBOC reduced the reserve requirement ratio of financial institutions by 50 bps (excluding institutions with an existing 5% reserve requirement ratio). The PBOC estimated that the move would reduce the weighted average reserve requirement ratios of financial institutions to 8.9%. The PBOC's stated goal was to reduce borrowing costs and support the economy.

Figure 3: Local Currency Treasury Bonds and Policy Bank Bonds Investor Profile

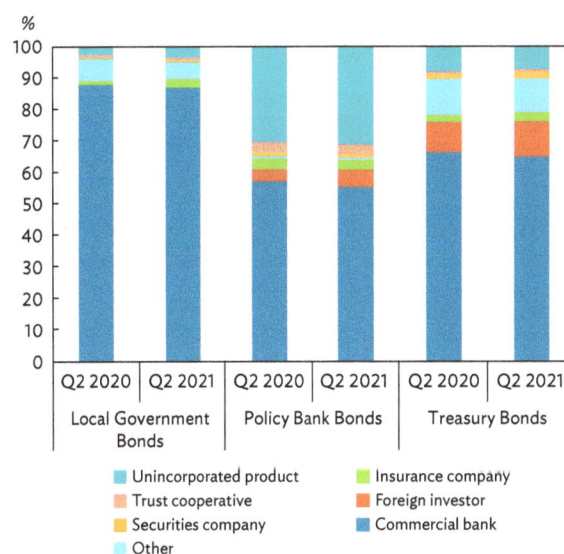

Q2 = second quarter.
Source: CEIC.

Table 5: Notional Values of the People's Republic of China's Interest Rate Swap Market in the Second Quarter of 2021

Interest Rate Swap Benchmarks	Notional Amount (CNY billion)	Share of Total Notional Amount (%)	Growth Rate (%)
	Q2 2021		q-o-q
7-Day Repo Rate	4,847.3	85.2	1.1
7-Day Repo Rate (Deposit Institutions)	2.2	0.04	8.9
Overnight SHIBOR	10.3	0.2	0.5
3-Month SHIBOR	800.1	14.1	1.2
1-Year Lending Rate	12.0	0.2	0.5
5-Year Lending Rate	1.9	0.0	0.3
10-Year Treasury Yield	5.3	0.1	0.5
China Development Bank 10-Year Bond Yield	4.8	0.1	0.4
10-Year Bond Yield/10-Year Government Bond Yield	4.5	0.1	0.4
3-Year AAA Short-Term Notes/ Government Debt	0.1	0.001	0.3
Total	5,688.4	100.0	6.1

CNY = Chinese yuan, q-o-q = quarter-on-quarter, Q2 = second quarter, Repo = repurchase, SHIBOR = Shanghai Interbank Offered Rate.
Note: Growth rate computed based on notional amounts.
Sources: *AsianBondsOnline* and *ChinaMoney*.

Hong Kong, China

Yield Movements

Hong Kong, China's local currency (LCY) bond yield curve exhibited mixed movements between 15 June and 15 August (**Figure 1**). The curve hardly moved at the shorter-end: yields were unchanged for bonds with maturities of 3 months or less, while yields dipped 1 basis point (bp) for bonds with maturities of between 6 months and 1 year. In contrast, the 2-year and 3-year tenors gained 2 bps and 7 bps, respectively. Yields fell an average of 8 bps for bonds with maturities of 10 years or more, shifting the curve slightly downward at the longer-end. On average, bond yields fell 1 bp across the curve. The spread between the 2-year and 10-year yields narrowed from 118 bps on 15 June to 109 bps on 15 August.

The yield movements of Hong Kong, China's LCY medium- to long-term government bonds broadly tracked the rate movements of the corresponding United States Treasuries during the review period. For both economies, risk-off sentiment drove long-term government bond yields down as the spread of the delta variant threatened the nascent economic recovery.

Hong Kong, China's inflation remained subdued as economic activities were still below pre-pandemic levels. Consumer price inflation accelerated to 3.7% year-on-year (y-o-y) in July from 0.7% y-o-y in June. The uptick in inflation in July was mainly due to a low base of comparison a year earlier, when a third wave of COVID-19 infections prompted government subsidies that drove prices down.

Hong Kong, China's gross domestic product expanded 7.6% y-o-y in the second quarter (Q2) of 2021 after rebounding to grow 8.0% y-o-y in the first quarter (Q1) of 2021. Consumption and investment demand gained momentum in Q2 2021 as the easing of social distancing measures revived consumer and investor sentiment. Private consumption rose 6.8% y-o-y in Q2 2021 versus 2.1% in Q1 2021. Investment growth jumped to 23.8% y-o-y in Q2 2021 from 4.8% y-o-y in the previous quarter. Exports of goods continued to be a main driver of economic growth, expanding 20.2% y-o-y in Q2 2021 after a 30.1% y-o-y rise in Q1 2021. Exports of services exhibited a modest recovery, rising 2.6% y-o-y in Q2 2021 after contracting 7.3% y-o-y in the prior quarter.

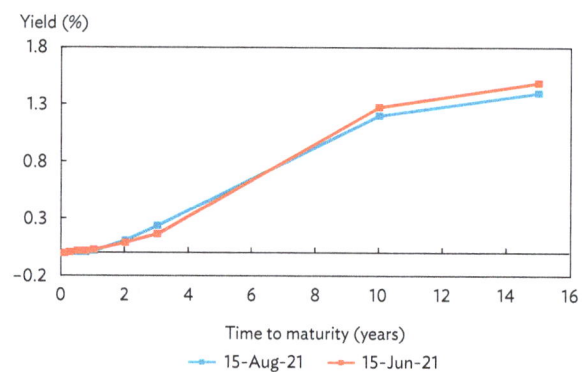

Figure 1: Hong Kong, China's Benchmark Yield Curve—Exchange Fund Bills and Notes

Source: Based on data from Bloomberg LP.

Hong Kong, China's track to economic recovery remains reliant on several factors, including the ongoing geopolitical tensions between the People's Republic of China and the United States, and the highly volatile trajectory of the global pandemic.

Size and Composition

Hong Kong, China's outstanding LCY bonds totaled HKD2,426.9 billion (USD312.5 billion) at the end of June (**Table 1**). The LCY bond market contracted 0.8% quarter-on-quarter (q-o-q) in Q2 2021, reversing the 1.7% q-o-q gain in Q1 2021. The contraction in the stock of outstanding bonds was driven by a decline in the corporate bond segment that outpaced the growth in the government bond segment. Government bonds accounted for 50.1% of total LCY bonds outstanding at the end of June, up from 48.6% at the end of March. On a y-o-y basis, growth in Hong Kong, China's LCY bond market moderated to 7.0% in Q2 2021 from 8.4% in the previous quarter.

Government bonds. LCY government bonds outstanding reached HKD1,215.7 billion at the end of June, with growth accelerating to 2.4% q-o-q in Q2 2021 from 0.2% q-o-q in Q1 2021. The growth was driven primarily by a 23.6% q-o-q expansion of Hong Kong Special Administrative Region (HKSAR) bonds. The stock of Exchange Fund Bills (EFBs) inched up 0.1% q-o-q, while the stock of Exchange Fund Notes (EFNs) fell 3.2% q-o-q

Table 1: Size and Composition of the Local Currency Bond Market in Hong Kong, China

| | Outstanding Amount (billion) | | | | | | Growth Rate (%) | | | |
| | Q2 2020 | | Q1 2021 | | Q2 2021 | | Q2 2020 | | Q2 2021 | |
	HKD	USD	HKD	USD	HKD	USD	q-o-q	y-o-y	q-o-q	y-o-y
Total	2,269	293	2,446	315	2,427	313	0.6	(0.7)	(0.8)	7.0
Government	1,156	149	1,187	153	1,216	157	(1.1)	(0.7)	2.4	5.1
Exchange Fund Bills	1,042	134	1,043	134	1,044	134	(1.7)	(0.003)	0.1	0.2
Exchange Fund Notes	26	3	25	3	24	3	(3.0)	(12.2)	(3.2)	(6.2)
HKSAR Bonds	89	11	119	15	147	19	6.4	(4.5)	23.6	66.4
Corporate	1,112	144	1,258	162	1,211	156	2.4	(0.8)	(3.7)	8.9

( ) = negative, HKD = Hong Kong dollar, HKSAR = Hong Kong Special Administrative Region, q-o-q = quarter-on-quarter, Q1 = first quarter, Q2 = second quarter, USD = United States dollar, y-o-y = year-on-year.
Notes:
1. Calculated using data from national sources.
2. Bloomberg LP end-of-period local currency–USD rates are used.
3. Growth rates are calculated from local currency base and do not include currency effects.
Source: Hong Kong Monetary Authority.

during the review period. On a y-o-y basis, growth in LCY government bonds outstanding quickened to 5.1% in Q2 2021 from 1.5% in Q1 2021.

Issuance of government bonds totaled HKD854.9 billion in Q2 2021 with the 4.5% q-o-q growth reversing the 5.6% q-o-q decline in the previous quarter. Strong issuance of HKSAR bonds largely drove the overall expansion in LCY government bond issuance.

Exchange Fund Bills. EFBs outstanding reached HKD1,044.2 billion at the end of June on growth of 0.1% q-o-q and 0.2% y-o-y. Issuance of EFBs totaled HKD825.5 billion in Q2 2021, rising 1.4% q-o-q.

Exchange Fund Notes. Since 2015, the Hong Kong Monetary Authority (HKMA) has limited its issuance of EFNs to 2-year tenors. In May, the HKMA issued 2-year EFNs worth HKD1.2 billion. Due to maturities, outstanding EFNs declined 3.2% q-o-q in Q2 2020, amounting to HKD24.2 billion at the end of June.

HKSAR bonds. Due to strong issuance, HKSAR bonds outstanding expanded 23.6% q-o-q in Q2 2021 to reach HKD147.3 billion at the end of June. The government issued a 4-year bond worth HKD4.0 billion in April, a 5-year bond worth HKD2.5 billion in May, and a 10-year bond worth HKD1.7 billion in June under the Institutional Bond Issuance Programme. The government also issued HKD20.0 billion of 3-year, inflation-linked retail bonds in June. On a y-o-y basis, HKSAR bonds outstanding expanded 66.4% in Q2 2021, up from 43.2% in the previous quarter.

Corporate bonds. Corporate bonds outstanding reached HKD1,211.2 billion at the end of June after a 3.7% q-o-q drop in Q2 2021 due to maturities and a decline in issuance. On a y-o-y basis, growth in the outstanding stock of corporate bonds moderated to 8.9% in Q2 2021 from 15.9% in Q1 2021.

Hong Kong, China's top 30 nonbank issuers had a combined HKD290.9 billion of bonds outstanding at the end of Q2 2021, accounting for 24.0% of the total LCY corporate bond market (**Table 2**). Hong Kong Mortgage Corporation remained the top issuer with HKD64.9 billion of bonds outstanding at the end of June. Sun Hung Kai & Co. and Hong Kong and China Gas Company were the next largest issuers with outstanding bond of HKD19.1 billion and HKD17.9 billion, respectively. The top 30 issuers were predominantly finance and real estate companies. A majority of the top 30 issuers were listed in the Hong Kong Stock Exchange and only three were government-owned corporations.

Issuance of corporate debt totaled HKD233.6 billion at the end of June. Issuance contracted 20.8% q-o-q in Q2 2021 as uncertainties about the negative impacts of new COVID-19 variants tempered demand for corporate debt.

Table 3 lists the largest corporate issuers in Q2 2021. Hong Kong Mortgage Corporation was the largest issuer with an aggregate HKD15.7 billion from 45 issuances, the largest of which was a 2.5-year bond worth HKD1.0 billion. The next largest issuer was CK Asset Holdings, which raised HKD3.8 billion from an issuance

Table 2: Top 30 Nonbank Corporate Issuers of Local Currency Corporate Bonds in Hong Kong, China

	Issuers	Outstanding Amount		State-Owned	Listed Company	Type of Industry
		LCY Bonds (HKD billion)	LCY Bonds (USD billion)			
1.	Hong Kong Mortgage Corporation	64.9	8.4	Yes	No	Finance
2.	Sun Hung Kai & Co.	19.1	2.5	No	Yes	Finance
3.	The Hong Kong and China Gas Company	17.9	2.3	No	Yes	Utilities
4.	New World Development	16.0	2.1	No	Yes	Diversified
5.	Link Holdings	12.9	1.7	No	Yes	Finance
6.	MTR	12.5	1.6	Yes	Yes	Transportation
7.	Hong Kong Land	12.5	1.6	No	No	Real Estate
8.	Hang Lung Properties	12.4	1.6	No	Yes	Real Estate
9.	Henderson Land Development	12.0	1.5	No	Yes	Real Estate
10.	Swire Pacific	11.6	1.5	No	Yes	Diversified
11.	CK Asset Holdings	10.0	1.3	No	Yes	Real Estate
12.	The Wharf Holdings	9.4	1.2	No	Yes	Finance
13.	Cathay Pacific	9.3	1.2	No	Yes	Transportation
14.	Airport Authority Hong Kong	8.9	1.1	Yes	No	Transportation
15.	Hong Kong Electric	8.5	1.1	No	No	Utilities
16.	CLP Power Hong Kong Financing	7.7	1.0	No	No	Finance
17.	Guotai Junan International Holdings	7.7	1.0	No	Yes	Finance
18.	Swire Properties	7.6	1.0	No	Yes	Diversified
19.	Hysan Development Corporation	5.7	0.7	No	Yes	Real Estate
20.	Future Days	4.2	0.5	No	No	Transportation
21.	Lethai Group	3.0	0.4	No	Yes	Real Estate
22.	AIA Group	2.4	0.3	No	Yes	Insurance
23.	China Dynamics Holdings	2.4	0.3	No	Yes	Diversified
24.	Champion REIT	2.3	0.3	No	Yes	Real Estate
25.	The 13 Holdings	2.2	0.3	No	Yes	Industrial
26.	IFC Development	2.0	0.3	No	No	Finance
27.	Nan Fung	1.8	0.2	No	No	Real Estate
28.	Wheelock and Company	1.5	0.2	No	Yes	Real Estate
29.	Emperor International Holdings	1.4	0.2	No	Yes	Real Estate
30.	Innovative Pharmaceutical Biotech	1.3	0.2	No	Yes	Health Care
	Total Top 30 Nonbank LCY Corporate Issuers	**290.9**	**37.5**			
	Total LCY Corporate Bonds	**1,211.2**	**156.0**			
	Top 30 as % of Total LCY Corporate Bonds	**24.0%**	**24.0%**			

HKD = Hong Kong dollar, LCY = local currency, REIT = real estate investment trust, USD = United States dollar.
Notes:
1. Data as of 30 June 2021.
2. State-owned firms are defined as those in which the government has more than a 50% ownership stake.
Source: *AsianBondsOnline* calculations based on Bloomberg LP data.

of a 3-year bond with a 0.62% coupon. Other notable issuers in Q2 2021 included New World Development, Sun Hung Kai & Co., MTR, and Guotai Junan International Holdings. The longest tenor issued during the quarter was a 30-year bond from New World Development.

Policy, Institutional, and Regulatory Developments

Hong Kong Monetary Authority Holds Countercyclical Capital Buffer at 1.0%

On 5 August, the HKMA announced that the countercyclical buffer (CCyB) would remain unchanged at 1.0%. The HKMA noted that while there have been initial signs of recovery, the economy continued to face uncertainties driven by the global pandemic. Thus, holding the CCyB steady and monitoring the economic situation for a few more quarters was deemed more appropriate. The CCyB is an integral part of the Basel III regulatory capital framework designed to increase the resilience of the banking sector during periods of excess credit growth. A lower CCyB releases additional liquidity into the banking system by raising banks' lending capacity to support the economy.

Table 3: Notable Local Currency Corporate Bond Issuances in the Second Quarter of 2021

Corporate Issuers	Coupon Rate (%)	Issued Amount (HKD billion)
Hong Kong Mortgage Corporation[a]		
9-month bond	zero	1.00
9-month bond	zero	1.00
1-year bond	0.27	0.70
2.5-year bond	0.70	1.00
3-year bond	0.80	0.70
5-year bond	0.42	0.92
5-year bond	1.07	0.40
10-year bond	1.71	0.30
CK Asset Holdings		
3-year bond	0.62	3.79
New World Development		
10-year bond	3.95	0.78
30-year bond	4.79	1.00
Sun Hung Kai & Co.		
3-year bond	0.70	0.70
7-year bond	1.90	0.80
MTR		
1-year bond	0.19	1.00
Guotai Junan International Holdings[a]		
1-year bond	0.60	0.30
1-year bond	0.80	0.25

HKD = Hong Kong dollar.
[a] Multiple issuance of the same tenor indicates issuance on different dates.
Source: Bloomberg LP.

Indonesia

Yield Movements

Local currency (LCY) government bond yield movements in Indonesia diverged across tenors between 15 June and 15 August. Excluding the 3-year tenor, bond yields fell from the 1-year through the 10-year maturities, shedding an average of 12 basis points (bps) (**Figure 1**). The largest decline was seen in the 1-year and 2-year tenors, which slipped by 19 bps each during the review period. In contrast, yields edged up marginally by an average of 3 bps for all maturities of 12 years or more except for the 16-year, which slipped 2 bps. The biggest yield uptick was recorded for the 12-year bond, which rose 7 bps. The 2-year and 10-year yield spread widened from 204 bps on 15 June to 219 bps on 15 August.

The decline in yields for maturities of 10 years or less largely reflected the weakening economic outlook as economic activities were once again halted by the reintroduction of mobility restrictions in July. The spike in COVID-19 cases due to the emergence of virus variants, particularly the more contagious delta variant, dampened economic recovery and dragged down investor sentiment. The ongoing uncertainties associated with the pandemic also led the Ministry of Finance to revise downward its economic growth projections for 2021 from a range of 4.5%–5.3% in February to 3.7%–4.5% in July.

Bank Indonesia has continued to maintain an accommodative monetary policy stance, similar with other central banks in emerging East Asia, to help propel economic growth. In its meeting on 18–19 August, Bank Indonesia's Board of Governors held steady the 7-day reverse repurchase rate at 3.50%, the deposit facility rate at 2.75%, and the lending facility rate at 4.25%. The central bank also continued to purchase government bonds during primary auctions as well as participate in green shoe options as part of burden-sharing agreement with the government to help fund the state budget. As of 16 August, Bank Indonesia's bond purchases had reached IDR132.0 trillion this year.

In August, Bank Indonesia announced that it will continue with its bond purchases this year, targeting to buy up to

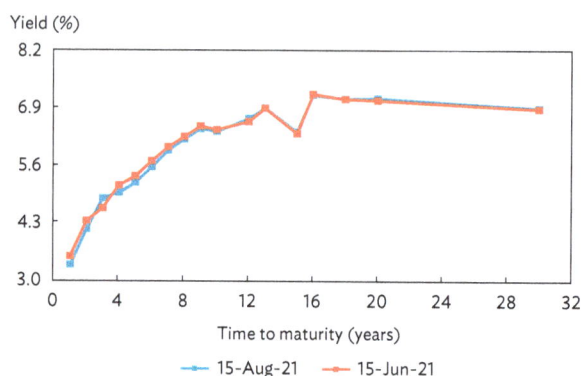

Figure 1: Indonesia's Benchmark Yield Curve—Local Currency Government Bonds

Source: Based on data from Bloomberg LP.

IDR215 trillion of tradable government bonds directly from the government. The burden-sharing agreement will also be extended until 2022 with planned bond purchases of up to IDR224 trillion.

Consumer sentiment has weakened, with inflation falling short of Bank Indonesia's target range of 2.0%–4.0% for 2021. Consumer prices rose 1.5% year-on-year (y-o-y) in July, up from 1.3% y-o-y in June.

Economic performance rebounded in the second quarter (Q2) of 2021, with gross domestic product (GDP) expanding for the first time since the outbreak of the pandemic after contracting for 4 quarters in a row. GDP growth climbed to 7.1% y-o-y in Q2 2021, following a 0.7% y-o-y decline in the first quarter (Q1) of 2021. Growth was buoyed by a recovery in private consumption (5.9% y-o-y) and investments(7.5% y-o-y), as well as faster expansions in government spending (8.1% y-o-y), exports (31.8% y-o-y), and imports (31.2% y-o-y). All industry sectors posted positive y-o-y growth in Q2 2021. The faster growth in Q2 2021 was fueled by the easing of mobility restrictions, which allowed for the opening of the economy as well as increased consumer spending related to Muslim religious festivities. However, the economic recovery was disrupted by the reimposition of mobility restrictions in July amid a surge in COVID-19 cases owing to delta variant infections.

Table 1: Size and Composition of the Local Currency Bond Market in Indonesia

	Outstanding Amount (billion)						Growth Rate (%)			
	Q2 2020		Q1 2021		Q2 2021		Q2 2020		Q2 2021	
	IDR	USD	IDR	USD	IDR	USD	q-o-q	y-o-y	q-o-q	y-o-y
Total	3,761,356	264	4,799,432	330	4,912,250	339	6.6	14.9	2.4	30.6
Government	3,331,641	234	4,366,500	301	4,489,539	310	8.0	16.6	2.8	34.8
Central Govt. Bonds	3,105,895	218	4,155,596	286	4,282,623	295	9.6	22.7	3.1	37.9
of which: Sukuk	579,263	41	765,420	53	740,172	51	21.1	37.9	(3.3)	27.8
Central Bank Bonds	49,624	3	54,927	4	58,670	4	2.5	(59.2)	6.8	18.2
of which: Sukuk	38,874	3	54,927	4	58,670	4	7.5	77.2	6.8	50.9
Nontradable Bonds	176,122	12	155,977	11	148,246	10	(13.7)	(14.0)	(5.0)	(15.8)
of which: Sukuk	37,274	3	35,684	2	33,106	2	(3.9)	(7.7)	(7.2)	(11.2)
Corporate	429,715	30	432,931	30	422,711	29	(3.0)	3.0	(2.4)	(1.6)
of which: Sukuk	29,382	2	31,172	2	31,672	2	(2.7)	21.8	1.6	7.8

( ) = negative, IDR = Indonesian rupiah, q-o-q = quarter-on-quarter, Q1 = first quarter, Q2 = second quarter, USD = United States dollar, y-o-y = year-on-year.
Notes:
1. Calculated using data from national sources.
2. Bloomberg LP end of period local currency–USD rates are used.
3. Growth rates are calculated from local currency base and do not include currency effects.
4. Sukuk refers to Islamic bonds.
Sources: Bank Indonesia; Directorate General of Budget Financing and Risk Management, Ministry of Finance; Indonesia Stock Exchange; and Bloomberg LP.

Size and Composition

Indonesia's LCY bond market growth decelerated to 2.4% quarter-on-quarter (q-o-q) in Q2 2021 from 6.2% q-o-q in Q1 2021 to reach a size of IDR4,912.3 trillion (USD338.8 billion) (**Table 1**). Central government bonds, comprising both Treasury bills and Treasury bonds, continued to drive growth, as the government issued additional bonds to help fund the budget deficit. Central bank bonds also contributed to the growth but to a smaller extent. In contrast, the stocks of nontradable bonds and corporate bonds posted q-o-q declines in Q2 2021. On a y-o-y basis, Indonesia accounted for the fastest LCY bond market growth in emerging East Asia in Q2 2021, albeit at a moderated pace of expansion of 30.6% versus 36.0% in the preceding quarter.

Among emerging East Asian peers, Indonesia's government bond segment continued to comprise the largest share of total bonds outstanding. At the end of June, government bonds represented a 91.4% share of the LCY bond market of Indonesia. This outsized government bond share vis-à-vis corporate bonds reflects how LCY bond financing remains an important funding source for the government in terms of economic development, infrastructure projects, and COVID-19-related stimulus and relief measures.

Conventional bonds continued to dominate Indonesia's LCY bond market, accounting for an 82.4% share of bonds outstanding at the end of June. While Indonesia remained home to the second-largest sukuk (Islamic bond) market in the region in Q2 2021, the share of sukuk to total bonds was only 17.6% at the end of June, down from 18.5% at the end of March and 18.2% at the end of June 2020.

Government bonds. At the end of June, total government bonds outstanding reached IDR4,489.5 trillion. Government bond market growth, however, moderated to 2.8% q-o-q in Q2 2021 from 6.7% q-o-q in Q1 2021. In the same period, growth also eased on a y-o-y basis to 34.8% from 41.5%.

Central government bonds. Central government bonds outstanding in Indonesia totaled IDR4,282.6 trillion at the end of June. This accounted for 95.4% of the total government bond stock. Growth of central government bonds eased to 3.1% q-o-q in Q2 2021 from 7.4% q-o-q in Q1 2021. Slower growth in bonds outstanding stemmed from the continued decline in issuance since Q1 2021, despite the government's adoption of a frontloading policy as in previous years. Compared with the same period in the previous year, central government bonds outstanding rose 37.9% y-o-y in Q2 2021, down from 46.7% y-o-y in Q1 2021.

Total issuance of Treasury bills and Treasury bonds reached IDR231.4 trillion in Q2 2021, down from IDR307.0 trillion in the preceding quarter. New issuance of central government bonds contracted 24.6% q-o-q in Q2 2021 following a 30.9% q-o-q decline in Q1 2021. The government has tapered its issuance due to excess funds from borrowing in 2020 and improved revenue collection in the first half of 2021. State revenue increased 9.1% y-o-y to IDR886.9 trillion in the first half of 2021, which was equivalent to 50.9% of the target indicated in the state budget.[7] In contrast, state spending totaled IDR1,170.1 trillion in the first half of the year, which was equivalent to 42.5% of the annual state budget. This resulted in a deficit of IDR283.2 trillion, or 1.7% of GDP, compared with the full-year budget deficit target for 2021 of 5.7%.

In August, however, the government revised upward its bond issuance plan for 2021 to support a wider budget deficit. The government estimated debt issuance for the year to reach IDR1,020.0 trillion compared with IDR958.1 trillion projected in July.

Central bank bonds. The outstanding amount of central bank bills and bonds rose to IDR58.7 trillion at the end of June. Growth rebounded to 6.8% q-o-q in Q2 2021, reversing the 0.9% q-o-q contraction in the previous quarter. Total central bank issuance rose to IDR309.5 trillion on growth of 79.7% q-o-q. Issuances during the quarter solely comprised Sukuk Bank Indonesia, as there has been no issuance of Sertifikat Bank Indonesia since April.

Corporate bonds. The outstanding amount of LCY corporate bonds fell to IDR422.7 trillion at the end of June, on contractions of 2.4% q-o-q and 1.6% y-o-y. The decline in the corporate bond stock in Q2 2021 stemmed from the continued slowdown in issuance and a higher volume of maturities during the quarter.

The 31 largest corporate bond issuers in Indonesia at the end of June are provided in **Table 2**.[8] The aggregate bonds outstanding of these 31 corporate entities reached IDR308.7 trillion, down from IDR311.5 trillion issued by the top 30 issuers at the end of March. As a share of total corporate bonds, the largest corporate bond issuers

accounted for 73.0% at the end of June, up from 72.0% at the end of March.

Leading the 31 firms on the list were corporates from the banking and financial industry. Other leading issuers included firms from the energy, telecommunications, construction, and manufacturing industries. Also included in the list are 19 state-owned institutions, of which 8 firms are ranked in the top 10, and 18 firms whose shares are listed in the Indonesia Stock Exchange.

At the end of June, the composition of the five-largest corporate bond issuers was similar with the list at the end of March. All five firms were state-owned institutions. Leading the list was energy firm Perusahaan Listrik Negara with bonds outstanding of IDR35.1 trillion, accounting for 8.3% of the total corporate bond stock at the end of June. In the second spot was Indonesia Eximbank with bonds outstanding of IDR23.1 trillion and a 5.5% share of the total. Next was Sarana Multi Infrastruktur with outstanding bonds of IDR20.5 trillion and a 4.9% share of the total. Rounding out the top five firms on the list were Bank Rakyat Indonesia and Sarana Multigriya Finansial.

Corporate bond sales in Q2 2021 totaled IDR18.8 trillion, down 8.5% q-o-q but up 108.3% y-o-y. Due to lingering uncertainties resulting from the COVID-19 pandemic, corporates opted to stay on the sidelines and reconsidered their borrowing plans. A total of 14 firms raised funds from the bond market in Q2 2021, a tad lower than the 16 firms in the prior quarter. This added 32 bond series to the corporate bond total at the end of June. Of this new series, four issues were structured as *sukuk mudharabah* (Islamic bonds backed by a profit-sharing scheme from a business venture or partnership) and two were structured as *sukuk ijarah* (Islamic bonds backed by lease agreements). The maturity distribution of the new corporate issues was concentrated in 3-year maturities (15 out of 32 new series) and 370-day bonds (11 out of 32 new series). The longest-dated corporate bond issued during the quarter was 7 years.

Two new corporate names also joined the list of bond issuers in Q2 2021. These were Integra Indocabinet and Adhi Commuter Properti. Both issues were priced

[7] *Antaranews.com.* 2021. Indonesia's Budget Deficit Reaches 1.72% of GDP in First Half: Govt. 5 July. https://en.antaranews.com/news/178338/indonesias-budget-deficit-reaches-172-of-gdp-in-first-half-govt.
[8] Two firms tied for the number 30 spot on the list.

Table 2: Top 31 Issuers of Local Currency Corporate Bonds in Indonesia

		Outstanding Amount				
	Issuers	LCY Bonds (IDR billion)	LCY Bonds (USD billion)	State-Owned	Listed Company	Type of Industry
1.	Perusahaan Listrik Negara	35,121	2.42	Yes	No	Energy
2.	Indonesia Eximbank	23,102	1.59	Yes	No	Banking
3.	Sarana Multi Infrastruktur	20,513	1.41	Yes	No	Finance
4.	Bank Rakyat Indonesia	16,619	1.15	Yes	Yes	Banking
5.	Sarana Multigriya Finansial	16,184	1.12	Yes	No	Finance
6.	Bank Tabungan Negara	14,675	1.01	Yes	Yes	Banking
7.	Bank Mandiri	14,000	0.97	Yes	Yes	Banking
8.	Pegadaian	12,919	0.89	Yes	No	Finance
9.	Indosat	11,149	0.77	No	Yes	Telecommunications
10.	Bank Pan Indonesia	9,927	0.68	No	Yes	Banking
11	Indah Kiat Pulp & Paper	9,505	0.66	No	Yes	Pulp and Paper
12.	Waskita Karya	9,402	0.65	Yes	Yes	Building Construction
13.	Pupuk Indonesia	9,046	0.62	Yes	No	Chemical Manufacturing
14.	Permodalan Nasional Madani	8,835	0.61	Yes	No	Finance
15.	Astra Sedaya Finance	8,206	0.57	No	No	Finance
16.	Semen Indonesia	7,078	0.49	Yes	Yes	Cement Manufacturing
17.	Tower Bersama Infrastructure	7,040	0.49	No	Yes	Telecommunications Infrastructure Provider
18.	Telkom Indonesia	7,000	0.48	Yes	Yes	Telecommunications
19.	Hutama Karya	6,500	0.45	Yes	No	Nonbuilding Construction
20.	Bank CIMB Niaga	6,484	0.45	No	Yes	Banking
21.	Adira Dinamika Multi Finance	6,328	0.44	No	Yes	Finance
22.	Federal International Finance	6,073	0.42	No	No	Finance
23.	Mandiri Tunas Finance	5,599	0.39	No	No	Finance
24.	Chandra Asri Petrochemical	5,489	0.38	No	Yes	Petrochemicals
25.	Bank Pembangunan Daerah Jawa Barat Dan Banten	5,248	0.36	Yes	Yes	Banking
26.	Wijaya Karya	5,000	0.34	Yes	Yes	Building Construction
27.	Bank Maybank Indonesia	4,849	0.33	No	Yes	Banking
28.	Sinar Mas Agro Resources and Technology	4,500	0.31	No	Yes	Food
29.	Adhi Karya	4,316	0.30	Yes	Yes	Building Construction
30.	Angkasa Pura II	4,000	0.28	Yes	No	Airport Management Services
31.	Kereta Api Indonesia	4,000	0.28	Yes	No	Transportation
	Total Top 31 LCY Corporate Issuers	308,707	21.29			
	Total LCY Corporate Bonds	422,711	29.15			
	Top 31 as % of Total LCY Corporate Bonds	73.0%	73.0%			

IDR = Indonesian rupiah, LCY = local currency, USD = United States dollar.
Notes:
1. Data as of 30 June 2021.
2. State-owned firms are defined as those in which the government has more than a 50% ownership stake.
Source: *AsianBondsOnline* calculations based on Indonesia Stock Exchange data.

at the tightest range, with their respective 3-year bonds each having a coupon rate of over 10.0%. Local rating agency Pemeringkatan Efek Indonesia rated the bond by Integra Indocabinet as idA– and that of Adhi Commuter Properti as idBBB. Most other 3-year bonds issued during the quarter had coupon rates of between 6.25% and 8.75%.

Table 3 lists the largest corporate bonds issued in Indonesia in Q2 2021. State-owned pawnshop Perum Pegadaian had the largest total issuance at IDR4.0 trillion issued in four tranches, including two issues of *sukuk mudharabah*. In the second spot was Astra Sedaya Finance with aggregate issuance of IDR2.5 trillion from a dual-tranche bond sale in April. Next was Bank Mandiri Taspen, which raised a total of IDR2.0 trillion from a dual-tranche bond sold in April.

Investor Profile

Foreign flows into the Indonesian bond market turned positive in Q2 2021, with net inflows reaching USD1.8 billion to reverse outflows of USD1.6 billion in Q1 2021. Net inflows were also recorded in April and June, which far exceeded the USD0.5 billion in net outflows posted in May. Foreign investor holdings of LCY government bonds fell to a share of 22.8% of the total market at the end of June from 22.9% at the end of March and from 30.2% at the end of June 2020 (**Figure 2**). In nominal terms, foreign holdings have been largely volatile this year.

Foreign investor appetite for long-term bonds has waned in 2021 due to uncertainty in the trajectory of economic recovery and volatility in financial markets. Bonds with maturities of more than 10 years accounted for only 26.6% of nonresident bond holdings at the end

Table 3: Notable Local Currency Corporate Bond Issuances in the Second Quarter of 2021

Corporate Issuers	Coupon Rate (%)	Issued Amount (IDR billion)
Perum Pegadaian		
370-day bond	4.85	2,173
370-day *sukuk mudharabah*	4.85	599
3-year bond	6.20	1,108
3-year *sukuk mudharabah*	6.20	166
Astra Sedaya Finance		
370-day bond	4.85	892
3-year bond	6.35	1,608
Bank Mandiri Taspen		
3-year bond	6.50	800
5-year bond	7.25	1,200
Federal International Finance		
370-day bond	4.60	628
3-year bond	6.25	872
Sinar Mas Agro Resources and Technology		
370-day bond	6.75	600
3-year bond	8.75	600
5-year bond	9.25	300

IDR = Indonesian rupiah.
Note: *Sukuk mudharabah* are Islamic bonds backed by a profit-sharing scheme from a business venture or partnership.
Source: Indonesia Stock Exchange.

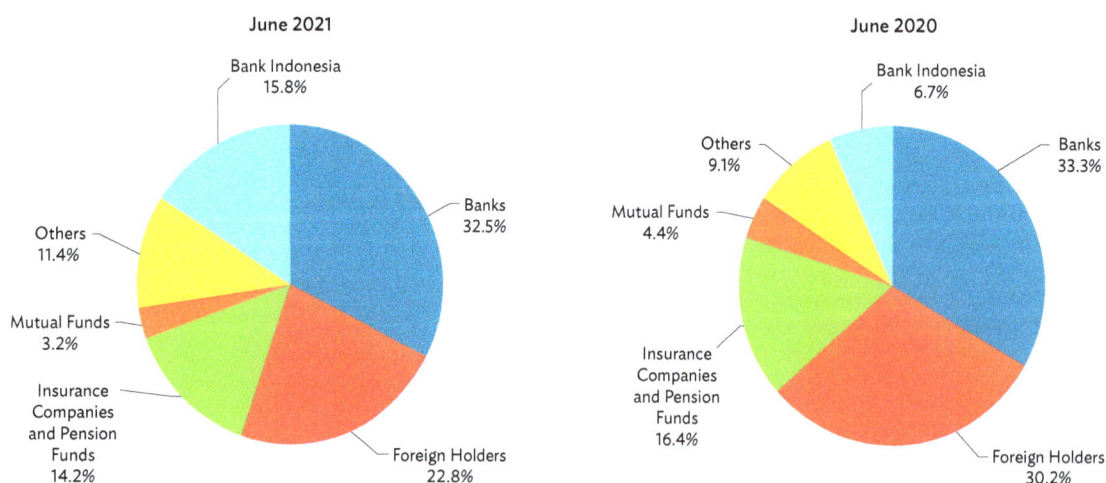

Figure 2: Local Currency Central Government Bonds Investor Profile

Source: Directorate General of Budget Financing and Risk Management, Ministry of Finance.

Figure 3: Foreign Holdings of Local Currency Central Government Bonds by Maturity

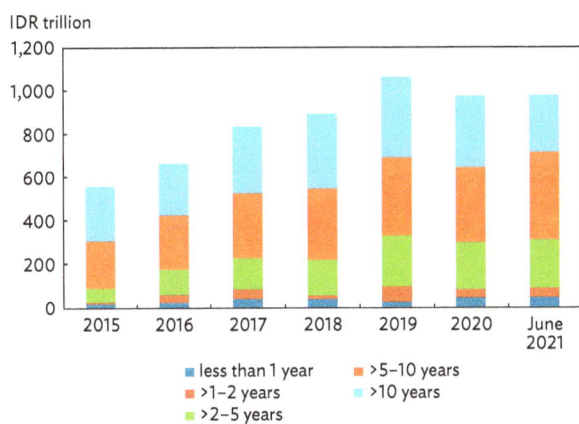

IDR trillion

Legend:
- less than 1 year
- >1–2 years
- >2–5 years
- >5–10 years
- >10 years

IDR = Indonesian rupiah.
Source: Directorate General of Budget Financing and Risk Management, Ministry of Finance.

of June (**Figure 3**). A steady decline in their holdings has been noted since January, at which time the maturity bucket of more than 10 years accounted for 34.1% of foreign holdings. In contrast, the share of bonds with maturities of more than 5 years to 10 years steadily rose to 41.6% at the end of June from only 35.4% at the end of January. This reflects the shift in foreign investor risk appetite for medium-dated tenors. Nonetheless, bonds with maturities of 1 year or less only accounted for 4.7% of total nonresident holdings at the end of June.

Among domestic investors, banking institutions had the largest holdings of government bonds. However, their holdings share slipped to 32.5% at the end of June from 33.3% a year earlier. Insurance companies and mutual funds also reduced their holdings of government bonds with their shares of outstanding bonds falling to 14.2% and 3.2%, respectively, at the end of June from 16.4% and 4.4% at the end of June 2020.

Bank Indonesia increased its holdings of government bonds during the review period. The central bank continued to purchase government bonds as part of a burden-sharing agreement with the government to help fund the state budget. Aside from bond purchases, Bank Indonesia also injected liquidity into the banking sector by lowering the reserve requirement ratio and engaging in monetary expansion. Central bank holdings of government bonds surged to 15.8% of the total at the end of June from 6.7% in the same period from a year earlier.

The only other investor group aside from Bank Indonesia that saw an increase in their holdings share of government bonds during the review period were individuals and other investors not elsewhere classified. Collectively, their holdings rose by 2.4 percentage points to 11.4% at the end of June from 9.1% a year earlier.

Policy, Institutional, and Regulatory Developments

Bank Indonesia Broadens Local Currency Settlement Framework with Bank Negara Malaysia and the Ministry of Finance, Japan

Effective 2 August, Bank Indonesia and Bank Negara Malaysia expanded their LCY settlement framework to encourage the use of Indonesian rupiah and Malaysian ringgit for the settlement of trade and direct investment transactions between Indonesia and Malaysia. The new policies in the expanded settlement framework are as follows: (i) inclusion of direct investments, income, and transfers as eligible transactions; (ii) inclusion of individuals as eligible participants; and (iii) simplified documentary requirements for tapping the framework. Both central banks also appointed additional banks to facilitate the LCY settlement framework.

Effective 5 August, Bank Indonesia and the Ministry of Finance, Japan relaxed some policies related to their existing Indonesian rupiah and Japanese yen settlement framework. This move was made to further support trade and investment activities between Indonesia and Japan. The policies that were relaxed include the (i) use of cross-currency swap and domestic nondeliverable forward transactions as hedging tools, (ii) removal of underlying documents for transactions of up to USD500,000 from the previous USD25,000, and (iii) expansion of eligible criteria for hedging transactions and extension of hedging maturities to more than 1 year.

Republic of Korea

Yield Movements

The Republic of Korea's local currency (LCY) government bond yield curve slightly flattened between 15 June and 15 August as yields for short-term to medium-term tenors rose, while those for long-term tenors fell (**Figure 1**). Correspondingly, the spread between the 2-year and 10-year tenors fell to 68 basis points (bps) from 91 bps during the review period. Yields for the 3-month and 6-month tenors rose 6 bps and 18 bps, respectively. Yields between the 1-year and 3-year tenors rose 9 bps on average, while that of the 5-year tenor fell 4 bps. Yields for long-term tenors of between 10 years and 50 years fell 19 bps on average.

Yields at the shorter-end of the curve rose on increased expectations of a rate hike by the Bank of Korea before the year ends. The expectations were driven by increased inflationary pressures as inflation has hovered above 2.0% since April, reaching a high of 2.6% in May and July. In addition, the need to arrest the rise in household debt and housing prices also contributed to market expectations of a rate hike. Subsequently on 26 August, the Bank of Korea decided to raise the base rate by 25 bps to 0.75%.

Meanwhile, yields at the longer-end of the curve fell, tracking the global downward trend in long-term yields on weakening optimism and expectations of a slowdown in the global economic recovery amid the rise in cases of the more transmissible delta variant of COVID-19. The resurgence in domestic cases and the slow vaccination rollout has resulted in the tightening and extension of social distancing measures in the Republic of Korea and is expected to dampen consumption. In addition, bond supply concerns eased as the government announced in June that the funding of the second supplementary budget for 2021 will not involve the issuance of additional government bonds. The National Assembly on 24 July passed a second supplementary budget of KRW34.9 trillion to support small businesses, households, and local governments, and for the procurement of additional vaccines.

On 26 August, the Bank of Korea decided to raise the base rate to 0.75%, after leaving it unchanged on its 15 July monetary policy meeting. The central bank noted the continued recovery in the domestic economy and

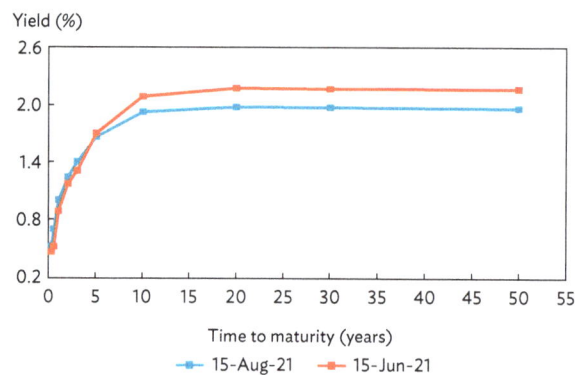

Figure 1: The Republic of Korea's Benchmark Yield Curve—Local Currency Government Bonds

Source: Based on data from Bloomberg LP.

maintained its economic growth forecast for 2021 at 4.0%. Meanwhile, 2021 inflation forecast was revised upward to 2.1% from May projection of 1.8%. Given these conditions, the Monetary Board stated that it will gradually adjust the degree of monetary policy accommodation, taking into consideration developments in COVID-19, risk of a buildup in financial imbalances, and monetary policy changes in advanced economies.

The Republic of Korea's economic growth accelerated to 6.0% y-o-y in the second quarter (Q2) of 2021 from 1.9% y-o-y in the first quarter (Q1), based on preliminary estimates by the Bank of Korea. The higher growth was driven by private consumption, government spending, and an acceleration in export growth. However, on a quarter-on-quarter (q-o-q) basis, domestic economic growth slowed to 0.8% in Q2 2021 from 1.7% in Q1 2021.

The Republic of Korea's LCY bond market continued to register high levels of foreign inflows in Q2 2021, with net inflows of KRW3,346 billion and KRW5,516 billion in the months of April and May, respectively. Foreign inflows surged to a record KRW9,387 billion in June and further to KRW9,290 billion in July. Investor confidence in the Republic of Korea's economic recovery and favorable external balances, and the high interest rate differential over United States (US) Treasuries drove this trend.

The Korean won was one of the weakest currencies in the region during the review period, depreciating

4.5% to KRW1,169.02 per USD1.0 as of 15 August. The resurgence in domestic cases and foreign selling of Korean equities contributed to the depreciation of the currency.

Size and Composition

The size of the Republic of Korea's LCY bond market increased to KRW2,756.4 trillion at the end of June on growth of 2.3% quarter-on-quarter (q-o-q) (**Table 1**), which is slightly lower than the 2.4% q-o-q expansion registered in the previous quarter. Growth for the quarter was largely driven by the government sector, while the corporate sector grew at a slower pace. From the same period in 2020, the Republic of Korea's bond market grew 7.9% y-o-y, slower than the 8.9% y-o-y growth posted in Q1 2021.

Government bonds. The outstanding size of the Republic of Korea's LCY government bond market rose 3.2% q-o-q to KRW1,158.3 trillion. Growth stemmed from the 5.0% q-o-q expansion in the stock of central government bonds to KRW807.7 trillion, which more than offset the decline in central bank bonds. Monetary Stabilization Bonds issued by the Bank of Korea declined 1.9% q-o-q to KRW154.2 trillion. Meanwhile, outstanding bonds issued by other government-owned entities inched up 0.3% q-o-q to KRW196.3 trillion.

Issuance of government bonds was up 11.1% q-o-q in Q2 2021 to KRW114.3 trillion, led by central government bonds, which rose 17.3% q-o-q to KRW59.1 trillion. This was consistent with the frontloading policy of the government, which announced plans to spend 67% of its 2021 budget in the first half of the year. The higher issuance for the quarter may also be attributed to the funding of the first supplementary budget of 2021 (KRW14.9 trillion) passed on March.

Corporate bonds. The Republic of Korea's LCY corporate bond market grew 1.6% q-o-q to KRW1,598.2 trillion at the end of June, with growth accelerating from the 1.2% q-o-q increase posted in Q1 2021. **Table 2** lists the top 30 LCY corporate bond issuers in the Republic of Korea at the end of June. The top 30's bonds outstanding reached an aggregate size of KRW955.4 trillion and comprised 59.8% of the total LCY corporate bond market. Financial companies such as banks and securities and investment firms continued to dominate the Top 30 list with a collective share of 64.1%. Korea Housing Finance Corporation remained the single-largest corporate bond issuer in the market with total bonds outstanding of KRW152.6 trillion and a 16.0% share of the top 30's aggregate bonds. Industrial Bank of Korea and Mirae Asset Securities were the next largest LCY corporate bond issuers with total bonds outstanding of KRW71.5 trillion and KRW62.6 trillion, respectively.

The higher q-o-q growth in the Republic of Korea's corporate bonds outstanding in Q2 2021 was driven by the 16.6% q-o-q surge in issuance to KRW150.5 trillion from KRW129.1 trillion in Q1 2021. Higher issuance volumes were registered in all categories—special public entities, financial debentures, and private companies—as institutions ramped up their issuance amid increased expectations of a rate hike before the year ends.

Table 1: Size and Composition of the Local Currency Bond Market in the Republic of Korea

| | Outstanding Amount (billion) | | | | | | Growth Rate (%) | | | |
| | Q2 2020 | | Q1 2021 | | Q2 2021 | | Q2 2020 | | Q2 2021 | |
	KRW	USD	KRW	USD	KRW	USD	q-o-q	y-o-y	q-o-q	y-o-y
Total	2,553,743	2,123	2,695,546	2,382	2,756,445	2,447	3.1	9.5	2.3	7.9
Government	1,038,139	863	1,122,368	992	1,158,252	1,028	4.6	9.7	3.2	11.6
Central Government Bonds	679,020	565	769,339	680	807,725	717	5.1	13.3	5.0	19.0
Central Bank Bonds	168,870	140	157,230	139	154,230	137	1.9	(1.6)	(1.9)	(8.7)
Others	190,249	158	195,799	173	196,297	174	5.3	8.5	0.3	3.2
Corporate	1,515,604	1,260	1,573,178	1,390	1,598,193	1,419	2.1	9.4	1.6	5.4

( ) = negative, KRW = Korean won, q-o-q = quarter-on-quarter, Q1 = first quarter, Q2 = second quarter, USD = United States dollar, y-o-y = year-on-year.
Notes:
1. Calculated using data from national sources.
2. Bloomberg LP end-of-period local currency–USD rates are used.
3. Growth rates are calculated from local currency base and do not include currency effects.
4. "Others" comprise Korea Development Bank Bonds, National Housing Bonds, and Seoul Metro Bonds.
5. Corporate bonds include equity-linked securities and derivatives-linked securities.
Sources: KG Zeroin Corporation and The Bank of Korea.

Table 2: Top 30 Issuers of Local Currency Corporate Bonds in the Republic of Korea

| Issuers | Outstanding Amount | | State-Owned | Listed on | | Type of Industry |
	LCY Bonds (KRW billion)	LCY Bonds (USD billion)		KOSPI	KOSDAQ	
1. Korea Housing Finance Corporation	152,640	135.5	Yes	No	No	Housing Finance
2. Industrial Bank of Korea	71,530	63.5	Yes	Yes	No	Banking
3. Mirae Asset Securities Co.	62,584	55.6	No	Yes	No	Securities
4. Korea Investment and Securities	58,252	51.7	No	No	No	Securities
5. KB Securities	50,252	44.6	No	No	No	Securities
6. Hana Financial Investment	49,716	44.1	No	No	No	Securities
7. NH Investment & Securities	35,070	31.1	Yes	Yes	No	Securities
8. Shinhan Investment Corporation	33,479	29.7	No	No	No	Securities
9. Korea Land & Housing Corporation	31,516	28.0	Yes	No	No	Real Estate
10. Samsung Securities	30,251	26.9	No	Yes	No	Securities
11. Shinhan Bank	29,612	26.3	No	No	No	Banking
12. Korea Electric Power Corporation	26,800	23.8	Yes	Yes	No	Electricity, Energy, and Power
13. Korea Expressway	25,150	22.3	Yes	No	No	Transport Infrastructure
14. Meritz Securities Co.	24,486	21.7	No	Yes	No	Securities
15. The Export-Import Bank of Korea	23,675	21.0	Yes	No	No	Banking
16. Woori Bank	21,310	18.9	Yes	Yes	No	Banking
17. KEB Hana Bank	20,665	18.3	No	No	No	Banking
18. Kookmin Bank	20,164	17.9	No	No	No	Banking
19. Korea National Railway	19,450	17.3	Yes	No	No	Transport Infrastructure
20. NongHyup Bank	18,530	16.5	Yes	No	No	Banking
21. Hanwha Investment and Securities	18,433	16.4	No	No	No	Securities
22. Korea SMEs and Startups Agency	18,418	16.4	Yes	No	No	SME Development
23. Shinyoung Securities	18,365	16.3	No	Yes	No	Securities
24. Shinhan Card	16,505	14.7	No	No	No	Credit Card
25. Hyundai Capital Services	14,425	12.8	No	No	No	Consumer Finance
26. KB Kookmin Bank Card	14,290	12.7	No	No	No	Consumer Finance
27. Standard Chartered Bank Korea	13,250	11.8	No	No	No	Banking
28. NongHyup	13,160	11.7	Yes	No	No	Banking
29. Samsung Card Co.	12,048	10.7	No	Yes	No	Credit Card
30. Korea Gas Corporation	11,369	10.1	Yes	Yes	No	Gas Utility
Total Top 30 LCY Corporate Issuers	955,394	848.3				
Total LCY Corporate Bonds	1,598,193	1,419.0				
Top 30 as % of Total LCY Corporate Bonds	59.8%	59.8%				

KOSDAQ = Korean Securities Dealers Automated Quotations, KOSPI = Korea Composite Stock Price Index, KRW = Korean won, LCY = local currency, SMEs = small and medium-sized enterprises, USD = United States dollar.
Notes:
1. Data as of 30 June 2021.
2. State-owned firms are defined as those in which the government has more than a 50% ownership stake.
3. Corporate bonds include equity-linked securities and derivatives-linked securities.
Sources: *AsianBondsOnline* calculations based on Bloomberg LP and KG Zeroin Corporation data.

Table 3: Notable Local Currency Corporate Bond Issuances in the Second Quarter of 2021

Corporate Issuers	Coupon Rate (%)	Issued Amount (KRW billion)	Corporate Issuers	Coupon Rate (%)	Issued Amount (KRW billion)
Shinhan Bank[a]			Nonghyup Bank[a]		
1-year bond	0.77	600	1-year bond	1.14	490
1-year bond	0.12	310	1-year bond	0.80	370
1-year bond	0.81	220	1-year bond	zero	360
1-year bond	0.82	200	1-year bond	zero	200
1-year bond	0.88	170	2-year bond	1.26	400
1-year bond	0.82	150	2-year bond	1.08	210
2-year bond	1.07	430	3-year bond	1.31	400
2-year bond	2.58	400	5-year bond	1.83	240
2-year bond	1.07	260	29-year bond	2.32	140
3-year bond	1.15	350	Sinbo Securitization Specialty[a]		
3-year bond	1.20	300	2-year bond	1.237	149
Woori Bank[a]			2-year bond	1.26	148
1-year bond	0.81	500	2-year bond	1.64	119
1-year bond	0.12	500	3-year bond	1.47	493
1-year bond	0.89	430	3-year bond	1.45	400
1-year bond	0.79	200	3-year bond	1.78	392
2-year bond	1.07	500	3-year bond	1.45	171
2-year bond	1.01	400	3-year bond	1.47	108
2-year bond	1.05	350			
10-year bond	2.64	300			

KRW = Korean won.
[a] Multiple issuance of the same tenor indicates issuance on different dates.
Source: Based on data from Bloomberg LP.

Table 3 lists the notable corporate bond issuances in Q2 2021. Financial firms such as Shinhan Bank, Woori Bank, Nonghyup Bank, and Sinbo Securitization had some of the largest aggregate issuance totals during the quarter.

Investor Profile

Insurance companies and pension funds continued to be the largest investor group in the Republic of Korea's LCY government bond market at the end of March 2021 with a share of 34.7%, which was almost at par with their 34.6% share in March 2020 (**Figure 2**). Banks surpassed the general government as the second-largest investor group at the end of March 2021. The share of banks rose to 18.3% (from 17.2% in March 2020) and the general government's share declined to 16.3% (from 18.1%). The share of other financial institutions remained the same at 14.9%, while nonfinancial corporations and households registered sharp declines. Foreign holdings of LCY government bonds registered the highest percentage increase during the review period, rising to 14.6% from 11.0%, as foreign bond inflows surged in Q1 2021.

Other financial institutions held the largest share of the Republic of Korea's LCY corporate bonds at the end of Q2 2021 with their share rising to 38.9% from 37.5% in the same period in 2020 (**Figure 3**). Meanwhile, the share of insurance companies and pension funds fell during the review period to 36.3% from 37.3%. The share of the general government was almost unchanged at 13.5% versus 13.6%, while the share of foreign holders remained negligible.

Foreign demand for the Republic of Korea's LCY bonds continued to remain high in Q2 2021, posting net inflows of KRW3,346 billion and KRW5,516 billion in the months of April and May, respectively, and reaching KRW9,387 billion in June and further to KRW9,290 billion in July (**Figure 4**). Strong foreign demand has been driven by the high interest rate differential of Korean LCY bonds over United States Treasuries. This was primarily due to a rise in domestic government bond yields, particularly for tenors of between 1 year and 5 years, on expectations of a rate hike later this year. Domestic bonds with remaining maturities of 1–5 years also registered the highest net foreign inflows during the review period (**Figure 5**). The Republic of Korea continued to be a safe haven relative

Figure 2: Local Currency Government Bonds Investor Profile

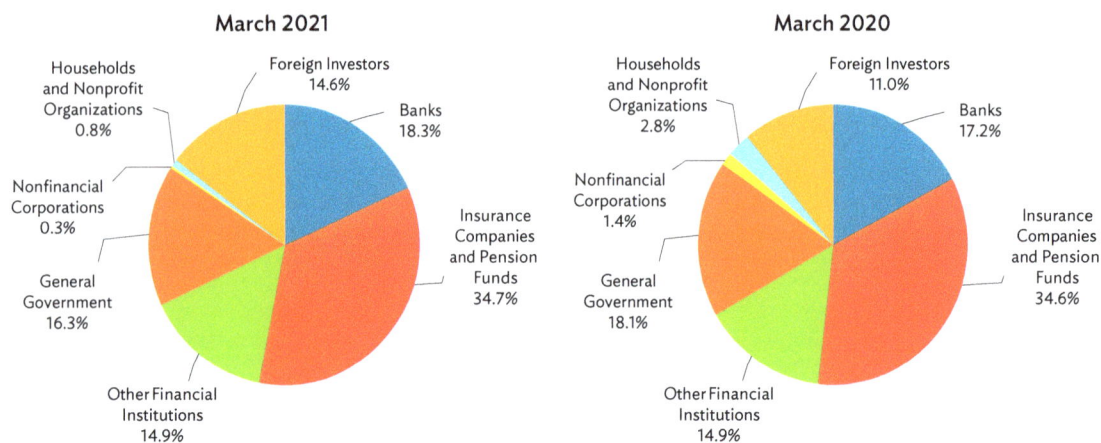

March 2021

Households and Nonprofit Organizations 0.8%
Foreign Investors 14.6%
Banks 18.3%
Insurance Companies and Pension Funds 34.7%
General Government 16.3%
Other Financial Institutions 14.9%
Nonfinancial Corporations 0.3%

March 2020

Households and Nonprofit Organizations 2.8%
Foreign Investors 11.0%
Banks 17.2%
Insurance Companies and Pension Funds 34.6%
General Government 18.1%
Other Financial Institutions 14.9%
Nonfinancial Corporations 1.4%

Source: *AsianBondsOnline* and The Bank of Korea.

Figure 3: Local Currency Corporate Bonds Investor Profile

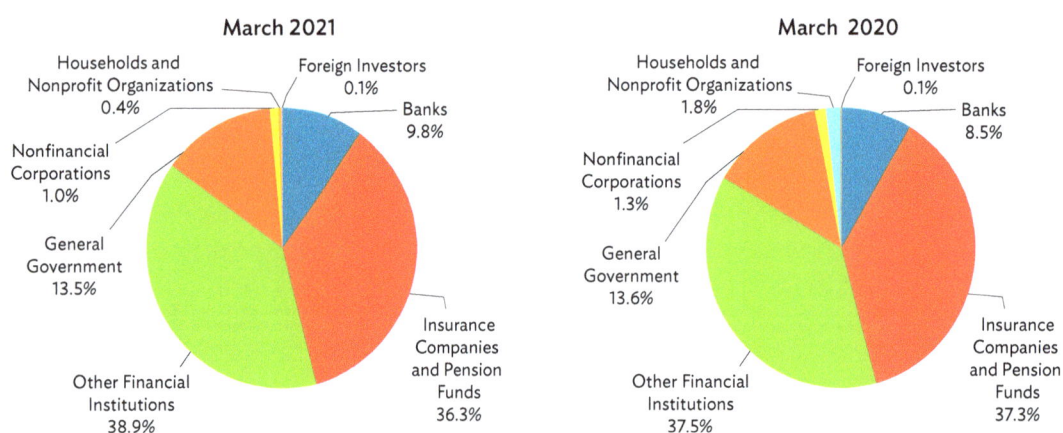

March 2021

Households and Nonprofit Organizations 0.4%
Foreign Investors 0.1%
Banks 9.8%
Insurance Companies and Pension Funds 36.3%
General Government 13.5%
Other Financial Institutions 38.9%
Nonfinancial Corporations 1.0%

March 2020

Households and Nonprofit Organizations 1.8%
Foreign Investors 0.1%
Banks 8.5%
Insurance Companies and Pension Funds 37.3%
General Government 13.6%
Other Financial Institutions 37.5%
Nonfinancial Corporations 1.3%

Source: *AsianBondsOnline* and The Bank of Korea.

to other bond markets in the region due to its strong domestic economic recovery and favorable external balances. The decline in the 5-year credit default swap spread from a peak of 26.0 bps in January to 18.5 bps at the end of July reflected strong investor confidence.

Ratings Update

On 21 July, Fitch Ratings affirmed the Republic of Korea's sovereign credit ratings at AA– with a stable outlook. The rating agency cited the Republic of Korea's "robust external finances, resilient macroeconomic performance, and modest fiscal headroom" as the reasons behind the rating affirmation. Downside risks remained following a

recent rise in domestic COVID-19 cases; however, the expanded vaccine rollout is expected to mitigate any new outbreak. In addition, the second supplementary budget is expected to support the recovery in consumption. Fitch Rating forecast that 2021 gross domestic product (GDP) growth will reach 4.5%. Meanwhile, the fiscal deficit is expected to widen to 4.4% of GDP in 2021. Despite the rise in government debt, the Republic of Korea's record of fiscal prudence, along with the government's proposal for a debt ceiling of 60% of GDP and an annual fiscal deficit limit of 3% of GDP, is expected to further support fiscal management. The rating agency also expects the Bank of Korea to hike policy rates by 25 bps in the second half of 2021 and by another 50 bps in 2022.

Figure 4: Net Foreign Investment in Local Currency Bonds in the Republic of Korea

KRW billion

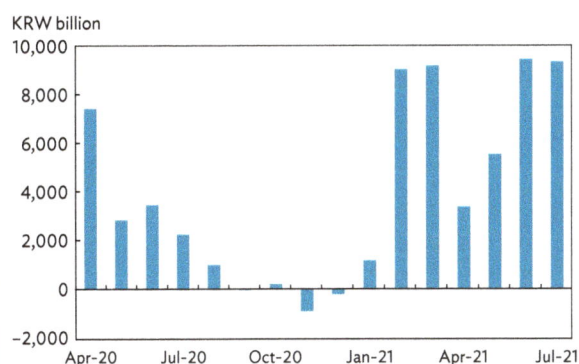

KRW = Korean won.
Source: Financial Supervisory Service.

Figure 5: Net Foreign Investment in Local Currency Bonds in the Republic of Korea by Remaining Maturity

KRW billion

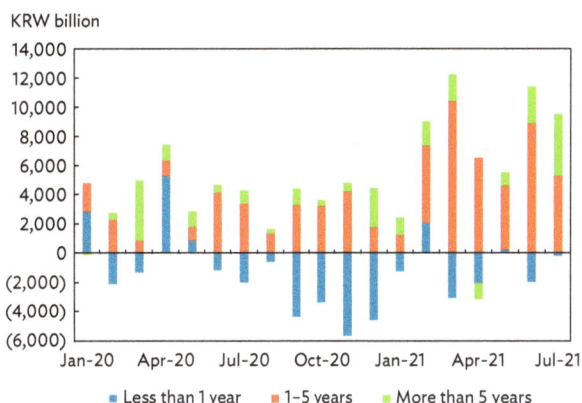

■ Less than 1 year ■ 1–5 years ■ More than 5 years

KRW = Korean won.
Source: Financial Supervisory Service.

Policy, Institutional, and Regulatory Developments

National Assembly Passes Second Supplementary Budget

On 24 July, the National Assembly passed the second supplementary budget for 2021 worth KRW34.9 trillion, which was KRW1.9 trillion higher than the proposed amount. This was the sixth supplementary budget related to the government's response to the pandemic since 2020: KRW14.9 trillion was allotted for pandemic relief packages, KRW12.6 trillion for local economic support and subsidies to local governments, KRW4.9 trillion for vaccine purchases and disease prevention efforts, and KRW2.5 trillion for employment support and low-income household aid. The supplementary budget brought the overall budget for 2021 to KRW604.9 trillion from an original amount of KRW558 trillion. The new 2021 budget is expected to produce a fiscal deficit equal to 4.4% of GDP and cumulative government debt equal to 47.2% of GDP.

The Bank of Korea Announces Changes to Monetary Stabilization Bonds Issuance System

On 2 August, the Bank of Korea announced changes to the issuance system of Monetary Stabilization Bonds (MSBs) to enhance liquidity management efficiency. Regular auctions of 182-day MSBs will be suspended given the introduction of 3-year MSBs. Meanwhile, the issuance of 1-year, 2-year, and 3-year MSBs will be held once a month. Issuance of 91-day MSBs—at auctions to be held once a week—will be slightly expanded to around KRW1 trillion. Finally, the issuance of 1-year and 2-year MSBs will be significantly reduced due to the issuance of 3-year MSBs. The new system will be implemented effective 1 September.

Malaysia

Yield Movements

Movements in Malaysia's local currency (LCY) government bond yields were mixed between 15 June and 15 August (**Figure 1**). Yields for the 1-month and 3-month tenors barely moved, increasing 0.3 basis points (bps) and 0.1 bps, respectively. At the shorter-end of the curve, the 6-month tenor and 1-year tenor declined 1 bp each, while the 2-year yield decreased 4 bps. Yields on tenors of 3 years to 7 years jumped an average of 10 bps, with the 5-year yield rising the most among all tenors with a 14-bps gain during the review period. The longer-end of the yield curve (9 years to 30 years) recorded declines, with the 20-year yield declining the most at 10 bps. During the review period, the yield spread between 2-year and 10-year government bonds slightly increased from 128 bps to 129 bps.

The mixed movement in yields reflected investors' cautious view of the economy as Malaysia and its neighboring economies continued to reel from the effects of the COVID-19 pandemic, with the spread of the delta variant and an increasing number of COVID-19 cases remaining a threat to the domestic and global economic recovery. Uncertainty in Malaysia's political landscape also affected Malaysia's financial markets, and the selling pressure in the belly of the yield curve may be attributed to risk-off sentiment among investors. On the other hand, the low long-term yields may be ascribed to the low-interest-rate environment as Bank Negara Malaysia (BNM) kept the overnight policy rate at 1.75% in July.

Aggravated by political uncertainty, the Malaysian ringgit weakened 2.8% against the United States (US) dollar during the review period to close at MYR4.2375 per USD1.0 dollar on 15 August.

On 8 July, the monetary policy committee of BNM maintained its policy rate at 1.75%. The decision came as the global economy continued to recover from the COVID-19 pandemic. On the domestic front, Malaysia's economic growth in the first quarter (Q1) of 2021 was better than expected, although this growth was slightly dampened in the second quarter (Q2) of 2021 as the economy was placed under another Movement Control Order to curb the spread of COVID-19 infections.

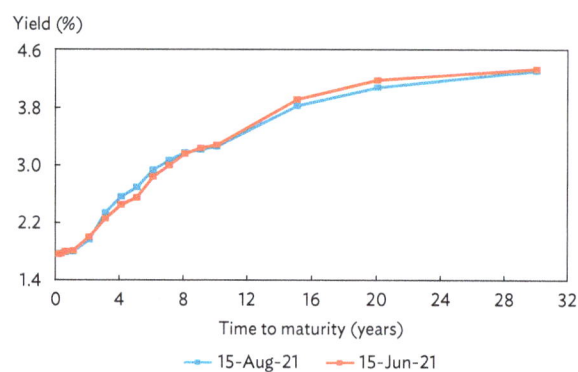

Figure 1: Malaysia's Benchmark Yield Curve— Local Currency Government Bonds

Source: Based on data from Bloomberg LP.

Malaysia's stimulus packages and strong external position are helping to support economic growth.

Malaysia's economy grew 16.1% year-on-year (y-o-y) on Q2 2021, reversing 4 straight quarters of contraction. Gross domestic product (GDP) growth was supported by expansions in the manufacturing and services sectors. At the same time, the significant growth in Q2 2021 was buoyed by a low base effect from Q2 2020 when GDP growth plunged owing to the first Movement Control Order implemented in March 2020 to curb the spread of COVID-19. On a quarter-on-quarter (q-o-q) basis, economic growth fell 2.0% during the quarter. In Q2 2021, the value of Malaysia's GDP remained lower than its pre-pandemic level in the fourth quarter of 2019. In August, BNM revised its expected full-year 2021 economic growth to 3.0%–4.0% from 6.0%–7.5%, mainly due to the effects of COVID-19 containment measures.

Consumer price inflation followed a downtrend, though remained elevated, during Q2 2021. From 4.7% y-o-y in April, prices of basic goods and services increased at a slower pace in May and June, recording inflation of 4.4% y-o-y and 3.4% y-o-y, respectively. Prices in April and May were elevated as increased demand from consumers coincided with Muslim festivities. The elevated inflation rates were also due to a low base effect from low retail fuel prices in 2020 and a lag in the effects of the government's tiered rebate of the electricity tariff implemented from April to December 2020. By July, inflation fell to 2.2% y-o-y. Malaysia's central bank expects consumer price inflation will fall between 2.5% and 4.0% for full-year 2021.

In June, the Government of Malaysia unveiled the National Recovery Plan, an exit strategy from the COVID-19 crisis. The plan consists of four phases. Movement from one phase to another is based on three thresholds: (i) number of daily COVID-19 infections, (ii) bed utilization rates in intensive care unit wards, and (iii) the percentage of the population that is fully vaccinated. Various restrictions on economic and social activities will be implemented during each phase, relaxing as the economy moves to latter phases. Malaysia was in Phase 1, the strictest phase, in June as a full Movement Control Order was implemented to curb rising COVID-19 cases. As of 4 August, seven states remained in Phase 1, while six states were in Phase 2, and three states had moved to Phase 3. By the end of October, 60% of Malaysia's population is expected to be fully vaccinated through the National COVID-19 Immunization Programme.

Size and Composition

The LCY bond market of Malaysia expanded 2.7% q-o-q in Q2 2021 to reach a size of MYR1,693.3 billion (USD408.1 billion) at the end of June, up from MYR1,648.9 billion at the end of Q1 2021 (**Table 1**). The Q2 2021 expansion was slightly slower than the

2.8% q-o-q growth recorded in Q1 2021. On an annual basis, the LCY bond market grew 8.9% y-o-y in Q2 2021, which was faster than the 7.9% y-o-y growth posted in the prior quarter. The growth may be attributed to expansions in both LCY government and corporate bonds, which accounted for 54.6% and 45.4%, respectively, of total LCY bonds outstanding at the end of June. At the end of the review period, total outstanding *sukuk* (Islamic bonds) reached MYR1,065.1 billion on growth of 2.3% q-o-q that was supported by increased stocks of government and corporate *sukuk*.

Issuance of LCY bonds in Q2 2021 increased 1.0% q-o-q to MYR101.2 billion from MYR100.2 billion in Q1 2021, driven by increased corporate bond issuance. The growth was partially offset by a decline in issuance of government bonds.

Government bonds. The LCY government bond market grew 3.9% q-o-q to a size of MYR924.1 billion at the end of Q2 2021 from MYR889.6 billion at the end of March. The Q2 2021 expansion was slower than the growth of 4.3% q-o-q in the previous quarter. The increase was due to the increase of 4.1% q-o-q in outstanding central government bonds, which comprised 97.4% of total outstanding LCY government bonds at the end of June, spurred by the increased stock of government bonds and Treasury bills. There were no outstanding central bank bills at the end of June, while the amount of outstanding

Table 1: Size and Composition of the Local Currency Bond Market in Malaysia

	Outstanding Amount (billion)						Growth Rate (%)			
	Q2 2020		Q1 2021		Q2 2021		Q2 2020		Q2 2021	
	MYR	USD	MYR	USD	MYR	USD	q-o-q	y-o-y	q-o-q	y-o-y
Total	1,555	363	1,649	398	1,693	408	1.8	4.5	2.7	8.9
Government	829	193	890	215	924	223	3.2	6.4	3.9	11.5
Central Government Bonds	797	186	865	209	900	217	4.0	7.4	4.1	12.9
of which: *Sukuk*	367	86	403	97	415	100	1.5	10.1	2.9	12.9
Central Bank Bills	5	1	1	0	0	0	(50.0)	(45.7)	(100.0)	(100.0)
of which: *Sukuk*	0	0	0	0	0	0	(100.0)	(100.0)	–	–
Sukuk Perumahan Kerajaan	27	6	24	6	24	6	0.0	(3.9)	0.0	(10.1)
Corporate	726	169	759	183	769	185	0.2	2.4	1.3	6.0
of which: *Sukuk*	582	136	614	148	626	151	0.9	5.0	2.0	7.6

( ) = negative, – = not applicable, MYR = Malaysian ringgit, q-o-q = quarter-on-quarter, Q1 = first quarter, Q2 = second quarter, USD = United States dollar, y-o-y = year-on-year.
Notes:
1. Calculated using data from national sources.
2. Bloomberg LP end-of-period local currency–USD rates are used.
3. Growth rates are calculated from local currency base and do not include currency effects.
4. *Sukuk* refers to Islamic bonds.
5. Sukuk Perumahan Kerajaan are Islamic bonds issued by the Government of Malaysia to refinance funding for housing loans to government employees and to extend new housing loans.
Sources: Bank Negara Malaysia Fully Automated System for Issuing/Tendering and Bloomberg LP.

Sukuk Perumahan Kerajaan, which comprised 2.6% of total outstanding LCY government bonds at the end of Q2 2021, was unchanged from Q1 2021.

LCY government bond issuance in Q2 2021 declined 1.8% q-o-q to MYR56.0 billion from MYR57.0 billion in Q1 2021. The reduced issuance was due to slightly lower issuances of government bonds and Treasury bills.

The total issuance of Malaysian Government Securities (conventional bonds) and Government Investment Issues (Islamic bonds) during the first half of 2021 increased compared to the first half of 2020 as Movement Control Orders restricted economic activities, and fiscal support was needed in response.

Corporate bonds. Outstanding LCY corporate bonds outstanding grew 1.3% q-o-q to MYR769.2 billion at the end of June from MYR759.3 billion at the end of March. Growth in Q2 2021 was faster than the 1.0% q-o-q growth logged in Q1 2021. The amount of outstanding corporate *sukuk* grew 2.0% q-o-q to MYR626.4 billion in Q2 2021 from MYR614.4 billion in Q1 2021, with growth also accelerating from 0.9% q-o-q in the previous quarter.

Malaysia's top 30 corporate bond issuers accounted for MYR456.4 billion of outstanding corporate bonds at the end of Q2 2021, representing 59.3% of the total LCY corporate bond market (**Table 2**). Government-owned Danainfra Nasional led all issuers with LCY corporate bonds outstanding amounting to MYR76.0 billion. Financial institutions had the largest sectoral share (52.9%) among all sectors represented in the top 30 list with MYR241.2 billion in LCY corporate bonds outstanding at the end of the review period.

LCY corporate bonds issued in Q2 2021 jumped 4.7% q-o-q to MYR45.2 billion from MYR43.2 billion in Q1 2021. The growth in Q2 2021 was a reversal from the decline of 25.8% q-o-q posted in the prior quarter. The expansion may be attributed to companies taking advantage of the low-interest-rate environment as BNM kept its overnight policy rate at 1.75% in July 2021 and the economy is expected to recover during the second half of the year.

In April, Infracap Resources, a special purpose vehicle of the Sarawak state government, issued a total of MYR5.8 billion of *sukuk murabahah,* an Islamic bond in which bondholders are entitled to a share of the revenues generated by the assets (**Table 3**). The issuance had 11 tranches with tenors ranging from 1 year to 15 years. Proceeds from the issuance will be used by the company to fund various Shariah-compliant purposes. Cagamas, the national mortgage corporation of Malaysia, issued three 2-year conventional medium-term notes during the quarter. A dual-tranche bond, both tranches with a coupon rate of 2.5%, was issued in May and its proceeds will be used in funding purchases from the financial system of housing loans. Cagamas' various Islamic medium-term notes were issued under its Medium-Term Note Programme. In May, Danainfra Nasional, which funds projects of the Government of Malaysia, issued five tranches of *sukuk murabahah* totaling MYR2.0 billion and with tenors ranging from 7 years to 30 years. Proceeds from this issuance will be used to fund Shariah-compliant expenses related to the Klang Valley Mass Rapid Transit Project.

Investor Profile

Foreign holdings of LCY government bonds in the Malaysian market rose throughout Q2 2021, with foreign investors holding MYR231.4 billion worth of LCY government bonds in April, MYR233.4 billion in May, and MYR233.8 billion in June (**Figure 2**). Net capital inflows into the bond market in April were MYR6.6 billion, declining to MYR2.0 billion and MYR0.4 billion in the succeeding 2 months. The tapered pace of buying from foreign investors may be attributed to investors' risk aversion due to the resurgence of COVID-19 infections in Malaysia and neighboring economies, which in turn lead the Government of Malaysia to institute again a nationwide Movement Control Order in June. Economic and political uncertainties contributed to foreigners' tepid enthusiasm for Malaysian government bonds. As a share of LCY government bonds, foreign holdings increased from 26.0% at the end of March to 26.6% at the end of April before gradually easing to 26.0% at the end of June.

At the end of March, investors in LCY government bonds were led by financial and social security institutions, holding 34.0% and 27.2% of the total, respectively (**Figure 3**). The holdings of financial institutions increased while those of social security institutions declined compared to the same month in 2020. The share of foreign holders increased to 25.6% during the review period from 21.8% a year prior. The holdings of insurance companies and BNM increased to 4.8% and 1.9% from 4.2% and 1.6%, respectively, between March 2020 and March 2021.

Table 2: Top 30 Issuers of Local Currency Corporate Bonds in Malaysia

	Issuers	Outstanding Amount		State-Owned	Listed Company	Type of Industry
		LCY Bonds (MYR billion)	LCY Bonds (USD billion)			
1.	Danainfra Nasional	76.0	18.3	Yes	No	Finance
2.	Prasarana	37.0	8.9	Yes	No	Transport, Storage, and Communications
3.	Lembaga Pembiayaan Perumahan Sektor Awam	34.2	8.2	Yes	No	Property and Real Estate
4.	Cagamas	30.3	7.3	Yes	No	Finance
5.	Project Lebuhraya Usahasama	28.9	7.0	No	No	Transport, Storage, and Communications
6.	Urusharta Jamaah	27.3	6.6	Yes	No	Finance
7.	Perbadanan Tabung Pendidikan Tinggi Nasional	24.3	5.9	Yes	No	Finance
8.	Pengurusan Air	18.3	4.4	Yes	No	Energy, Gas, and Water
9.	CIMB Bank	13.4	3.2	Yes	No	Finance
10.	Maybank Islamic	13.0	3.1	No	Yes	Banking
11.	Malayan Banking	12.1	2.9	No	Yes	Banking
12.	Sarawak Energy	12.0	2.9	Yes	No	Energy, Gas, and Water
13.	Khazanah	11.9	2.9	Yes	No	Finance
14.	CIMB Group Holdings	11.6	2.8	Yes	No	Finance
15.	Tenaga Nasional	10.3	2.5	No	Yes	Energy, Gas, and Water
16.	Danga Capital	10.0	2.4	Yes	No	Finance
17.	Jimah East Power	8.9	2.2	Yes	No	Energy, Gas, and Water
18.	Danum Capital	8.4	2.0	No	No	Finance
19.	Public Bank	6.9	1.7	No	No	Banking
20.	Bank Pembangunan Malaysia	6.8	1.6	Yes	No	Banking
21.	Sapura TMC	6.4	1.5	No	No	Finance
22.	YTL Power International	6.1	1.5	No	Yes	Energy, Gas, and Water
23.	Bakun Hydro Power Generation	5.9	1.4	No	No	Energy, Gas, and Water
24.	Infracap Resources	5.8	1.4	Yes	No	Finance
25.	GOVCO Holdings	5.7	1.4	Yes	No	Finance
26.	Turus Pesawat	5.3	1.3	Yes	No	Transport, Storage, and Communications
27.	GENM Capital	5.3	1.3	No	No	Finance
28.	EDRA Energy	5.1	1.2	No	Yes	Energy, Gas, and Water
29.	1Malaysia Development	5.0	1.2	Yes	No	Finance
30.	Kuala Lumpur Kepong	4.6	1.1	No	Yes	Energy, Gas, and Water
	Total Top 30 LCY Corporate Issuers	456.4	110.0			
	Total LCY Corporate Bonds	769.2	185.4			
	Top 30 as % of Total LCY Corporate Bonds	59.3%	59.3%			

LCY = local currency, MYR = Malaysian ringgit, USD = United States dollar.
Notes:
1. Data as of 30 June 2021.
2. State-owned firms are defined as those in which the government has more than a 50% ownership stake.
Source: *AsianBondsOnline* calculations based on Bank Negara Malaysia Fully Automated System for Issuing/Tendering data.

Table 3: Notable Local Currency Corporate Bond Issuances in the Second Quarter of 2021

Corporate Issuers	Coupon Rate (%)	Issued Amount (MYR million)
Infracap Resources		
1-year sukuk murabahah	2.83	900
3-year sukuk murabahah	3.11	350
5-year sukuk murabahah	3.69	450
7-year sukuk murabahah	4.12	500
8-year sukuk murabahah	4.23	400
10-year sukuk murabahah	4.40	600
11-year sukuk murabahah	4.50	300
12-year sukuk murabahah	4.60	400
13-year sukuk murabahah	4.70	300
14-year sukuk murabahah	4.80	450
15-year sukuk murabahah	4.90	1,100
Cagamas		
2-year Islamic MTN	2.48	600
2-year Islamic MTN	2.41	200
2-year MTN	2.50	700
2-year MTN	2.50	800
2-year MTN	2.41	700
3-year Islamic MTN	2.78	400
5-year Islamic MTN	3.15	350
Danainfra Nasional		
7-year sukuk murabahah	3.25	300
15-year sukuk murabahah	4.10	400
20-year sukuk murabahah	4.47	400
25-year sukuk murabahah	4.56	400
30-year sukuk murabahah	4.64	500

MTN = medium-term note, MYR = Malaysian ringgit.
Notes:
1. Sukuk murabahah are Islamic bonds in which bondholders are entitled to a share of the revenues generated by the assets.
2. Multiple issuances of the same tenor indicates issuance on different dates.
Source: Bank Negara Malaysia Bond Info Hub.

Figure 2: Foreign Holdings and Capital Flows in the Malaysian Local Currency Government Bond Market

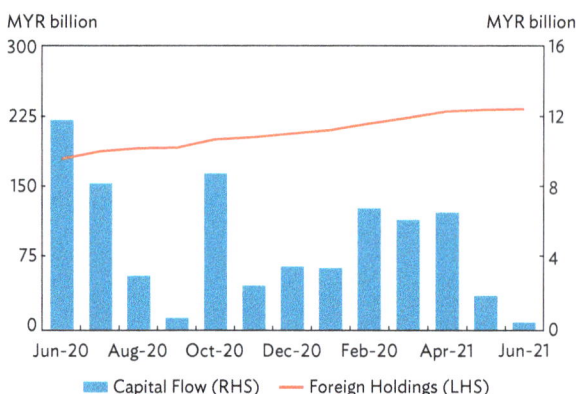

LHS = left-hand side, MYR = Malaysian ringgit, RHS = right-hand side.
Notes:
1. Figures exclude foreign holdings of Bank Negara Malaysia bills.
2. Month-on-month changes in foreign holdings of local currency government bonds were used as a proxy for bond flows.
Source: Based on data from Bloomberg LP.

Ratings Update

Rating and Investment Information Affirms Malaysia's Credit Rating with Stable Outlook

On 2 June, Rating and Investment Information affirmed Malaysia's A+ foreign and local currency issuer ratings with a stable outlook for both ratings. The affirmation came as the rating agency expects Malaysia's economy to recover this year supported by

Figure 3: Local Currency Government Bonds Investor Profile

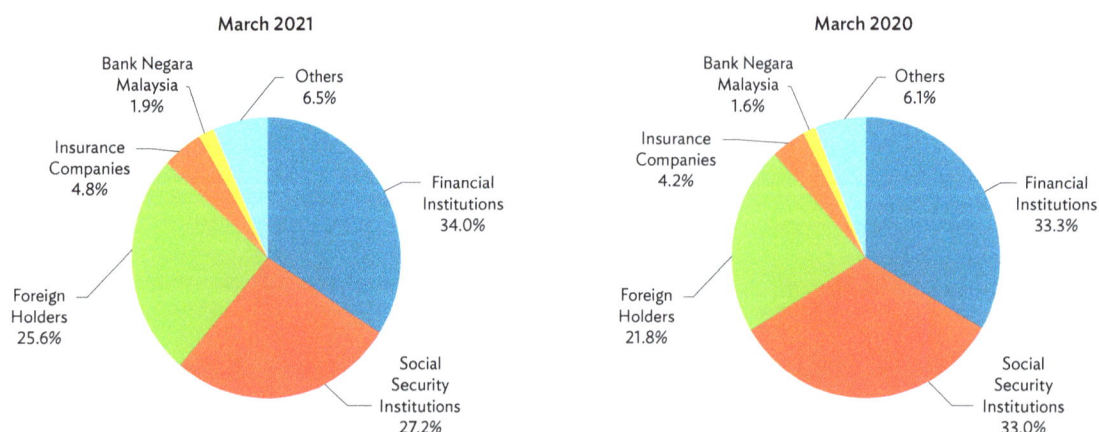

Note: "Others" include statutory bodies, nominees and trustee companies, and cooperatives and unclassified items.
Source: Bank Negara Malaysia.

its relatively advanced diversified industries. R&I also viewed Malaysia's government debt ratio as manageable albeit at an elevated level. Finally, R&I affirmed the credit ratings due to the economy's external stability as evidenced by current account surpluses and ample international reserves.

S&P Global Ratings Affirms Malaysia's Credit Rating with Negative Outlook

On 22 June, S&P Global Ratings affirmed the foreign currency long-term issuer rating of A– for Malaysia with a negative outlook. The affirmation of the rating was attributed to Malaysia's strong external position, flexible monetary policy, and the government's track record of having the ability to sustain economic growth and demonstrating resiliency during economic downturns. The rating agency attributes the negative outlook to Malaysia's high fiscal deficit and debt ratio. A slow economic recovery and political uncertainties are seen to prevent the government's ability to consolidate its finances.

Fitch Ratings Affirms Malaysia's Credit Rating with Stable Outlook

On 18 July, Fitch Ratings affirmed the long-term foreign currency issuer default rating of Malaysia at BBB+, maintaining its stable outlook. The affirmation came as the rating agency sees the economy recovering in 2021 from the contraction recorded in 2020. Despite increased government debt due to expenses related to the COVID-19 response, Malaysia's debt ratio is expected to decline starting in 2022. Fitch Ratings also sees a gradual reduction in the fiscal deficit. Supporting the affirmation are Malaysia's consistent annual current account surplus and the central bank's monetary policy, which the rating agency views as supportive of economic activities.

Policy, Institutional, and Regulatory Developments

Bank Negara Malaysia and Bank Indonesia Expand Local Currency Settlement Framework

On 2 August, BNM and Bank Indonesia expanded their LCY settlement framework. The framework aims to encourage investors to use Malaysian ringgit and Indonesian rupiah in settlements of financial transactions between the two economies. Aside from trade settlement, the expanded framework included in its list of eligible transactions direct investments, income, and transfer settlements. Individuals were included in the expanded framework's eligible users. Its foreign exchange policy has also been streamlined to attract more investors. With the expanded framework, the central banks of Malaysia and Indonesia included in their list more qualified banks that are allowed to execute the framework.

Bank Negara Malaysia Revises Reference Rate Framework

On 11 August, BNM released its revised Reference Rate Framework, effective 1 August 2022. In the revised version, all financial institutions will use a common rate, the standardized base rate, as the reference rate for new issuances of floating-rate notes and refinancing of existing loans in Malaysia. This replaces the current use of a base rate that differs across financial institutions. Furthermore, the standardized base rate will be linked to the overnight policy rate. The revision allows consumers to understand better the changes in their loan repayments. This will also facilitate the transmission of the policy rate to the broader economy.

Philippines

Yield Movements

The yields of local currency (LCY) government bonds in the Philippines fell for all tenors between 15 June and 15 August except for bonds with 7-year and 10-year maturities (**Figure 1**). On average, yields dropped 10 basis points (bps) for all bonds that saw declines. The yield on the 1-year tenor had the smallest decrease at 1 bp, while the 4-year tenor had the largest drop at 15 bps. On the other hand, yields on bonds with 7-year and 10-year maturities climbed 4 bps and 7 bps, respectively. The movements caused the yield spread between the 2-year and 10-year tenors to widen during the review period from 184 bps to 202 bps.

High liquidity in the market and sustained demand for government bonds, along with recent developments in the economy, prompted the downward movement of yields during the review period.

Inflation concerns had dissipated as consumer prices eased further to a 7-month low in July, falling to 4.0% year-on-year (y-o-y) from 4.1% y-o-y in June. It was the first month in 2021 that the inflation rate fell within the full-year target of the Bangko Sentral ng Pilipinas (BSP) of 2.0%–4.0. Transportation largely contributed to the downward adjustment of overall prices. On the other hand, prices of the heavily weighted food and nonalcoholic beverages group remained elevated. The resulting year-to-date inflation remained above the BSP target at 4.4%. In August, the BSP raised its inflation forecast to 4.1% from 4.0% for 2021 and to 3.1% from 3.0% for 2022. The upward revisions could point to higher bond yields ahead.

The BSP continued its accommodative monetary policy stance, keeping the policy rate steady at 2.00% in its monetary policy meeting on 12 August. The decision came on the back of renewed risk to the ongoing economic recovery amid a rising number of COVID-19 cases. According to the BSP, it will continue to implement monetary policy support as long as necessary for the economic recovery to gain more traction. Meanwhile, while the inflation forecast for 2021 was shifted slightly upward, the risks associated with it were broadly balanced to warrant the current policy setting to remain unchanged. Prior to the policy meeting, the BSP hinted that a lowering

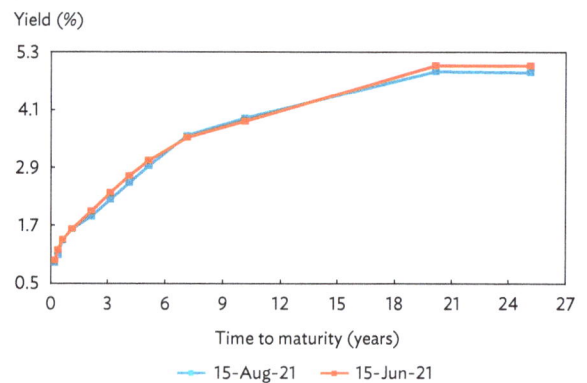

Figure 1: Philippines' Benchmark Yield Curve—Local Currency Government Bonds

Source: Based on data from Bloomberg LP.

of the reserve requirement ratio was possible, which may have also contributed to the downward pressure on yields. This possibility was dismissed later by the BSP, stating that a cut would be untimely.

The reimposition of the strictest mobility controls in early August to curb the spread of the delta variant of the COVID-19 virus threatened recovery prospects, leading to a decline in yields even as gross domestic product (GDP) posted growth in the second quarter (Q2) of 2021. The Philippines ended its recession in Q2 2021 as the economy expanded 11.8% y-o-y during the quarter. The Philippines had experienced 5 consecutive quarters of GDP decline, with the largest contraction (–17.0%) occurring in Q2 2020 at the height of the pandemic and the associated quarantine measures that brought the economy to a standstill. While the double-digit growth was impressive, it is largely a result of a low base effect. On a quarterly basis, GDP contracted 1.3% quarter-on-quarter (q-o-q) in Q2 2021, reflecting the impact of stricter mobility restrictions reimposed in the National Capital Region and surrounding provinces from March through May. GDP in the first half of 2021 expanded 3.7% y-o-y after the negative growth in the first quarter (Q1) of 2021 was revised up to –3.9% y-o-y from –4.2% y-o-y. In August, the government downgraded the growth target for full-year 2021 to 4.0%–5.0% from an earlier target of 6.0%–7.0% in May.

The Philippine peso began weakening against the United States (US) dollar in the middle of June. It traded at PHP50.5 per USD1.0 on 15 August, having lost 5.1% from 15 June. The domestic currency's depreciation was largely due to comments from the US Federal Reserve related to unwinding its loose monetary policy, with hints of tapering to its monthly asset purchases by the end of the year. This was compounded by a flight to safety among investors amid worries over rising COVID-19 cases.

Size and Composition

The Philippine LCY bond market expanded in Q2 2021 by 2.5% q-o-q to reach a size of PHP9,351.0 billion (USD191.6 billion) at the end of June, decelerating from growth of 6.5% q-o-q in Q1 2021 (**Table 1**). The quarterly growth was driven solely by the government segment as the corporate segment contracted during the quarter. On an annual basis, the LCY bond market expanded 25.1% y-o-y. Government bonds accounted for 83.8% of the total bond market at the end of June, while corporate bonds accounted for 16.2%.

Government bonds. Total LCY government bonds outstanding expanded 3.9% q-o-q to PHP7,833.9 billion in Q2 2021, which was slower than the growth of 8.4% q-o-q in the previous quarter. The increase in market size was mainly driven by Treasury bonds and augmented by BSP bills.

Outstanding Treasury bonds amounted to PHP6,351.0 billion in Q2 2021 on growth of 3.6% q-o-q, decelerating from 7.2% q-o-q growth in Q1 2021. The faster growth in the previous quarter was due to the large sale of Retail Treasury Bonds (RTBs), which inflated the market's size in that period. On the other hand, Treasury bills outstanding declined 2.5% q-o-q to PHP1,023.1 billion in Q2 2021 because maturities during the quarter offset new issuances.

Securities issuance from the BSP also contributed to the government bond market's growth, with its outstanding bonds increasing 34.5% q-o-q to reach PHP400 billion at the end of June. Outstanding debt from government-related entities fell 9.1% q-o-q due to bond maturities and the absence of issuance during the quarter.

Total securities issuances from the government segment declined 3.5% q-o-q to PHP2,056.4 billion in Q2 2021. The overall quarterly drop was due to lower Treasury bond issuance during the quarter, which offset the growth in Treasury bills and BSP bills.

Debt raised via Treasury bonds in Q2 2021 amounted to PHP332.0 billion, which was only about half the amount issued in Q1 2021. The quarterly decline was due to a high base in Q1 2021 when PHP463.3 billion in RTBs were issued. Without the RTBs, Treasury bond issuance in Q2 2021 was higher than in Q1 2020 as the Bureau of the Treasury (BTr) increased its borrowing

Table 1: Size and Composition of the Local Currency Bond Market in the Philippines

| | Outstanding Amount (billion) | | | | | | Growth Rate (%) | | | |
| | Q2 2020 | | Q1 2021 | | Q2 2021 | | Q2 2020 | | Q2 2021 | |
	PHP	USD	PHP	USD	PHP	USD	q-o-q	y-o-y	q-o-q	y-o-y
Total	7,477	150	9,122	188	9,351	192	5.2	11.5	2.5	25.1
Government	5,904	119	7,543	155	7,834	160	6.8	11.6	3.9	32.7
Treasury Bills	797	16	1,049	22	1,023	21	43.1	22.1	(2.5)	28.4
Treasury Bonds	5,068	102	6,130	126	6,351	130	2.8	9.8	3.6	25.3
Central Bank Securities	0	0	297	6	400	8	–	–	34.5	–
Others	40	1	66	1	60	1	(0.02)	83.3	(9.1)	50.2
Corporate	1,573	32	1,579	33	1,517	31	(0.4)	11.0	(3.9)	(3.6)

( ) = negative, – = not applicable, PHP = Philippine peso, q-o-q = quarter-on-quarter, Q1 = first quarter, Q2 = second quarter, USD = United States dollar, y-o-y = year-on-year.
Notes:
1. Calculated using data from national sources.
2. Bloomberg end-of-period local currency–USD rates are used.
3. Growth rates are calculated from local currency base and do not include currency effects.
4. "Others" comprise bonds issued by government agencies, entities, and corporations for which repayment is guaranteed by the Government of the Philippines. This includes bonds issued by Power Sector Assets and Liabilities Management and the National Food Authority, among others.
5. Peso Global Bonds (PHP-denominated bonds payable in USD) are not included.
Sources: Bloomberg LP and Bureau of the Treasury.

target of the said securities to PHP280.0 billion in Q2 2021 from PHP180.0 billion in the previous quarter; the programmed issuance was fully awarded. Notably in June, the BTr increased its Treasury bond sales target to PHP140.0 billion, double the monthly target in April and May. The BTr had received a good reception on long tenors in previous auctions as investors sought better yields, thus prompting the adjustment.

Treasury bill issuance amounted to PHP427.4 billion in Q1 2021 on growth of 14.7% q-o-q. The increase was due to larger offer volumes from the BTr during the quarter that were fully awarded, while the opening of the tap facility to accommodate the demand resulted in higher-than-programmed sales of the short-term debt sales.

The government continued to ramp up borrowing from the market to fund its widening budget gap in response to COVID-19 and associated economic recovery plans. Preference for safe-haven assets like government securities remained high on the back of the uncertainties brought about by the pandemic and boosted by abundant market liquidity.

In Q2 2021, the Philippines also tapped the international bond market twice for its fund mobilization. In April, the Philippines successfully returned to the Japanese yen bond market with the issuance of a JPY55.0 billion 3-year, zero-coupon samurai bond. In the same month, the Philippines also issued the largest EUR-denominated bond in a three-tranche sale. A total of EUR2.1 billion was raised, comprising a 4-year bond (EUR650.0 million with a 0.25% coupon), 12-year bond (EUR650.0 billion with a 1.25% coupon), and a 20-year bond (EUR850.0 billion with a 1.75% coupon). The success of the two international debt sales underscored investor confidence in the Philippines' credit soundness.

The issuance of BSP bills climbed 14.0% q-o-q to PHP1,250.0 billion in Q2 2021. The central bank increased its volume offer and auctions were all met with strong demand, which was indicative of market liquidity remaining high. There was no securities issuance from government-related entities during the quarter.

The government plans to borrow PHP3.0 trillion this year to fund its budget deficit.

Corporate bonds. Debt outstanding in the corporate sector declined 3.9% q-o-q in Q2 2021 to PHP1,517.1 billion after dropping 2.0% q-o-q in Q1 2021. The decline was underpinned by the maturation of bonds amid low issuance volume during the quarter.

The banking sector remained the largest segment of the LCY corporate bond market with a share of 41.0% at the end of June, which was almost unchanged from the end of June 2020 (**Figure 2**). Property companies and utilities firms remained in the second and third spots, respectively, comprising 25.1% and 14.5% of the market. The former's share increased over the year in review while the latter's was unchanged. The holding firms, transport, and telecommunications sector saw lower shares in June 2021 versus a year earlier, while the share of "others" went up.

Figure 2: Local Currency Corporate Bonds Outstanding by Sector

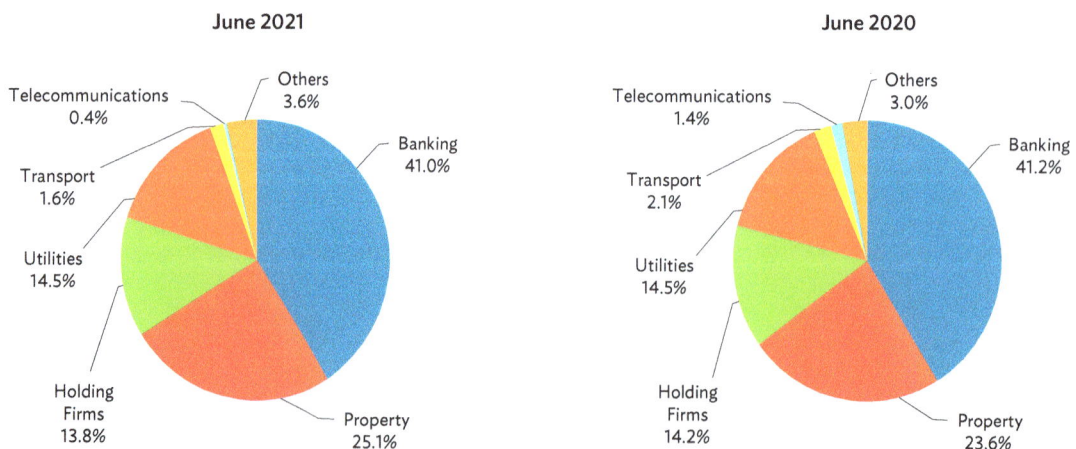

June 2021

- Telecommunications 0.4%
- Others 3.6%
- Banking 41.0%
- Transport 1.6%
- Utilities 14.5%
- Holding Firms 13.8%
- Property 25.1%

June 2020

- Telecommunications 1.4%
- Others 3.0%
- Banking 41.2%
- Transport 2.1%
- Utilities 14.5%
- Holding Firms 14.2%
- Property 23.6%

Source: Based on data from Bloomberg LP.

The aggregate debt outstanding of the top 30 corporate issuers amounted to PHP1,360.6 billion at the end of June, or 89.7% of the total corporate bond market (**Table 2**). The banking sector comprised the largest share at 43.8% (PHP596.4 billion). This was followed by holdings firms and property firms with shares of 20.7% (PHP281.9 billion) and 18.0% (PHP244.7 billion), respectively. Ayala Land, Metropolitan Bank and Trust Co., and BDO Unibank remained the top three issuers with outstanding debt at the end of June of over PHP100 billion each.

Table 2: Top 30 Issuers of Local Currency Corporate Bonds in the Philippines

	Issuers	Outstanding Amount		State-Owned	Listed Company	Type of Industry
		LCY Bonds (PHP billion)	LCY Bonds (USD billion)			
1.	Ayala Land	123.9	2.5	No	Yes	Property
2.	Metropolitan Bank and Trust Co.	121.8	2.5	No	Yes	Banking
3.	BDO Unibank	109.9	2.3	No	Yes	Banking
4.	SM Prime Holdings	95.7	2.0	No	Yes	Holding Firms
5.	Bank of the Philippine Islands	86.1	1.8	No	Yes	Banking
6.	SMC Global Power	80.0	1.6	No	No	Electricity, Energy, and Power
7.	China Bank	61.2	1.3	No	Yes	Banking
8.	San Miguel	60.0	1.2	No	Yes	Holding Firms
9.	Rizal Commercial Banking Corporation	55.1	1.1	No	Yes	Banking
10.	Security Bank	48.3	1.0	No	Yes	Banking
11.	Aboitiz Power	48.0	1.0	No	Yes	Electricity, Energy, and Power
12.	SM Investments	43.3	0.9	No	Yes	Holding Firms
13.	Petron	42.9	0.9	No	Yes	Electricity, Energy, and Power
14.	Vista Land	42.8	0.9	No	Yes	Property
15.	Ayala Corporation	40.0	0.8	No	Yes	Holding Firms
16.	Philippine National Bank	31.8	0.7	No	Yes	Banking
17.	Maynilad	28.1	0.6	No	No	Water
18.	Aboitiz Equity Ventures	27.9	0.6	No	Yes	Holding Firms
19.	Filinvest Land	25.8	0.5	No	Yes	Property
20.	Philippine Savings Bank	25.4	0.5	No	Yes	Banking
21.	Robinsons Land	25.2	0.5	No	Yes	Property
22.	Union Bank of the Philippines	24.6	0.5	No	Yes	Banking
23.	East West Banking	16.2	0.3	No	Yes	Banking
24.	Robinsons Bank	16.0	0.3	No	No	Banking
25.	GT Capital	15.1	0.3	No	Yes	Holding Firms
26.	Doubledragon	15.0	0.3	No	Yes	Property
27.	San Miguel Food and Beverage	15.0	0.3	No	Yes	Food and Beverage
28.	Megaworld	12.0	0.2	No	Yes	Property
29.	Puregold	12.0	0.2	No	Yes	Whole and Retail Trading
30.	MTD Manila Expressway	11.5	0.2	No	No	Infrastructure
	Total Top 30 LCY Corporate Issuers	**1,360.6**	**27.9**			
	Total LCY Corporate Bonds	**1,517.1**	**31.1**			
	Top 30 as % of Total LCY Corporate Bonds	**89.7%**	**89.7%**			

LCY = local currency, PHP = Philippine peso, USD = United States dollar.
Notes:
1. Data as of 30 June 2021.
2. State-owned firms are defined as those in which the government has more than a 50% ownership stake.
Source: *AsianBondsOnline* calculations based on Bloomberg LP data.

Issuance activity in the corporate sector in Q2 2021 remained weak, declining by 20.2% q-o-q, following a drop of 0.2% q-o-q in the previous quarter. While the number of corporate issuers during the quarter was the same as in Q1 2021, the total volume fell to PHP47.0 billion.

The reduced debt sales from the corporate sector were due to economic prospects remaining gloomy amid a resurgence of COVID-19 cases that negatively affected business and consumer confidence. This prompted firms to hold off on expanding or operating above pre-COVID-19 pandemic levels that would require capital mobilization. **Table 3** lists all issuances in Q2 2021. The majority were 3-year to 5-year tenors, led by Metropolitan Bank and Trust Co. with a PHP19.0 billion single issuance.

While corporate issuance in the domestic market was meek, two firms turned to the international debt market to generate funds. In April, Petron issued USD-denominated perpetual bonds amounting to USD550.0 million with a 5.95% coupon. In June, SMC Global Power raised USD600.0 billion through its perpetual bond issuance denominated in US dollars and carrying a coupon of 5.45%. Proceeds from the international issuances will be used mainly for debt repayment and general corporate purposes.

Table 3: Notable Local Currency Corporate Bond Issuances in the Second Quarter of 2021

Corporate Issuers	Coupon Rate (%)	Issued Amount (PHP billion)
Metropolitan Bank and Trust Co.		
5-year bond	3.60	19.00
Ayala Land		
4-year bond	3.63	10.00
Ayala Corporation		
3-year bond	3.03	4.00
5-year bond	3.79	6.00
Energy Development Corporation		
3-year bond	2.86	2.50
5-year bond	3.73	2.50
AllHome		
4-year bond	5.00	2.00
Cirtek Holdings		
6-month bond	zero coupon	0.31
1-year bond	zero coupon	0.70

PHP = Philippine peso.
Source: Based on data from Bloomberg LP.

Investor Profile

The investor landscape for LCY government bonds in June was changed from a year earlier (**Figure 3**). Banks and investment houses were the largest investor group in LCY government bonds at the end of June, with their

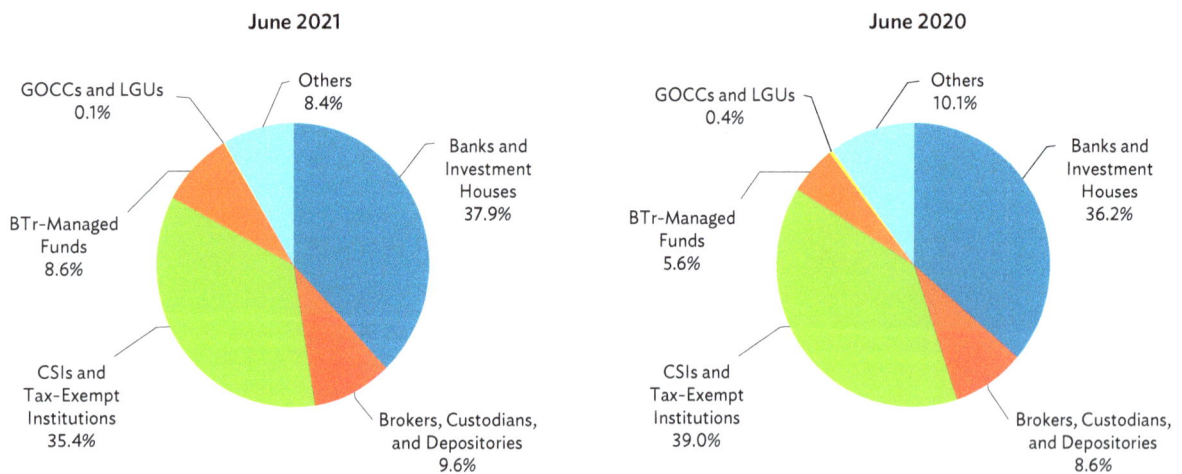

Figure 3: Local Currency Government Bonds Investor Profile

BTr = Bureau of the Treasury, CSI = contractual savings institution, GOCC = government-owned or -controlled corporation, LGU = local government unit.
Source: Bureau of the Treasury.

market share climbing to 37.9% from 36.2% in June 2020. Banks and investment houses overtook contractual savings and tax-exempt institutions as the largest investor group, whose market share declined to 35.4% from 39.0% during the review period. Brokers, custodians, and depositories (9.6%); BTr-managed funds (8.6%); and "other" investor group (8.4%) were the third-, fourth-, and fifth-largest investor groups by market share at the end of June, respectively. Government-owned or -controlled corporations and local government units remained the investor group with the smallest holdings of government bonds, with their share declining to 0.1% from 0.4% during the review period.

Ratings Update

On 12 July, Fitch Ratings affirmed the Philippines' sovereign credit at BBB but revised the outlook to negative from stable. According to the rating agency, the affirmation reflected the economy's strong external buffers and government debt levels remaining below the median of similarly rated peers. The negative outlook reflected risks to the credit profile resulting from the adverse impact of the pandemic to the economy as well as challenges to fiscal consolidation. A rating downgrade remained possible if there were a sustained rise in the debt-to-GDP ratio, weaker medium-term macroeconomic prospects, and a deterioration of external position. On the other hand, enhancements to fiscal finances that would put the debt-to-GDP ratio on a downward trajectory and a strengthening of governance standards could lead to a rating upgrade.

Policy, Institutional, and Regulatory Developments

Bureau of the Treasury Plans to Borrow PHP685 Billion in the Third Quarter of 2021

The BTr planned to borrow PHP235 billion from the domestic debt market in July, comprising of PHP60 billion of Treasury bills and PHP175 billion of Treasury bonds. Less borrowing was set for August at PHP200 billion: PHP60 billion of Treasury bills and PHP140 billion of Treasury bonds. In September, the borrowing plan was set to PHP250 billion, comprising PHP75 billion of Treasury bills and PHP175 billion of Treasury bonds. The borrowing program in Q3 2021, totaling PHP685 billion, upsized the

offer volume for longer-tenor securities, as the BTr tried to extend its maturity profile amid strong market liquidity and low interest rates.

Bangko Sentral ng Pilipinas Approves PHP540 Billion Loan to the Central Government

In July, the BSP approved another PHP540 billion short-term loan to the Government of the Philippines. It was the fourth time since March 2020 that the central bank extended credit to the government as a form of assistance to increase funds for the pandemic response. The government had repaid in June the loan drawn from the BSP in January, which amounted to PHP540 billion. The Bayanihan to Recover as One Act (Republic Act No. 11494) allowed direct provisional advances from the central bank of up to PHP850 billion.

Bangko Sentral ng Pilipinas Eases Foreign Exchange Regulations

On 10 August, the BSP amended the foreign exchange (FX) regulations to allow access to FX without prior BSP approval in select trade and nontrade current account transactions. According to the BSP, the amendment will promote ease of use of FX resources of the banking system and further simplify procedures and documentary requirements for FX transactions. These transactions include (i) the sale of FX by banks without prior BSP approval involving payments for e-commerce; living allowance and medical expenses of dependents abroad; and importation of goods with services covered by engineering, procurement, and construction contracts among others; (ii) FX derivatives transactions to be entered into by nonbank government entities; and (iii) use of peso receipts relating to trade transactions to fund the peso deposit accounts of nonresidents. The reform took effect 15 banking days after its publication.

Singapore

Yield Movements

Singapore's local currency (LCY) government bond yields increased for all tenors between 15 June and 15 August except for the 3-month and 6-month tenors, which were unchanged (**Figure 1**). The 15-year yield also barely moved, increasing only 0.2 basis points (bps). The 10-year yield registered the highest increase during the review period with a jump of 4 bps. The remaining tenors increased an average of 1 bp. During the review period, the yield spread between 2-year and 10-year government bonds expanded from 107 bps to 110 bps.

The tepid demand for Singapore government bonds may be attributed to investors staying on the sideline and being cautiously optimistic as the increasing number of cases of COVID-19 and the spread of its delta variant remained a threat to global and local economic progress. Investor optimism was restrained even as the government increased its economic growth forecast for full-year 2021.

The risk-off sentiment caused by the pandemic also took its toll on the Singapore dollar as the currency weakened 2.0% during the review period against the United States (US) dollar, reaching SGD1.355 per USD1.0 on 15 August. Fitch Solutions, a subsidiary of rating agency Fitch Ratings, announced toward the end of July that it expects the Singapore dollar to trade between SGD1.35 and SGD1.38 per USD1.0 for the remainder of 2021 due to a resurgence of COVID-19 cases across the region.

Singapore's economy grew 14.7% year-on-year (y-o-y) in the second quarter (Q2) of 2021, extending the 1.5% y-o-y growth recorded in the first quarter (Q1). The growth was due to improvements in the performance of all sectors contributing to Singapore's gross domestic product (GDP). At the same time, the rapid pace of y-o-y expansion was due to a low base effect from Q2 2020 when Singapore's GDP growth plunged 13.3% y-o-y due to Circuit Breaker measures that were implemented in April to arrest the spread of COVID-19. On a quarter-on-quarter (q-o-q) basis, Singapore's economy contracted 1.8% in Q2 2021. The value of Singapore's GDP in Q2 2021 was still lower compared

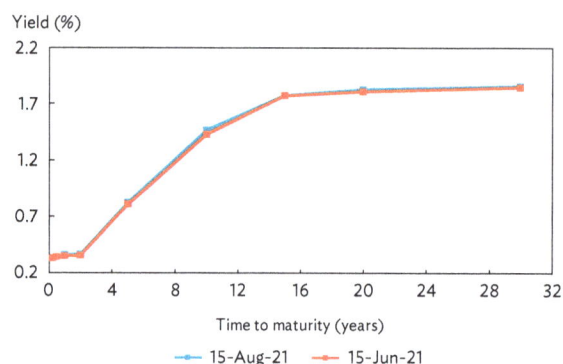

Figure 1: Singapore's Benchmark Yield Curve—Local Currency Government Bonds

Source: Based on data from Bloomberg LP.

to its value pre-pandemic in Q2 2019. In August, the Ministry of Trade and Industry upgraded its economic growth forecast to 6.0%–7.0% for full-year 2021 from 4.0%–6.0% as announced in May. The upgrade was due to Singapore's stronger-than-expected growth and improvements in the global economy (albeit with continued exposure to downside risks).

Prices of basic goods and services in Singapore increased 2.1% y-o-y in April, while consumer price inflation was at 2.4% y-o-y in both May and June. In July, Monetary Authority of Singapore (MAS) revised its full-year 2021 inflation forecast to 1.0%–2.0% from the 0.5%–1.5% forecast announced in the prior month. The higher forecast can be attributed to the effects of increased inflation among Singapore's trading partners. On the domestic front, tightened measures under Phase 2 (Heightened Alert) COVID-19 restrictions might also affect consumer sentiments.

Singapore was placed under Phase 2 (Heightened Alert) from 22 July to 18 August. The city-state experienced an elevated number of new cases in July. Under Phase 2, the number of people allowed to gather and the operating capacity of various businesses were reduced, and the removal of masks during allowed events is prohibited. Under the national vaccination program, 63% of Singapore's population has been fully vaccinated as of 2 August.

Table 1: Size and Composition of the Local Currency Bond Market in Singapore

| | Outstanding Amount (billion) | | | | | | Growth Rate (%) | | | |
| | Q2 2020 | | Q1 2021 | | Q2 2021 | | Q2 2020 | | Q2 2021 | |
	SGD	USD	SGD	USD	SGD	USD	q-o-q	y-o-y	q-o-q	y-o-y
Total	474	340	522	388	555	412	2.9	12.4	6.3	17.1
Government	306	219	349	260	366	272	4.4	16.5	4.8	19.7
SGS Bills and Bonds	195	140	203	151	207	154	3.7	50.5	1.7	6.2
MAS Bills	111	80	146	109	159	118	5.7	(16.5)	9.0	43.3
Corporate	168	121	173	129	189	141	0.3	5.7	9.3	12.3

( ) = negative, MAS = Monetary Authority of Singapore, q-o-q = quarter-on-quarter, Q1 = first quarter, Q2 = second quarter, SGD = Singapore dollar, SGS = Singapore Government Securities, USD = United States dollar, y-o-y = year-on-year.
Notes:
1. Government bonds are calculated using data from national sources. Corporate bonds are based on *AsianBondsOnline* estimates.
2. SGS bills and bonds do not include the special issue of SGS held by the Singapore Central Provident Fund.
3. Bloomberg LP end-of-period local currency–USD rates are used.
4. Growth rates are calculated from local currency base and do not include currency effects.
Sources: Bloomberg LP, Monetary Authority of Singapore, and Singapore Government Securities.

Size and Composition

The LCY bond market of Singapore expanded 6.3% q-o-q in Q2 2021, increasing to a size of SGD555.0 billion (USD412.5 billion) at the end of June from SGD522.2 billion at the end of March 2021 (**Table 1**). The rate of expansion in Q2 2021 was an acceleration from growth of 3.8% q-o-q in the previous quarter. On an annual basis, the LCY bond market grew 17.1% y-o-y in Q2 2021, up from the 13.4% y-o-y growth recorded in Q1 2021. The expansion was attributed to the growth in both LCY government and corporate bonds, which accounted for 65.9% and 34.1%, respectively, of total outstanding LCY bonds at the end of the review period.

LCY bond issuance in Q2 2021 jumped 15.3% q-o-q to SGD261.4 billion in Q2 2021 from SGD226.7 billion in Q1 2021 due to increased government and corporate bond issuances. Q2 2021 growth was notably faster than the expansion of 4.7% q-o-q posted in the prior quarter.

Government bonds. In Q2 2021, LCY government bonds outstanding increased 4.8% q-o-q to SGD365.9 billion from SGD349.2 billion in Q1 2021. However, growth in Q2 2021 was slower than the increase of 6.0% q-o-q logged in the previous quarter. Singapore Government Securities bills and bonds, which comprised 56.5% of total LCY government bonds outstanding at the end of June, grew 1.7% q-o-q. MAS bills, which comprised 43.5% of all LCY government bonds outstanding, jumped 9.0% q-o-q on growth in the stock of MAS floating-rate notes.

Issuance of LCY government bonds increased 11.8% q-o-q in Q2 2021. Issuances of Treasury bills and bonds increased 25.2% q-o-q due to the reopening of more tenors of Treasury bonds. Central bank bills jumped 9.6% q-o-q as MAS started issuing 2-year floating-rate notes in June to promote use of the Singapore Overnight Rate Average as Singapore's new interest rate benchmark.

Corporate bonds. In Q2 2021, LCY corporate bonds outstanding increased 9.3% q-o-q to SGD189.1 billion from SGD173.0 billion in the previous quarter. The growth was a reversal from the decline of 0.3% q-o-q in Q1 2021 and can be attributed partly to many companies issuing perpetual bonds to lock in low interest rates amid concerns over rising benchmark interest rates.

The top 30 LCY corporate bond issuers in Singapore had combined bonds outstanding of SGD102.3 billion, or 54.1% of the total LCY corporate bond market, at the end of June (**Table 2**). Government-owned Housing & Development Board remained the largest issuer with outstanding LCY corporate bonds amounting to SGD26.1 billion. Real estate companies comprised the largest sectoral share (43.4%) among the top 30 issuers of LCY corporate bonds with SGD44.4 billion of aggregate LCY corporate bonds outstanding at the end of the review period.

In Q2 2021, issuance of LCY corporate bonds surged to SGD12.0 billion, an expansion of 228.3% q-o-q from SGD3.7 billion in the previous quarter. The growth reversed 3 consecutive quarters of decline in corporate bond issuance. The jump in LCY corporate bond

Table 2: Top 30 Issuers of Local Currency Corporate Bonds in Singapore

	Issuers	Outstanding Amount		State-Owned	Listed Company	Type of Industry
		LCY Bonds (SGD billion)	LCY Bonds (USD billion)			
1.	Housing & Development Board	26.1	19.4	Yes	No	Real Estate
2.	Singapore Airlines	14.7	10.9	Yes	Yes	Transportation
3.	Land Transport Authority	9.5	7.0	Yes	No	Transportation
4.	CapitaLand	5.6	4.1	Yes	Yes	Real Estate
5.	Frasers Property	4.0	3.0	No	Yes	Real Estate
6.	United Overseas Bank	4.0	3.0	No	Yes	Banking
7.	Sembcorp Industries	3.3	2.4	No	Yes	Diversified
8.	Temasek Financial	3.1	2.3	Yes	No	Finance
9.	DBS Bank	2.9	2.1	No	Yes	Banking
10.	Mapletree Treasury Services	2.7	2.0	No	No	Finance
11.	Keppel Corporation	2.2	1.6	No	Yes	Diversified
12.	City Developments Limited	2.1	1.5	No	Yes	Real Estate
13.	CapitaLand Mall Trust	2.0	1.5	No	No	Finance
14.	Olam International	1.8	1.4	No	Yes	Consumer Goods
15.	Oversea-Chinese Banking Corporation	1.7	1.3	No	Yes	Banking
16.	Shangri-La Hotel	1.5	1.1	No	Yes	Real Estate
17.	Suntec Real Estate Investment Trust	1.5	1.1	No	Yes	Real Estate
18.	Ascendas Real Estate Investment Trust	1.5	1.1	No	Yes	Finance
19.	Singtel Group Treasury	1.4	1.0	No	No	Finance
20.	NTUC Income	1.4	1.0	No	No	Finance
21.	Singapore Technologies Telemedia	1.2	0.9	Yes	No	Utilities
22.	GuocoLand Limited IHT	1.1	0.8	No	No	Real Estate
23.	Public Utilities Board	1.0	0.7	Yes	No	Utilities
24.	Ascott Residence	1.0	0.7	No	Yes	Real Estate
25.	National University of Singapore	1.0	0.7	No	No	Education
26.	Singapore Press Holdings	1.0	0.7	No	Yes	Communications
27.	StarHub	0.9	0.7	No	Yes	Diversified
28.	Keppel Land International	0.9	0.7	No	No	Real Estate
29.	Hyflux	0.9	0.7	No	Yes	Utilities
30.	Mapletree Commercial Trust	0.8	0.6	No	Yes	Real Estate
	Total Top 30 LCY Corporate Issuers	**102.3**	**76.1**			
	Total LCY Corporate Bonds	**189.1**	**140.5**			
	Top 30 as % of Total LCY Corporate Bonds	**54.1%**	**54.1%**			

LCY = local currency, SGD = Singapore dollar, USD = United States dollar.
Notes:
1. Data as of 30 June 2021.
2. State-owned firms are defined as those in which the government has more than a 50% ownership stake.
Source: *AsianBondsOnline* calculations based on Bloomberg LP data.

issuances was due to a huge issuance by flagship carrier Singapore Airlines, which in June issued a zero-coupon, 9-year mandatory convertible bond worth SGD6.2 billion (**Table 3**). Singapore Airlines will use the additional liquidity to manage its capital structure to address challenges to the airline industry brought about by the COVID-19 pandemic.

Table 3: Notable Local Currency Corporate Bond Issuances in the Second Quarter of 2021

Corporate Issuers	Coupon Rate (%)	Issued Amount (SGD million)
Singapore Airlines		
9-year bond	zero	6,196.8
Singtel Group Treasury		
Perpetual bond	3.300	1,000.0
United Overseas Bank		
Perpetual bond	2.550	600.0
Mapletree Industrial Trust		
Perpetual bond	3.150	300.0
Keppel Infrastructure Trust		
Perpetual bond	4.300	300.0
Mapletree North Asia Commercial Trust		
Perpetual bond	3.500	250.0
Lendlease Global Commercial REIT		
Perpetual bond	4.200	200.0
Suntec REIT		
Perpetual bond	4.250	150.0

REIT = Real Estate Investment Trust, SGD = Singapore dollar.
Source: Bloomberg LP.

Multiple companies issued perpetual bonds in Q2 2021 with coupon rates ranging from 2.55% to 4.30%. In April, Singtel Group Treasury, a subsidiary of telecommunications conglomerate Singapore Telecommunications, issued the largest perpetual bond during the quarter at SGD1.0 billion. With a coupon rate of 3.3%, proceeds from the perpetual security will be used to fund ordinary business expenses. In June, the perpetual bond issuance with the highest coupon rate during the review period came from Keppel Infrastructure Trust. Proceeds from its SGD300.0 million issuance with a 4.3% coupon will be used to refinance the company's borrowings and to fund general corporate purposes.

Policy, Institutional, and Regulatory Developments

Monetary Authority of Singapore to Issue Infrastructure Bonds in October

MAS announced on 3 August that it would issue infrastructure bonds called Singapore Government Securities (Infrastructure) beginning 1 October. The first issuance of this kind will be a 30-year benchmark bond and the maiden issuance under the Significant Infrastructure Government Loan Act, which was passed by Singapore's Parliament on 10 May to fund major long-term infrastructure projects.

Thailand

Yield Movements

Between 15 June and 15 August, Thailand's local currency (LCY) government bond yield curve flattened, with yields slightly rising at the shorter-end but moving significantly downward at the longer-end (**Figure 1**). Bonds with maturities of less than 1 year gained an average of 2 basis points (bps), while bonds with maturities of 1 year or longer shed an average of 22 bps. The 6-year tenor showed the steepest decline at 36 bps. The 2-year tenor dropped 5 bps, while the 10-year tenor fell 30 bps. As a result, the spread between the 2-year and the 10-year tenors narrowed from 135 bps on 15 June to 110 bps on 15 August.

The overall decline in Thai LCY bond yields, particularly medium- and long-term yields, tracked the regional decline in government bond yields amid the resurgence of COVID-19 cases brought about by the spread of the highly contagious delta variant. Thailand experienced a third wave of COVID-19 infections beginning in April, which disrupted plans to revive tourism. The overall decline in yields also reflected expectations of a protracted recovery, as the global resurgence of virus cases and the resulting movement restrictions pose downside risks to Thailand's tourism-reliant economy.

A rise in net inflows of foreign funds also contributed to the decline in yields. The Thai bond market saw robust inflows amounting to THB51.7 billion during the review period, buoyed by favorable sentiment as Fitch Ratings affirmed Thailand's BBB+ rating in June.

Thailand's economy, which fell into recession in the first quarter (Q1) of 2020 amid the onset of the global pandemic, showed initial signs of recovery in the second quarter (Q2) of 2021. Gross domestic product rose 7.5% year-on-year (y-o-y) in Q2 2021 after a 2.6% y-o-y contraction in the previous quarter. The robust growth was partly due to a low base in the previous year when the economy contracted heavily during the first wave of the pandemic. Private consumption rose 4.6% y-o-y in Q2 2021 after a 0.3% y-o-y decline in the previous quarter. Government expenditure increased 1.1% y-o-y in Q2 2021 versus 2.1% y-o-y in the previous quarter. Investment growth accelerated to 8.1% y-o-y in Q2 2021

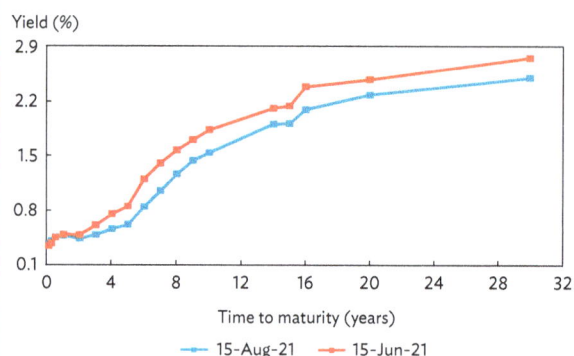

Figure 1: Thailand's Benchmark Yield Curve— Local Currency Government Bonds

Sources: Based on data from Bloomberg LP and Thai Bond Market Association.

from 7.3% y-o-y in the prior quarter. Exports of goods and services rebounded, rising 27.5% y-o-y in Q2 2021 after contracting 10.5% y-o-y in Q1 2021.

Thailand's growth outlook remained fragile as a third wave of COVID-19 outbreaks delayed the reopening of the economy to tourism and prompted a return of movement restrictions. In August, the National Economic and Social Development Council lowered its GDP growth forecast for full-year 2021 to 0.7%–1.2% from a 1.5%–2.5% forecast announced in May.

Thailand's consumer price inflation slowed to 0.5% y-o-y in July from 1.3% y-o-y in June due primarily to government subsidies on utilities. Core inflation, which excludes volatile fresh food and energy prices, eased to 0.1% y-o-y in July from 0.5% y-o-y in June. Headline inflation from April to June was within the Bank of Thailand's target range of 1.0%–3.0%, but fell short of the target in July. The Bank of Thailand (BOT) expects headline inflation to remain within the target rate for the rest of 2021.

The BOT's monetary policy remained accommodative. On 4 August, the Monetary Policy Committee of the BOT voted to maintain the policy rate at 0.5%. The committee viewed that the risks to the economic outlook remained high due to the resurgence of COVID-19, but most members deemed that financial measures would be more effective than a further rate reduction. Since the onset of

Table 1: Size and Composition of the Local Currency Bond Market in Thailand

| | Outstanding Amount (billion) | | | | | | Growth Rate (%) | | | |
| | Q2 2020 | | Q1 2021 | | Q2 2021 | | Q2 2020 | | Q2 2021 | |
	THB	USD	THB	USD	THB	USD	q-o-q	y-o-y	q-o-q	y-o-y
Total	13,449	435	13,842	443	14,203	443	2.1	3.2	2.6	5.6
Government	9,732	315	10,152	325	10,324	322	4.1	4.4	1.7	6.1
Government Bonds and Treasury Bills	5,306	172	6,349	203	6,485	202	4.5	11.6	2.1	22.2
Central Bank Bonds	3,633	118	2,911	93	2,917	91	4.0	(3.7)	0.2	(19.7)
State-Owned Enterprise and Other Bonds	793	26	892	29	921	29	1.4	(0.1)	3.2	16.2
Corporate	3,716	120	3,690	118	3,880	121	(2.6)	(0.03)	5.1	4.4

( ) = negative, q-o-q = quarter-on-quarter, Q1 = first quarter, Q2 = second quarter, THB = Thai baht, USD = United States dollar, y-o-y = year-on-year.
Notes:
1. Calculated using data from national sources.
2. Bloomberg LP end-of-period local currency–USD rates are used.
3. Growth rates are calculated from local currency base and do not include currency effects.
Source: Bank of Thailand.

the pandemic, the BOT has reduced its policy rate by a total of 75 bps.

Size and Composition

Thailand's LCY bonds outstanding totaled THB14,203.5 billion (USD443.4 billion) at the end of June (**Table 1**). The bond market expanded 2.6% quarter-on-quarter (q-o-q) in Q2 2021, reversing the 0.6% q-o-q decline in Q1 2021. Both the government and corporate segments contributed to the overall expansion in the LCY bond market. On a y-o-y basis, the growth of outstanding LCY bonds picked up, rising 5.6% in Q2 2021 versus 5.1% in the previous quarter. Government bonds continued to dominate the Thai LCY bond market, accounting for 72.7% of total bonds outstanding at the end of June.

Government bonds. The size of the LCY government bond market reached THB10,323.6 billion at the end of June, with the 1.7% q-o-q growth in Q2 2021 reversing the 0.8% q-o-q decline in Q1 2021. All components of government bonds contributed to the growth, led by state-owned enterprise and other bonds, which rose 3.2% q-o-q in Q2 2021. The outstanding stock of government bonds and Treasury bills increased 2.1% q-o-q, while BOT bonds outstanding inched up 0.2% q-o-q during the review quarter. On a y-o-y basis, the growth of total government bonds outstanding eased to 6.1%% in Q2 2021 from 8.5% in Q1 2021.

The issuance of government bonds totaled THB1,730.1 billion in Q2 2021, rising 2.6% q-o-q after a 13.6% q-o-q decline in the previous quarter. The

growth was solely driven by a 7.0% q-o-q rise in BOT bonds issuance. To promote the development of a new reference rate, the BOT terminated its issuance of Bangkok Interbank Offered Rate-lined floating-rate bonds in Q1 2021. The monthly issuance of Thai Overnight Repurchase Rate-lined floating-rate bonds started in March, boosting total BOT issuance in Q2 2021. Meanwhile, issuance of government bonds and Treasury bills contracted 3.7% q-o-q, while issuance of state-owned enterprise and other bonds dropped 17.7% q-o-q in Q2 2021. On a y-o-y basis, issuance of total government bonds contracted 20.8% in Q2 2021 following a 17.0% decline in the previous quarter.

Corporate bonds. Outstanding corporate bonds amounted to THB3,879.9 billion at the end of June, rebounding 5.1% q-o-q in Q2 2021 after a marginal 0.1% q-o-q dip in the previous quarter. The growth was driven by robust issuance of corporate debt during the review period.

The LCY bonds outstanding of the top 30 corporate issuers totaled THB2,297.1 billion at the end of June, accounting for 59.2% of the Thai corporate bond market (**Table 2**). Food and beverage, commerce, banking, and finance and securities firms held over half of the top 30 issuers' outstanding bond stock. The majority of the top 30 issuers were listed on the Thai Stock Exchange, while only four were state-owned firms. CP ALL remained the top issuer, with an outstanding bond stock of THB249.7 billion at the end of June. Thai Beverage and Siam Cement were the next largest issuers, with outstanding bond stocks of THB173.1 billion and THB165.0 billion, respectively.

Table 2: Top 30 Issuers of Local Currency Corporate Bonds in Thailand

	Issuers	Outstanding Amount		State-Owned	Listed Company	Type of Industry
		LCY Bonds (THB billion)	LCY Bonds (USD billion)			
1.	CP ALL	249.7	7.8	No	Yes	Commerce
2.	Thai Beverage	173.1	5.4	No	No	Food and Beverage
3.	Siam Cement	165.0	5.2	Yes	Yes	Construction Material
4.	Charoen Pokphand Foods	139.7	4.4	No	Yes	Food and Beverage
5.	True Corp	135.7	4.2	No	No	Communications
6.	Berli Jucker	121.6	3.8	No	Yes	Commerce
7.	True Move H Universal Communication	117.0	3.7	No	No	Communication
8.	Bank of Ayudhya	108.8	3.4	No	Yes	Banking
9.	PTT	91.6	2.9	Yes	Yes	Energy and Utilities
10.	Toyota Leasing Thailand	77.6	2.4	No	No	Finance and Securities
11.	Indorama Ventures	66.5	2.1	No	Yes	Petrochemicals and Chemicals
12.	CPF Thailand	64.1	2.0	No	No	Food and Beverage
13.	Bangkok Commercial Asset Management	60.2	1.9	No	Yes	Finance and Securities
14.	Minor International	58.1	1.8	No	Yes	Hospitality and Leisure
15.	PTT Global Chemical	51.7	1.6	No	Yes	Petrochemicals and Chemicals
16.	Frasers Property Thailand	47.3	1.5	No	Yes	Property and Construction
17.	Banpu	45.3	1.4	No	Yes	Energy and Utilities
18.	Global Power Synergy	45.0	1.4	No	Yes	Energy and Utilities
19.	Krungthai Card	45.0	1.4	Yes	Yes	Banking
20.	Krung Thai Bank	44.0	1.4	Yes	Yes	Banking
21.	Muangthai Capital	43.7	1.4	No	Yes	Finance and Securities
22.	TPI Polene	43.1	1.3	No	Yes	Property and Construction
23.	ICBC Thai Leasing	41.5	1.3	No	No	Finance and Securities
24.	CH Karnchang	40.9	1.3	No	Yes	Property and Construction
25.	Bangkok Expressway & Metro	40.1	1.3	No	Yes	Transportation and Logistics
26.	Sansiri	39.0	1.2	No	Yes	Property and Construction
27.	dtac TriNet	37.5	1.2	No	Yes	Communications
28.	Land & Houses	35.6	1.1	No	Yes	Property and Construction
29.	TMB Bank	35.4	1.1	No	Yes	Banking
30.	Bangchak	33.5	1.0	No	Yes	Energy and Utilities
	Total Top 30 LCY Corporate Issuers	**2,297.1**	**71.7**			
	Total LCY Corporate Bonds	**3,879.9**	**121.1**			
	Top 30 as % of Total LCY Corporate Bonds	**59.2%**	**59.2%**			

LCY = local currency, THB = Thai baht, USD = United States dollar.
Notes:
1. Data as of 30 June 2021.
2. State-owned firms are defined as those in which the government has more than a 50% ownership stake.
Source: *AsianBondsOnline* calculations based on Bloomberg LP data.

Table 3: Notable Local Currency Corporate Bond Issuances in the Second Quarter of 2021

Corporate Issuers	Coupon Rate (%)	Issued Amount (THB billion)
CP ALL		
2-year bond	1.53	3.0
3-year bond	1.76	3.0
4-year bond	2.14	6.5
5-year bond	3.00	17.8
7-year bond	3.40	7.4
10-year bond	3.90	21.4
12-year bond	4.20	7.0
Thai Beverage[a]		
2-year bond	1.17	7.5
3-year bond	1.45	7.0
3-year bond	1.21	8.0
4-year bond	2.07	11.5
5-year bond	2.43	11.0
8-year bond	2.71	1.5
10-year bond	3.03	1.5
True Corp		
1.8-year bond	2.95	2.9
3-year bond	3.50	4.4
3.8-year bond	3.85	4.2
4.8-year bond	4.20	3.9
5.8-year bond	4.55	6.6

THB = Thai baht.
a Multiple issuance of the same tenor indicates issuance on different dates.
Source: Bloomberg LP.

Corporate debt issuance totaled THB477.2 billion in Q2 2021, up from THB294.8 in Q1 2021. Issuance growth jumped to 61.9% q-o-q in Q2 2021 from 6.4% q-o-q in the previous quarter. Firms tapped the bond market to raise funds for working capital and debt refinancing, taking advantage of the low-interest-rate environment.

Table 3 lists the top corporate issuers in Q2 2021. CP ALL issued the largest amount of corporate debt in Q2 2021, raising a total of THB66.0 billion from a multitranche issuance of bonds with tenors ranging from 2 years to 12 years and coupons ranging from 1.53% to 4.20%. Thai Beverage was the second-largest issuer during the quarter, with total issuance amounting to TH48.0 billion from bonds with tenors ranging from 2 years to 10 years and carrying coupons ranging from 1.17% to 3.03%. True Corp was the third-largest issuer with total issuance of THB22.0 billion from bonds with tenors ranging from 1.8 years to 5.8 years and carrying coupons ranging from 2.95% to 4.55%.

Investor Profile

Central government bonds. Between June 2020 and June 2021, the combined share of the four largest holders of LCY government bonds declined slightly to 89.5% from 90.4% (**Figure 2**). Financial corporations continued to hold the largest share of government bonds,

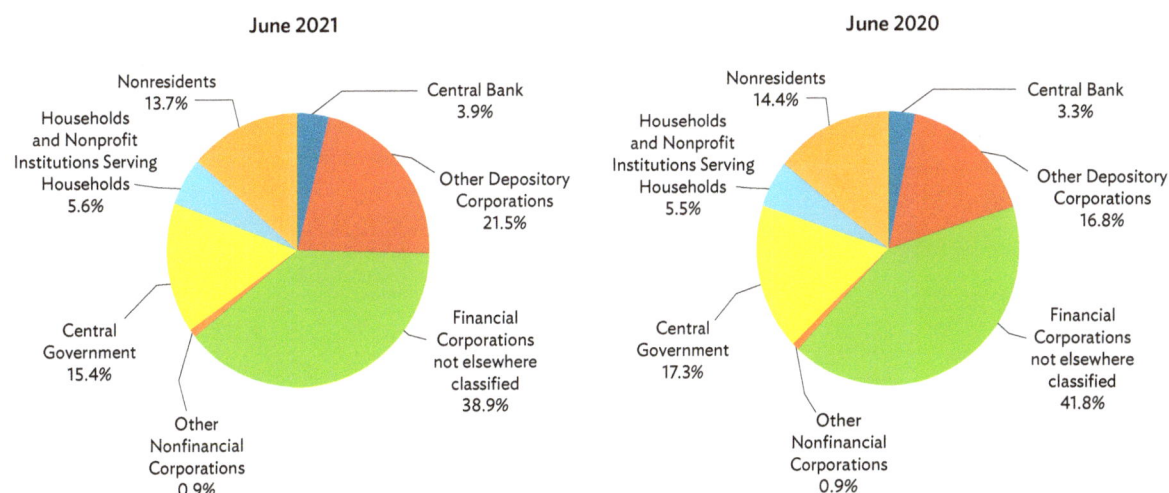

Figure 2: Local Currency Government Bonds Investor Profile

June 2021

Nonresidents 13.7%
Central Bank 3.9%
Households and Nonprofit Institutions Serving Households 5.6%
Other Depository Corporations 21.5%
Central Government 15.4%
Financial Corporations not elsewhere classified 38.9%
Other Nonfinancial Corporations 0.9%

June 2020

Nonresidents 14.4%
Central Bank 3.3%
Households and Nonprofit Institutions Serving Households 5.5%
Other Depository Corporations 16.8%
Central Government 17.3%
Financial Corporations not elsewhere classified 41.8%
Other Nonfinancial Corporations 0.9%

Note: Government bonds include Treasury bills and bonds.
Source: AsianBondsOnline and Bank of Thailand.

although their share fell to 38.9% at the end of June 2021 from 41.8% a year earlier. In contrast, the share of other depository corporations increased to 21.5% from 16.8% between June 2020 and June 2021. The share held by the central government decreased to 15.4% from 17.3% during the same period. Nonresident holdings inched down to 13.7% in June 2021 from 14.4% a year earlier. The BOT's holdings of government bonds rose slightly to 3.9% in June 2021 from 3.3% a year earlier, as the central bank purchased government bonds to stabilize the market amid uncertainties during the prolonged pandemic.

Central bank bonds. Between June 2020 and June 2021, the combined share of the four largest holders of BOT bonds slipped to 96.2% from 96.7% (**Figure 3**). Other depository corporations held the largest share of BOT bonds, although their share dropped to 37.8% from 45.2% during the review period. Financial corporations remained the second-largest holder of BOT bonds, with 33.9% of total holdings at the end of June, up from 28.4% a year earlier. The BOT's holdings of its LCY bonds rose to 14.6% from 13.2% during the same period. The central government's share was stable at 10.0% between June 2020 and June 2021. Nonresidents continued to hold a marginal share of BOT bonds at 0.7% in June 2021, down from 1.2% a year earlier.

Net inflows from foreign investors to the Thai LCY bond market soared to THB83.7 billion in Q2 2021 from

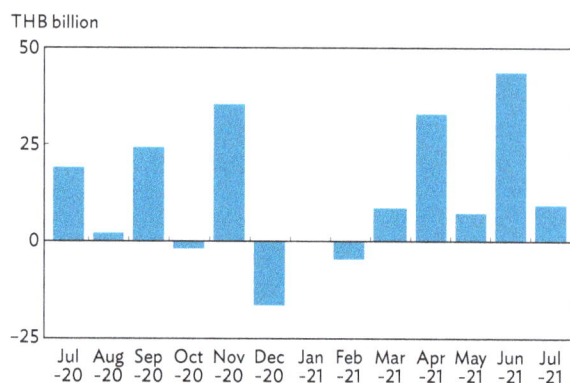

Figure 4: Foreign Investor Net Trading of Local Currency Bonds in Thailand

THB = Thai baht.
Source: Thai Bond Market Association.

THB4.0 billion in the previous quarter (**Figure 4**). The uptick in foreign investment flows to the Thai sovereign bond market was driven by an increase in demand for emerging market bonds as investors sought to diversify portfolios amid low global yields. The Thai bond market has recorded monthly net inflows of foreign capital since March 2021, peaking at THB43.6 billion in June amid investor optimism as the government ramped up its mass vaccination program. Net inflows dropped to THB9.3 billion in July as the spread of the delta variant in the region dampened investor sentiment.

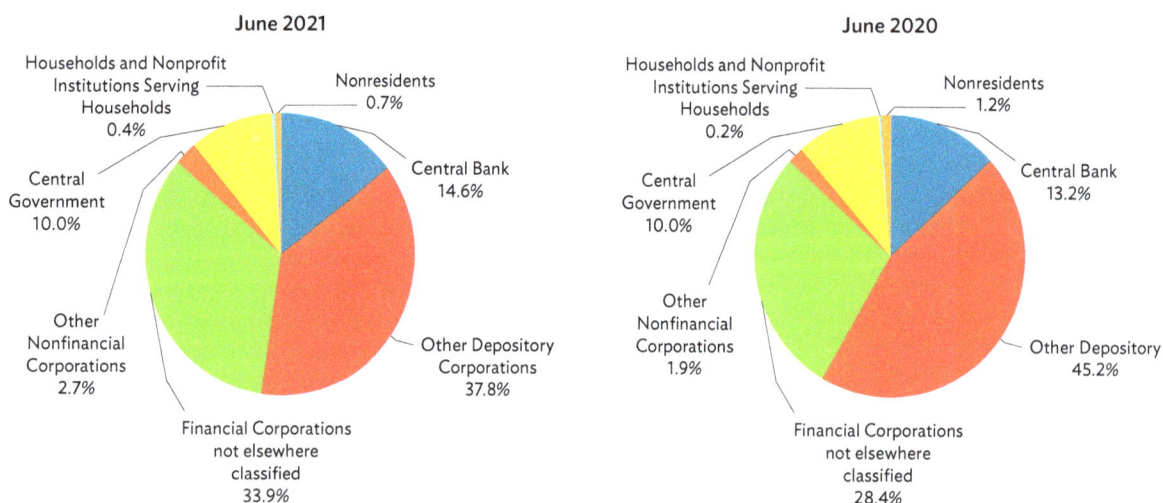

Figure 3: Local Currency Central Bank Securities Investor Profile

Source: Bank of Thailand.

Ratings Update

On 18 June, Fitch Ratings affirmed Thailand's long-term foreign currency issuer default rating at BBB+ with a stable outlook. The rating was based on the assessment that Thailand's robust external position and public finances would continue to cushion against any downside risks from a protracted economic recovery from the global pandemic. Fitch Ratings viewed that the debt incurred to finance the government's fiscal response to the pandemic was sustainable in the medium-term based on Thailand's record in managing its public finances.

Policy, Institutional, and Regulatory Developments

Cabinet Approves Emergency Decree for Additional THB500 Billion of Borrowing

In June, Thailand's House of Representatives approved an executive decree authorizing the Ministry of Finance to borrow up to an additional THB500 billion for relief measures in response to the impacts of COVID-19. Up to THB30 billion will be allocated for the Ministry of Public Health. The rest of the loan amount was earmarked for assistance to individuals (THB300 billion) and businesses (THB170 billion) affected by the pandemic.

Japan and Thailand Renew Bilateral Swap Agreement

On 23 July, the Bank of Japan and the BOT renewed the existing Bilateral Swap Agreement (BSA) between Japan and Thailand. The agreement allows the two central banks to exchange their domestic currencies for United States dollars. It also allows the BOT to swap Thai baht for Japanese yen. The size of the BSA was left unchanged at up to USD3.0 billion or its equivalent in Japanese yen. The renewed BSA incorporates a precautionary scheme, as well as amendments to align it with recent changes in the Chiang Mai Initiative Multilateralization Agreement.

Viet Nam

Yield Movements

The yields of local currency (LCY) government bonds in Viet Nam declined for all tenors between 15 June and 15 August, shifting the yield curve downward (**Figure 1**). Yields fell 11 basis points (bps) on average across the curve. The smallest drop was seen for the 2-year tenor (3 bps), while the largest drop was for the 15-year tenor (18 bps). The yield spread between the 2-year and 10-year tenors narrowed during the review period from 152 bps to 145 bps.

The downward movement of the yield curve reflected risk aversion amid renewed uncertainties posed by the more contagious variants of COVID-19, and abundant liquidity in the market. This resulted in the continued preference for safe-haven assets like government securities. The accommodative monetary policy of the State Bank of Vietnam (SBV) and inflation remaining low also offset any upward pressure on the bond yields.

The SBV announced that it would keep its accommodative monetary policy stance and dismissed speculation it would adopt a looser policy approach in the near term.[9] The central bank stated that the timing of any adjustment to the policy rate will be properly assessed based on the actual situation. With sufficient liquidity, low credit demand, and the pandemic still underway, the SBV determined that easing monetary policy further would be inappropriate at present. Thus, the key policy rate remained at 4.00% after the SBV had reduced it by a total of 200 bps in 2020 to support the economy.

The prices of consumer goods in Viet Nam inched up by 2.8% year-on-year (y-o-y) in August, accelerating from a 2.6% y-o-y gain in July. The upward movement in prices was largely driven by food and foodstuffs due to increased stockpiling and higher cost of transportation as the government has limited the mobility of the population. Year-to-date through the end of August, consumer price inflation was 1.8% y-o-y, far below the government ceiling of 4.0% for 2021.

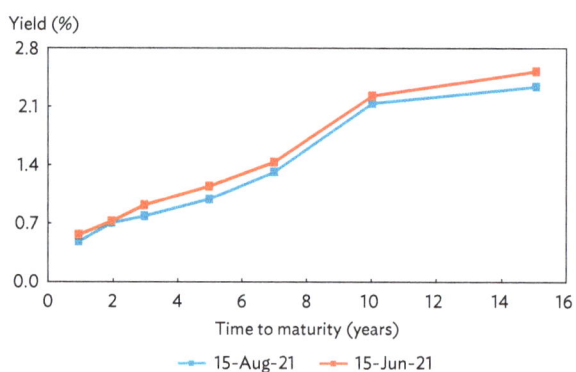

Figure 1: Viet Nam's Benchmark Yield Curve—Local Currency Government Bonds

Source: Based on data from Bloomberg LP.

Viet Nam's economy continued to expand as its gross domestic product grew 6.6% y-o-y in the second quarter (Q2) of 2021, accelerating from 4.5% y-o-y growth in Q1 2021 and significantly higher than the 0.4% y-o-y increase in Q2 2020. The domestic economy managed to sustain its growth despite the resurgence of COVID-19 cases in April. The government is targeting annual gross domestic product growth of 6.5% for full-year 2021.

The Vietnamese dong remained relatively steady against the United States dollar from the start of the year through the middle of August. The domestic currency traded at VND22,822.0 per USD1.0 on 15 August, reflecting a year-to-date appreciation of 1.2%. The stability of the dong was supported by inflows of worker remittances and foreign direct investment, as well as the adequate foreign reserve position of the central bank.

Size and Composition

The LCY bond market in Viet Nam expanded 6.1% quarter-on-quarter (q-o-q) to VND1,759.0 trillion (USD76.5 billion) at the end of Q2 2021, reversing the previous quarter's contraction of 0.3% q-o-q (**Table 1**). The quarterly growth was mainly driven by the corporate sector as outstanding government debt slightly decreased.

[9] *Hanoi Times*. 2021. Policy Rate Cut Not in Sight at Present: C. Bank. 11 August. http://hanoitimes.vn/policy-rate-cut-not-in-sight-at-present-cbank-318340.html.

Table 1: Size and Composition of the Local Currency Bond Market in Viet Nam

| | Outstanding Amount (billion) | | | | | | Growth Rate (%) | | | |
| | Q2 2020 | | Q1 2021 | | Q2 2021 | | Q2 2020 | | Q2 2021 | |
	VND	USD	VND	USD	VND	USD	q-o-q	y-o-y	q-o-q	y-o-y
Total	1,379,762	59	1,658,262	72	1,758,977	76	(1.2)	11.7	6.1	27.5
Government	1,183,518	51	1,364,303	59	1,357,573	59	(7.6)	5.0	(0.5)	14.7
Treasury Bonds	1,039,610	45	1,220,377	53	1,221,237	53	4.9	11.5	0.1	17.5
Central Bank Bills	0	0	0	0	0	0	(100.0)	(100.0)	–	–
Government-Guaranteed and Municipal Bonds	143,908	6	143,927	6	136,337	6	(6.1)	(11.5)	(5.3)	(5.3)
Corporate	196,244	8	293,959	13	401,404	17	70.3	81.8	36.6	104.5

( ) = negative, – = not applicable, q-o-q = quarter-on-quarter, Q1 = first quarter, Q2 = second quarter, USD = United States dollar, VND = Vietnamese dong, y-o-y = year-on-year.
Notes:
1. Bloomberg LP end-of-period local currency–USD rates are used.
2. Growth rates are calculated from local currency base and do not include currency effects.
Sources: Bloomberg LP and Vietnam Bond Market Association.

Government bonds accounted for 77.2% of Viet Nam's bond market at the end of June, while corporate bonds comprised 22.8%. On an annual basis, the bond market expanded 27.5% y-o-y in Q2 2021, up from a gain of 18.7% y-o-y in Q1 2021.

Government bonds. The government bond market slightly contracted 0.5% q-o-q in Q1 2021, trimming the government's outstanding debt to VND1,357.6 trillion. A smaller amount of government-guaranteed and municipal bonds outstanding and the absence of central bank bills offset the marginal increase in Treasury bonds.

Treasury bonds outstanding increased 0.1% q-o-q to VND1,221.2 trillion in Q2 2021 after dropping 0.6% q-o-q in the preceding quarter. The expansion occurred due to large bond sales from the State Treasury of Vietnam amounting to VND102.3 trillion, which exceeded the programmed VND100.0 trillion issuance and more than offset the considerable amount of maturing securities during the quarter.

Outstanding government-guaranteed and municipal bonds declined 5.3% q-o-q to VND136.3 trillion due to maturities and the absence of issuance in this government bond segment in Q2 2021. There were no outstanding central bank bills at the end of Q2 2021 as the SBV remained committed to supporting liquidity in the market.

Corporate bonds. Corporate bonds surged on 36.6% q-o-q growth in Q2 2021, up from a 3.3% q-o-q

gain in Q1 2021, raising the total amount of corporate bonds outstanding to VND401.4 trillion at the end of June. The growth was underpinned by sizable debt sales from the corporate sector during the quarter. Bonds are still an attractive channel for firms to raise funds, especially with the SBV's strict control of credit in potentially risky sectors like property. Moreover, higher debt sales from the banking sector that helped banks increase their capital base boosted issuance from the corporate sector.[10]

The top 30 LCY corporate issuers had aggregate bonds outstanding of VND257.8 trillion at the end of June, or 64.2% of the total corporate bond market (**Table 2**). Banks dominated the list with cumulative outstanding bonds equal to VND172.1 trillion, comprising a 66.7% share of the top 30's outstanding bonds. Property firms were the next most prolific issuers with VND52.6 trillion in bonds outstanding, or 20.4% of the top 30's total debt. The Bank for Investment and Development of Vietnam remained the single-largest issuer at the end of Q2 2021 with outstanding debt of VND25.9 trillion, up from VND22.0 trillion at the end of Q1 2021.

Issuance from the corporate sector in Q2 2021 climbed to VND112.6 trillion, about six times the debt sales in Q1 2021. There were 75 corporate bond issuers in Q2 2021, more than doubling the number in the previous quarter. A majority of issuers were from the property (28 issuers) and banking (15 issuers) sectors. In terms of sales, banks dominated the debt market, raising an aggregate VND64.9 trillion during the quarter,

---

[10] *Vietnam News*. 2021. Banks Boost Fundraising Through Bonds. 7 June. https://vietnamnews.vn/economy/967735/banks-boost-fundraising-through-bonds.html.

Table 2: Top 30 Issuers of Local Currency Corporate Bonds in Viet Nam

	Issuers	Outstanding Amount		State-Owned	Listed Company	Type of Industry
		LCY Bonds (VND billion)	LCY Bonds (USD billion)			
1.	Bank for Investment and Development of Vietnam	25,902	1.13	Yes	Yes	Banking
2.	Ho Chi Minh City Development Joint Stock Commercial Bank	18,348	0.80	No	Yes	Banking
3.	Vietnam Prosperity Joint Stock Commercial Bank	18,050	0.78	No	Yes	Banking
4.	Masan Group	16,900	0.73	No	Yes	Finance
5.	Asia Commercial Joint Stock Bank	16,500	0.72	No	Yes	Banking
6.	Tien Phong Commercial Joint Stock Bank	15,649	0.68	No	Yes	Banking
7.	Vietnam International Joint Stock Commercial Bank	15,393	0.67	No	Yes	Banking
8.	Lien Viet Post Joint Stock Commercial Bank	14,100	0.61	No	Yes	Banking
9.	Vietnam Joint Stock Commercial Bank for Industry and Trade	10,435	0.45	Yes	Yes	Banking
10.	Vinhomes Joint Stock Company	8,890	0.39	No	Yes	Property
11.	Orient Commercial Joint Stock Bank	8,635	0.38	No	No	Banking
12.	Saigon Glory Company Limited	8,000	0.35	No	No	Property
13.	Sovico Group Joint Stock Company	7,550	0.33	No	Yes	Property
14.	Bac A Commercial Joint Stock Bank	6,140	0.27	No	Yes	Banking
15.	Golden Hill Real Estate JSC	5,701	0.25	No	No	Property
16.	Vietnam Maritime Joint Stock Commercial Bank	5,699	0.25	No	Yes	Banking
17.	Vingroup	5,425	0.24	No	Yes	Property
18.	Vietnam Technological and Commercial Joint Stock Bank	5,000	0.22	No	Yes	Banking
19.	Saigon - Hanoi Commercial Bank	4,600	0.20	No	Yes	Banking
20.	Trung Nam Dak Lak 1 Wind Power JSC	4,500	0.20	No	No	Energy
21.	Phu My Hung Corporation	4,497	0.20	No	No	Property
22	Ho Chi Minh City Infrastructure Investment Joint Stock Company	4,370	0.19	No	Yes	Construction
23.	Nui Phao Mining and Processing Co., Ltd.	4,310	0.19	No	No	Mining
24.	NoVa Real Estate Investment Corporation JSC	3,907	0.17	No	Yes	Property
25.	Orient Commercial Joint Stock Bank	3,900	0.17	No	Yes	Banking
26.	An Binh Commercial Joint Stock Bank	3,700	0.16	No	No	Banking
27.	Vincom Retail Joint Stock Company	3,050	0.13	No	Yes	Retail Trading
28.	Tuong Minh Investment and Real Estate Company Limited	2,950	0.13	No	No	Property
29.	TNL Investment and Leasing Joint Stock Company	2,926	0.13	No	No	Property
30.	Phu Long Real Estate Joint Stock Company	2,800	0.12	No	No	Property
	Total Top 30 LCY Corporate Issuers	**257,826**	**11.21**			
	Total LCY Corporate Bonds	**401,404**	**17.45**			
	Top 30 as % of Total LCY Corporate Bonds	**64.2%**	**64.2%**			

LCY = local currency, USD = United States dollar, VND = Vietnamese dong.
Notes:
1. Data as of 30 June 2021.
2. State-owned firms are defined as those in which the government has more than a 50% ownership stake.
Sources: *AsianBondsOnline* calculations based on Bloomberg LP and Vietnam Bond Market Association data.

which accounted for 57.8% of total issuance; property firms were second, raising VND26.5 trillion. Notable bond issuances during the quarter are listed in **Table 3**. Golden Hill Real Estate JSC topped the list with a VND5,700.6 trillion issuance of 3-year bonds.

Table 3: Notable Local Currency Corporate Bond Issuances in the Second Quarter of 2021

Corporate Issuers	Coupon Rate (%)	Issued Amount (VND billion)
Golden Hill Real Estate JSC		
3-year bond	–	5,701
Asia Commercial Joint Stock Bank[a]		
3-year bond	–	2,500
3-year bond	–	2,500
3-year bond	–	2,000
3-year bond	–	2,000
Voyage Investment		
4-year bond	–	2,300
Ho Chi Minh City Development Joint Stock Commercial Bank[a]		
3-year bond	–	2,000
3-year bond	–	2,000
Trung Nam Group		
3-year bond	–	2,000

– = not available, VND = Vietnamese dong.
[a] Multiple issuance of the same tenor indicates issuance on different dates.
Sources: Vietnam Bond Market Association.

In Q2 2021, two firms tapped the international bond market to raise funds. In April, Vingroup raised USD500.0 million in its first international bond issuance. The corporate security has a 5-year maturity and a coupon of 3.0%. Proceeds will be used to pay loans and increase the capital of its subsidiaries. In May, BIM Land had its inaugural issuance of a USD-denominated bond worth USD200.0 million and with a maturity of 5 years and a coupon of 7.38%. It was the first corporate green bond issued by a domestic firm outside of Viet Nam. The proceeds will be used to fund Excellence in Design for Greater Efficiencies-certified real estate projects.

Investor Profile

Government securities outstanding were held almost entirely by insurance firms and banks at the end of June, which together accounted for 99.1% of the total holdings. Insurance firms held 57.1% of government securities, up from 55.4% at the end of June 2020, while banks held 42.0%, down from 43.3% during the same period. The remaining outstanding bonds were held by securities companies, investment funds, offshore investors, and other investors. Foreign investors held 0.8% of government securities at the end of June, increasing from 0.6% a year earlier. Viet Nam's LCY bond market continued to have the smallest foreign holdings share among all emerging East Asian economies.

Figure 2: Local Currency Government Bonds Investor Profile

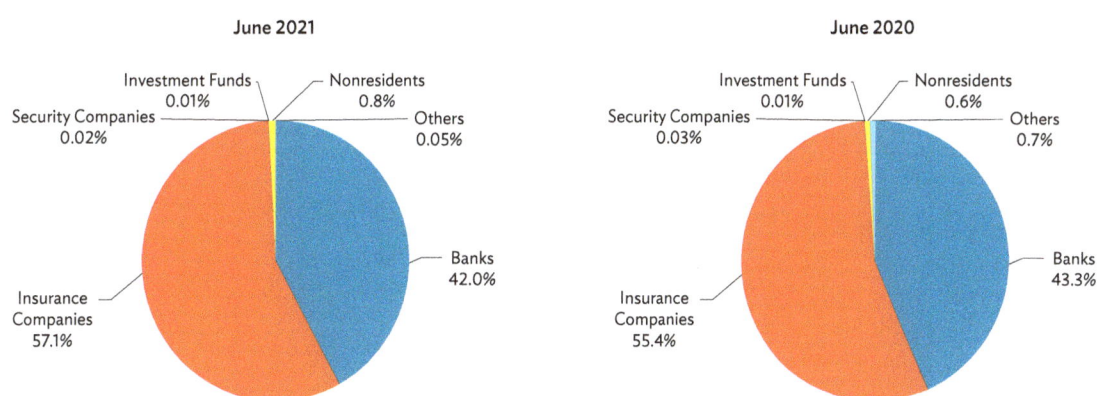

June 2021

Investment Funds 0.01%
Nonresidents 0.8%
Security Companies 0.02%
Others 0.05%
Banks 42.0%
Insurance Companies 57.1%

June 2020

Investment Funds 0.01%
Nonresidents 0.6%
Security Companies 0.03%
Others 0.7%
Banks 43.3%
Insurance Companies 55.4%

Source: Ministry of Finance, Government of Viet Nam.

Policy, Institutional, and Regulatory Developments

Hanoi Stock Exchange Launches 10-Year Government Bond Futures

On 28 June, the Hanoi Stock Exchange launched the 10-year government bond futures, which will be traded on the exchange's derivatives market. The base asset of the derivatives product is a 10-year government bond issued by the State Treasury of Viet Nam amounting to VND100,000 and with an annual interest rate of 5.0%. According to the Hanoi Stock Exchange, the new bond futures product aims to diversify derivatives securities in the market and provide more risk prevention tools for long-term government bonds. The 10-year government bond futures is the third derivatives product in the Vietnamese bond market, following the VN30 Index and 5-year government bond futures.

www.ingramcontent.com/pod-product-compliance
Lightning Source LLC
Chambersburg PA
CBHW042036220326
41599CB00045BA/7474